Persuasive Messages

Persuasive Messages

The Process of Influence

William L. Benoit and Pamela J. Benoit

Blackwell Publishing

BLACKWELL PUBLISHING
350 Main Street, Malden, MA 02148-5020, USA
9600 Garsington Road, Oxford OX4 2DQ, UK
550 Swanston Street, Carlton, Victoria 3053, Australia

First published 2008 by Blackwell Publishing Ltd

1   2008

Library of Congress Cataloging-in-Publication Data

Benoit, William L.
     Persuasive messages : the process of influence / William L. Benoit and Pamela J. Benoit.
       p. cm.
     Includes bibliographical references and index.
     ISBN 978-1-4051-5820-6 (hardcover : alk. paper) – ISBN 978-1-4051-5821-3 (pbk. : alk. paper)
1.Persuasion (Rhetoric) 2. Persuasion (Psychology) 3. Social influence. 4. Attitude change. I. Benoit, Pamela J., 1954– II. Title
     HM1196.B46 2008 153.8'52–dc22

                                    2007028074

A catalogue record for this title is available from the British Library.

Set in 10.5/13pt Minion
by SPi Publisher Services, Pondicherry, India

For further information on
Blackwell Publishing, visit our website:
www.blackwellpublishing.com

Contents

Figures

Tables

Boxes

Preface

This book is a guide to successful persuasion. It is primarily designed to help you become better, or more successful, persuaders. The book offers practical advice on refining your purpose, understanding your audience, and designing a persuasive message.

We wrote the book for several reasons. First, we wanted to provide a balance between theory and research on the one hand and practical advice on the other. We wanted our book to be firmly grounded in what researchers have found, but we also wanted to offer specific advice to help readers apply that sometimes abstract body of knowledge about persuasion. We also believe that the audience must construe and interpret persuasive messages: meanings are found in people, although messages are a way to encourage the audience to have certain ideas rather than others. This leads us to adopt the cognitive response model generally (and the elaboration likelihood model specifically) as a perspective for understanding persuasion. Our goal was to cover the same ideas found in other persuasion books, but to do so from a different perspective.

The book is divided into four parts. The first part includes four chapters. Chapter 1 explains that persuasion touches all of our lives, from business to ordinary life. It defines key concepts and discusses the relationship between attitudes and behavior. Chapter 2 explains an important theory of persuasion, the cognitive response model (elaboration likelihood model). We will refer to this theory at various points in the text, so it provides an important background for this book. Chapter 3 discusses the nature and effects of the source of persuasive messages. Chapter 4 discusses the nature of ethics in persuasion. The next two parts are in many ways the heart of this book. Part II is devoted to helping you design effective persuasive messages. Its chapters will help you learn about refining your purpose, understanding and adapting to your audience (chapter 5), organizing your message (chapter 6), selecting ideas and support for your message (chapter 7), putting your ideas into words (chapter 8), and dealing with hostile and multiple audiences (chapter 9). Part III discusses three other important theories of persuasion: consistency (chapter 10), social judgment/

involvement (chapter 11), and reasoned action (chapter 12). The last part of the book introduces the idea of being critical consumers of persuasive messages, discussing persuasion in advertising (chapter 13) and in politics (chapter 14).

We have worked diligently to relate these concepts to our intended readers. Although not every example used to illustrate the ideas in this book concerns students or college life, many of them were chosen with students in mind. We have also tried very hard to make clear how you, as persuaders, can use the ideas from this book in the messages you create to achieve your goals.

In chapter 14 we sometimes illustrate our points with excerpts from presidential TV spots. These quotations are from actual ads; however, we provided no reference for ads because they are not available in libraries. For the rest, all other passages without cited sources are hypothetical illustrations and not direct quotations.

At the end of each chapter is a glossary, which includes brief definitions of terms or words that have been set in bold in the text.

A book like this inevitably relies on the work of others who have written on persuasion before. We want to acknowledge four scholars who were particularly influential: Richard Petty and John Cacioppo (who developed the elaboration likelihood model), Ruth Anne Clark (who wrote a very useful book on persuasive speaking), and Richard Johanessen (who wrote on ethics and communication). We also want to thank Dennis Barnes and Maurice Parisien, who offered particularly useful advice for the chapter on advertising, Jon Hess, who provided comments on the chapter on ethics, and Jen Benoit, our daughter, who provides important support for us in many ways. Jayne Henson worked on the glossaries. Our students over the years have had an important impact on what and how we teach (including, of course, persuasion). We also appreciate the feedback from teachers who completed a survey on the topics they cover in their persuasion classes.

Part I

Attitudes and Persuasion

Chapter 1

The Importance of Persuasion

Chapter Contents

Why Study Persuasion?

College students sometimes try to persuade their parents to buy them new clothes, a laptop, or a car. They may try to persuade parents to foot the bill for a Spring Break trip. Friends persuade each other about the merits of a new musical group or a particular movie. Students persuade one another about where to live on campus, which bars are the most fun, or what to do on the weekend. Spouses influence one another's ideas about where to go for dinner, which car or minivan to buy, or how to redecorate a room in the house. Persuasion abounds in interpersonal or dyadic relationships.

There are thousands of committees which discuss problems, make decisions, and then either recommend or implement action to address those problems. In those groups the committee members use persuasion to propose and support their ideas to other committee members, hoping to influence the outcome of the committee's discussion. When the committee reports to a superior in the organization, it seeks to persuade that person to implement the group's recommendations. When committees implement their suggestions, they often must persuade others to cooperate. Committees or group projects are common in the classroom, in the workplace, and in government (and can be found in other contexts, such as academia). Members of committees constantly attempt to persuade one another – as well as the people to whom they report and the other people with whom they work. If you reflect on this question, you have probably experienced many groups in which persuasion occurred.

In larger groups, such as school board meetings, parents stand up and speak for or against such ideas as outcome-based education, prayer in schools, or whether a student should be suspended for having an over-the-counter pain reliever in a backpack. Print media (newspapers, magazines, direct mailing) as well as electronic media (radio, television, the world wide web) positively thrive on advertisements that attempt to persuade consumers to buy certain goods and services. These examples illustrate just a few of the wide variety of situations you are likely to encounter in which persuasion flourishes. Thinking about the varied contexts in which communication occurs quickly reveals that persuasion exists throughout all human activity.

We can also see that persuasion pervades our lives by thinking about the activities that make up our daily lives. Persuasion is a part of education and learning. A college recruiter, alum, or parent may try to persuade you to attend his or her school. Once at school, students persuade their friends when to take classes (e.g. in the morning or afternoon) and which classes or professors to take (or which ones to avoid). Academic advisors and professors attempt to persuade students which major to select, which classes to take, and whether to go to graduate or professional school. Students try to persuade professors to accept an assignment late, to change a grade, or to permit the student to take a test early. Faculty members are asked to write letters of recommendation encouraging (persuading) employers to hire their graduates. Persuasion is a pervasive part of education.

Persuasion also lurks "behind the scenes" in academia. Faculty members suggest to one another what courses a department should offer, when to offer them, and who should teach them. Faculty members persuade each other which courses should be required and which should be considered electives. This example could easily be spun out further (for example, faculty members persuade their deans to let them add or replace faculty, or they persuade promotion and tenure committees to award tenure to faculty members; deans persuade provosts to increase their budgets; presidents of state-supported schools persuade legislators to increase their budgets). Persuasion is an important part of education in many ways that might not be readily apparent.

Persuasion is also a large part of the working world. During employment interviews, applicants want to persuade the employer or recruiter to offer them jobs. When demand for employees outstrips supply, employers work to persuade applicants to accept job offers. At work, employees constantly persuade co-workers about projects, bosses about promotions (or raises, vacations, or other perks), and customers about the company's products or services. Workers may even try to persuade subordinates what to do or how to do it (rather than ordering them), in an effort to improve morale. Furthermore, many professions – for instance sales, politics, and the law – are essentially about nothing but persuading others. Thus, persuasion is widespread in the workplace.

Persuasion is also a part of recreation and relaxation. We persuade our families, roommates, and friends that we should go out to eat, and what kind of food to eat tonight. We persuade our friends that we ought to go see (or rent) a movie, and then which film to watch. Of course movies, whether seen in the theater or at home on rental tapes, contain previews that attempt to persuade us to see other movies (and, sometimes, to buy the soundtrack CD). We tell our friends about a new store or radio station or webpage that they really should check out. It seems that human beings do very little that does not involve persuasion in some fashion.

So we persuade each other while learning, working, and socializing. And this is not all! Most church services involve sermons, which clearly are persuasive messages aimed at the congregation. The fact is, most of us have never thought about just how much of our lives is spent in persuading or being persuaded. Rosseli, Skelly, and Mackie (1995: 163) estimated that people are "exposed to 300–400 persuasive messages a day from the mass media alone." That figure has surely not dropped since they conducted their study.

It is important to realize that the fact that you so often persuade (and are targets of persuasion) does not mean you are already experts in persuasion. Of course, you have learned something about persuasive strategies through trial and error. However, literally thousands of scholars in disciplines such as communication, psychology, and advertising have systematically studied persuasion for many, many years. In fact, rhetoricians or philosophers such as Aristotle have written about how to persuade others since four centuries before the Christian era. Practitioners, such as lawyers, politicians, and advertisers have also devoted an incredible amount of time and effort to understanding persuasion "in the real world." Cicero, who lived about three hundred years after Aristotle, was one of the greatest orators in ancient Rome. He was also an accomplished lawyer and was elected consul in Rome, a position roughly analogous to that of President of the United States. Cicero wrote several books on rhetoric or persuasion. More recently, social scientists have conducted tens of thousands of experiments into the nature of persuasion or attitude change. Thus, there is an incredible wealth of knowledge about persuasion which has accumulated over literally thousands of years, from scholars and practitioners, in a variety of disciplines. There is much that is useful to be learned about persuasion.

It is important to realize that persuasion affects us in two very different ways. We may try to persuade others (we are the sources or senders of persuasive messages) and other people may attempt to persuade us (we are the targets or receivers of persuasive messages). Although we rarely have the opportunity to persuade others via the mass media, that is a context in which others develop vast numbers of persuasive messages aimed at us. In other contexts, as in the give-and-take of a conversation, we are both the sources and targets of persuasive messages. When two friends discuss the best movie, each one is alternatively a **persuader**, or source who creates short persuasive messages (about which movies are best), and an **audience**, or target of the messages from the other person. A moment's reflection should convince you that understanding what persuasive communication is, and how it works, can be very important in both situations. Whenever we want to influence others through messages (speaking, writing, or using pictures and symbols), we need to understand how persuasion works in order to increase the likelihood that our messages will be successful. However, it is also important for us to understand that persuasion is aimed at us, so that other people may not unduly influence us. Informed consumers of persuasive messages ought to be able to ask themselves, "Should I be responding positively to this message?" "Does this advertisement give me a good reason to buy this product?" Understanding how persuasion works is useful to us because we both send messages as sources and receive persuasive messages as audiences or targets.

Persuasion Is an Alternative to Apathy or Coercion

Not only is persuasion present almost everywhere in human social activity, but persuasion can be a positive force. We frequently think about persuasion as propaganda, manipulation, or verbal trickery. It can be misused, like any other tool (and we will devote chapter 4 to ethical concerns). But persuasion should be thought of as a means to accomplishing something you (the persuader) want. If there is a goal that you want to accomplish – to make someone, say, go out on a date; let you hand in an assignment late; give you a raise; have your suggestion included in a report; buy your company's product; or vote for you – that goal often depends on the actions of others. To obtain the cooperation of other people, you have only a few basic choices.

First, you can do nothing – have an attitude of **apathy** – ignoring your wants, needs, and desires and hoping that someone else will notice what you (secretly) want and spontaneously do it. Doing nothing gives up control of your own life, allowing your wants to go unmet, or met only at the whim of others. If a person wishes her roommate would not let dirty dishes sit in the sink for days, she could hope her roommate will realize how much better it would be to clean up after a meal more quickly. This approach (well, really a non-approach) is not likely to be very satisfying or very effective (if she does not say something about those dirty dishes, her roommate is unlikely to wash them any sooner). Of course, there are times when we must realize that what we want is impossible or impractical and asking for it can be a waste of time. It can even be counter-productive if we make obviously unreasonable requests, if we make reasonable requests to people whom we know to be unreasonable, or if we make requests to those who do not have the power to grant our requests. These kinds of messages can irritate others and possibly even backfire. Still, while there are some specific situations in which it is better to do nothing, as a general strategy for trying to achieve our wants doing nothing is simply not very productive.

Second, you can use force, violence, or threats – that is, **coercion** – to get your own way. That frustrated roommate could threaten to throw into the trash any dishes which sit in the sink for more than a day. She could threaten not to pay her half of the rent unless dishes are washed in a timely fashion. Assuming a person has both the ability and the willingness to follow through, coercion can be a means of obtaining what you want. If the dirty dishes belong to her instead of the roommate, or if she is worried about eviction for non-payment of rent, these might be empty (and ineffective) threats. But even if you are willing to follow through, coercion has a variety of drawbacks as a method of getting what you want. First, there can be both moral and legal problems with using force to get others to comply with our wishes. Furthermore, coercion can cause others to be difficult or slow in satisfying our demands, to do a poor job on purpose, and to dislike us and possibly retaliate against us. Creating bad feelings can be especially unfortunate if we have to work with those whom we are coercing. Some people just become obstinate in the face of threats, so it does not always work. Even when coercion works, it is not likely to be pleasant. Furthermore, if you lose your power or authority, are not willing to follow through and punish those you threaten, or cannot observe others' behavior to make certain they comply, threats can be ineffectual.

Third, one can use persuasion to try to satisfy wants and needs. This is far more likely to succeed than doing nothing (apathy). It may not always work better than coercion – but even coercion does not always work, and this book is about how you can make your attempts at persuasion more likely to be successful. Most importantly, when it does work, the people we persuade will cooperate willingly. This will make us more popular, or better liked, than if we use coercion. And, if others are doing what we want them to do willingly, they may do a better job than when they are being coerced.

So, not only is persuasion everywhere, but it is one of only three basic options for getting others to help satisfy our needs, wants, and desires. Arguably, persuasion is the best way for us to obtain the cooperation of others in achieving our goals. Persuasion is a way for us to exert influence or control over our own lives, so we have some measure of control rather than feeling helpless. Of course, like any other tool, it is not always appropriate. Sometimes we have authority over others, and giving them a simple or direct order, with its implicit threat for noncompliance, is the best thing to so. Persuasion can be abused, as demagogues like Hitler and con artists who trick the elderly out of their life savings show. Still, persuasion can be used for good as well as evil – and it can be used against con artists and demagogues – and it is usually better than the alternatives for getting our own way.

Key Concepts in Persuasion

We define **persuasion** as a process in which a source (persuader) uses a message to achieve a goal by creating, changing, or reinforcing the attitudes of others (the audience). This definition has four important components, each discussed separately.

Persuasion is goal-directed

The first characteristic is that persuasion is goal-oriented, a means to an end. You can use persuasion when you want to influence an audience. Persuasion can be useful when you have a need or desire which you cannot satisfy by yourself (or which would be more easily or more quickly satisfied with the help of others). This means that the audience consists of people you believe can help you achieve your goal. Your persuasive message is intended to encourage your audience to comply with your wishes. For example, suppose that you decide that your family needs a new computer at home. If you and your spouse have an understanding that these kinds of purchases are not made unilaterally, you need to persuade your spouse to agree that you should get a new home computer. In this case, your goal is to buy a new computer. Because you have this understanding about purchases, satisfying your goal requires the cooperation of another person, your spouse. Your persuasive message, therefore, is the means to your goal: You want to use a persuasive message to convince your audience that you should realize this goal.

Some goals do not require the cooperation of others. For example, a person who is bored might decide to watch television, play a video-game, or walk over to the swimming pool for a swim. Ordinarily, persuasion is not needed in those situations (although you may have to persuade someone else to let you use the television, for example, if it is already being watched). But if you want to ease your boredom by going to see a movie with a friend, then you must persuade your friend to go along. So, often the goals that we want to attain are possible, but require the cooperation of others. When we have a goal that others might be willing to help obtain, identification of that goal is the first step in persuasion. We must know what we want before we can hope to achieve it. Do you want another person to go out on a date? Do you want a professor to change your grade? Do you want to sell your product to a customer? Do you want someone to vote for you?

We do want to note that some goals are unrealistic: You may want someone to give you a million dollars, you might want world peace today, you could want to fly on the next space shuttle mission. It is not likely that persuasion will help you achieve these goals.

The persuader must identify the right audience, the group of people who can help us achieve our goal. The audience is the recipient of the completed persuasive message, so in a sense it is the last part of the process of persuasion. However, an important principle (discussed further in chapter 5) is that a given persuasive message probably will not be equally persuasive for everyone. This means that, when developing your messages, you should think about the nature of your specific audience and what ideas might appeal to them. The audience must be a group that you can communicate with (you have to be able to get your message to them). Tom, who wants new clothes, would probably have more trouble getting to talk to a bank loan officer than to Jill, the small-business owner. The audience must also have what it takes to achieve your purpose, the means to obtain your goal. For example, your audience may have information, or money, or power that you need to achieve that goal. But for persuasion to truly be successful the audience must be able to grant your wish.

Persuasion is a process

Another important feature of persuasion is that it is a process. Persuasion begins with a person (the source or persuader), who has a goal. The source then creates a message which, in the source's opinion, will encourage others (the audience) to accomplish the source's goal. This message must be delivered to the audience, those who can help achieve the speaker's goal. If the message is effective, then the audience will comply with the speaker's wishes.

Box 1.1 The process of persuasion

Source > Message   > Audience [attitudes]   > Outcome: ultimate goal
(me)   > (reasons to buy) > (customer: pro-DVD attitude) > (customer buys DVD)

For example, consider a sales person, Peg, who wants to persuade a customer to buy a DVD player. Box 1.1 shows a simplified version of this process. In this illustration, Peg uses a message to convey ideas about why the customer should buy a DVD player (or a particular DVD player). Peg hopes that this message (or a series of short messages as they talk back and forth in their conversation) will change the customers' mind, so that, instead of being undecided about buying a DVD player, the customer will decide to buy one today. It is important to realize that, in a very real sense, Peg has two goals. Her ultimate goal is to convince this customer to buy a DVD player. However, to accomplish that goal, she must persuade the customer to change his mind. Her customer probably does not already have a favorable attitude towards buying the DVD player (or he would not need to use persuasion). So Peg hopes that, if she can change the customer's mind (change his attitude toward buying a DVD player today), her ultimate goal will be accomplished and the customer will buy a DVD player. Changing the other person's mind (or attitudes) is the means to achieving the persuader's goal (selling the product). Persuasive messages have the potential to change attitudes and thereby to influence behavior.

For some goals, a simple request might be enough to achieve your goal. "Honey, the Superbowl starts in five minutes. Can I have the remote control?" For other goals, you will have to work to convince the audience to do what you want. It is very important to realize that it may not be enough to tell them why you want them to do something. Of course, the banker knows why Jill wants a loan: Being able to buy more stock for her shelves can make Jill higher profits. But she must convince the banker that this would be a good loan (one that will make money for the bank), that Jill will be able to pay back the loan with interest, and on time. Persuaders can be more successful when they can make the audience want to help achieve their own goals. You must appeal to our audience's self-interests, not your own. You can increase your chances of convincing them to help if you know your audience. Knowing what the audience knows, what interests the audience, what is important to them, and their attitudes on our topic, can be very helpful.

The message has to be conveyed to the audience. In interpersonal relations, this simply means meeting (or calling, or sending mail or email to) the other person. Other messages, like advertisements, require more elaborate preparation and distribution arrangements. But persuasion cannot possibly be successful if the message does not reach its intended audience.

So persuasion is a process that begins with a source and a goal. The persuader identifies an audience who has the ability or power to help accomplish that goal. Then he or she creates a message containing reasons that encourage the audience to comply with his or her request. Then the persuader communicates the persuasive message to the audience. Hopefully, the message will successfully persuade the audience to do what the persuader asks, and his or her goal will be satisfied.

Persuasion involves people

We may say that "the dark clouds persuaded me to get my umbrella," or that "Fido scratched the screen door and persuaded me to let him inside." However, this book is focused on situations in which one person (or a group of people) attempt to influence an audience. We do not mean to say that these uses of the word "persuasion" are wrong, but that when we use the word, we intend to refer to messages created by people (persuaders, sources) for other people (audiences).

Persuasion can create, change, or reinforce attitudes

Persuasive messages are designed to reinforce, create, or change the attitudes or behaviors of individuals. To understand this part of the definition, we need to understand the nature of attitudes.

Attitudes are the key to successful persuasion. An **attitude** is a cognition (a thought, a mental construct) which is developed through experience, is evaluative, and influences our behavior. Because they are cognitions or thoughts, attitudes are not directly observable. They are learned (we are not born with attitudes), which means that they develop (and change) as we experience the world, both directly and as we learn about it from other people. Attitudes are evaluative, which means we are favorably or unfavorably inclined toward the object of an attitude (if we have a favorable attitude toward a musical group, this simply means we like that group or enjoy its music). Finally, attitudes influence (but do not necessarily determine) our behavior. If we like a group, we are likely to buy CDs by that group, although we will not do so if we are broke.

Attitudes have two key parts: beliefs and values. A **belief** is a description of the world and of the people, places, things, and relationships in it. Roughly, a belief is a fact, something that is either true or false. These are examples of beliefs:

- The University of Minnesota enrolls more than 60,000 students.
- Los Angeles has a higher violent crime rate than New York City.
- The capital of Illinois is Chicago (this belief is wrong, but it is still a belief).
- Connecticut has the highest per capita state tax rate in the country.
- The moon is made of green cheese (another false belief).

Beliefs are potentially verifiable, or verifiable in principle. Now that we have visited the moon and brought back moon rocks for study, we have indisputable evidence that the last belief was false. However, before the age of space travel, this belief could not be tested directly, so it was potentially verifiable. For a statement to qualify as a belief, we must be able, at least in principle, to verify whether it is true or false.

The second part of an attitude is a value. **Values** are judgments of worth. Because they are judgments, they are subjective and are neither true nor false. Of course, some people hold a given value so strongly that they believe it is true. Examples of values include:

- Harvard University provides high quality education.
- Cities with high violent crime rates are terrible places to live.
- Connecticut is the most beautiful state in the Union.
- The best college degrees are ones with the most job offers.
- Chicago's blues clubs are the finest anywhere.
- Saturn is the most interesting planet.
- It is a waste of time to dream about the moon.
- Attending football games is the right way to show school spirit.

We can make arguments about these value statements. We could point to evidence about the number and salary of jobs obtained by Harvard University graduates – or we could point to the number of Nobel Prize winners on the faculty – to try to show that Harvard's education is the best. We can, for example, argue that Chicago's blues clubs are the finest because of which bands play there, and try to persuade people that the blues musicians who play in Chicago are more accomplished than other musicians. But none of these statements can be objectively verified as true or false in the same way beliefs can be verified. Reasonable people do not disagree about whether Chicago is the capital of Illinois, but reasonable people could disagree about whether Chicago blues are better than, say, Delta blues.

This analysis of attitudes into beliefs and values leads to several important propositions. First, it is important to understand that beliefs and values work together to form attitudes. Consider the statements shown in box 1.2, representing cognitions or thoughts from Cheryl.

Box 1.2   Cheryl's thoughts about Terrence Jones

Terrence Jones is a rap musician. (= belief)

+

Rap is the best kind of music. (= value)

=

Positive attitude toward Terrence Jones the musician. (= attitude)

This favorable attitude toward Jones makes it more likely that Cheryl would attend Jones' concerts or buy his CDs. However, Cheryl must have both a belief and a value to have an attitude (and the belief must be related to the value). Only if she accepts the belief that Jones is a rap musician and embraces the value that rap is better would she have a positive attitude. If Cheryl likes rap (has the value) but does not know whether Jones is rap, rock, or pop (lacks the corresponding belief), she does not have enough information to form a favorable or unfavorable attitude toward Jones. A value that rap is the best type of music cannot help her form an attitude about Jones unless she knows whether he does rap. On the other hand, if Cheryl knows Jones is a rapper (has the belief) but does not think that rap is the best kind of music (lacks the corresponding value), she still cannot have a favorable or unfavorable attitude toward Jones. Only if she knows his style of music (belief) and she has preferences about different kinds of music (value) is it possible for Cheryl to have an attitude about Jones as a musician.

Second, when you want to change someone's attitude, you can try to change either the belief or the value but not both. For example, take the example about Terrence Jones, in which Cheryl has a positive attitude toward Jones. If one of her friends develops a message that successfully changes her belief, the result is as shown in box 1.3. This persuasive message successfully changed her attitude, from one that is favorable toward Jones to an unfavorable attitude, by changing the belief.

Box 1.3 Cheryl's thoughts about Terrence Jones after her belief has changed

Terrence Jones is a rock musician. (= belief)
Rap is the best kind of music. (= value)
Negative attitude toward Terrence Jones the musician. (= attitude)

On the other hand, if one of Cheryl's friends creates a message that successfully changes my value, the outcome would be as shown in box 1.4. Here again, the new attitude after this successful persuasive message is unfavorable toward Jones, but this time Cheryl's attitude changed because her friend changed her value.

Box 1.4 Cheryl's thoughts about Terrence Jones after her value has changed

Terrence Jones is a rap musician. (= belief)
Rock is the best kind of music. (= value)
Negative attitude toward Terrence Jones the musician. (= attitude)

However, if a third friend designs a message that changes both her belief and her value, Cheryl's attitude will remain unchanged (see box 1.5). Although Cheryl now holds her positive attitude for quite different reasons from before, she still has a positive attitude toward Jones after this third persuasive message. So, when you use persuasion, you can try to change an attitude (and, hopefully, subsequent behavior) by changing either the belief or the value component of an attitude – but not both.

Box 1.5   Cheryl's thoughts about Terrence Jones after her belief and value have changed

Terrence Jones is a rock musician. (= belief)
Rock is the best kind of music. (= value)
Positive attitude toward Terrence Jones the musician. (= attitude)

A third principle is that most attitudes are made up of a collection of belief/value pairs. The attitude is influenced by the number of positive belief/value pairs and the number of negative belief/value pairs (as well as by how important each belief/value pair is to the person). So let us consider Steve's attitude about a car, the Mini-Cooper (box 1.6).

Box 1.6   Steve's attitude toward the Mini-Cooper

The Mini Cooper is a sporty car. (= belief)
Sporty cars are the best! (= value)
I really like the Mini Cooper. (= attitude)

This belief/value pair, by itself, tends to lead to a positive attitude. But Steve also knows other things about this car. It is so small that it has little cargo room (box 1.7).

Box 1.7   Steve's belief and value about cargo room in the Mini-Cooper

The Mini Cooper has almost no room for cargo. (= belief)
Cargo space is very important to me in a car. (= value)

Price is also a consideration for Steve (box 1.8).

Box 1.8   Steve's belief and value about the cost of a Mini-Cooper

The Mini Cooper is relatively inexpensive. (= belief)
I prefer an inexpensive car. (= value)

It should be clear that Steve could have other belief/value pairs (about such ideas as gas mileage, anti-lock brakes, air bags, car audio) that would go together to shape his attitude toward this car. When Steve considers all of the belief/value pairs about the Mini Cooper together, he may end up with an attitude that is positive or negative depending on the make-up of the belief/value pairs he holds. The overall attitude will be positive if most of the belief/value pairs are positive, or if the belief/value pairs that matter most to him are positive (e.g. cost might be more important to Steve than cargo room).

The point is, if a target audience member has many favorable belief/value pairs and few or no unfavorable ones, changing a single belief or value may not change the overall attitude very much. In general, the more a person knows about an attitude topic like a car or a politician (roughly, the more belief/value pairs he or she has), the more difficult it will be to create a substantial change in their attitude. The complexity of some attitudes (along with the fact that some attitude changes tend to be temporary) is one of the reasons why many persuaders develop advertising campaigns which repeat a message several times and/or use several different messages. For example, during a campaign, politicians seem to run an ad over and over (repetition). They also usually make more than one ad, discussing different issues, telling us about themselves and/or their opponent (different messages). The complexity of most attitudes also means that we need to have realistic expectations about what a persuasive message can be expected to accomplish.

We will talk about the audience, and audience analysis, in chapter 5. However, the idea that most attitudes are made up of groups of belief/value pairs shows how important it is for a persuader to understand the audience. You need to know what beliefs and values, relevant to your persuasive goal, the audience accepts. If you are lucky, your target audience will already hold some belief/value pairs that help with your goal (e.g. if you want their attitude to be positive and they already have some positive belief/value pairs). If so, you do not want to change them accidentally! You also need to know which belief/value pairs are opposed to your goal, so you can try to change either the belief or the value. You can also change an attitude by adding new belief/value pairs ("Did you know that the Mini Cooper comes with heated seats? [belief] "That would be so nice in the winter" [value]). However, this will only help if the information really is new; restating what the audience already knows is not likely to help your cause very much. Again, knowing what beliefs and values your audience holds – which ones are helpful to your goal, which ones are harmful to your goal, and which ones are the beliefs or values the audience does not yet have – will help you discover ways to try to persuade them. If you know that Steve is worried about cargo space when he takes long trips, you could inform him about the Mini Cooper's optional (cool-looking) car-top carrier.

With this understanding of the nature of attitudes, we can turn to the three purposes of persuasion. Persuasive messages can have three purposes. They can:

- reinforce the audience's attitudes and/or behavior;
- create audience attitudes and/or behavior;
- change the audience's attitudes and/or behavior.

Sometimes persuasive messages are intended to reinforce what an audience already believes, or the behaviors an audience is already likely to enact. For example, many political advertisements are aimed at reinforcing voters who have already decided to vote for a candidate – they strengthen the audience's existing attitudes. Advertisers spend a large part of their advertising budgets to reinforce current customers, so they will repeat their buying behavior.

A form of reinforcement is **resistance**, in which you attempt to strengthen existing attitudes so that they will resist, or stand up to, persuasive messages from others which try to change those attitudes. Those who sell goods and services are concerned that their competitors will steal away customers. General Motors would surely like to increase its share of the automobile sales market, but it also does not want to lose any of its current customers to Ford, Chrysler, or other automakers. Similarly, political candidates have opponents, so they both want to attract additional supporters and to key current supporters from bolting to the other candidate. William McGuire (1964) developed an important theory of resistance, **inoculation theory**, which is based on a disease metaphor (we use inoculations to increase resistance to infection; McGuire discusses how messages which refute opposing ideas and arguments can inoculate an audience against being "infected" with a contrary persuasive message).

Messages which create an attitude, or behavior, are planned for audiences who do not have pre-existing attitudes or behaviors related to the topic. Audiences may be neutral, or may have little knowledge of the issue. In these cases, the speaker's challenge is to build an attitude or generate an action where apathy or a lack of awareness previously existed. For example, a speaker gave a speech on United Nations relief efforts in Africa. On the basis of conversations with members of the audience, it becomes clear that they have very little knowledge of, or interest in, this topic because most of the audience sees it as only remotely related to their own interests. To be persuasive, the speaker must first find a way to build interest for the topic and then educate this audience. Such efforts are necessary steps in creating a positive attitude for these relief efforts or in generating any action in support of the United Nation's efforts.

Other messages are designed to change an audience's attitudes or behavior. A speaker may know that the audience downloads music files and may want to convince them to stop using their university accounts to access these files. This persuasive message is designed to convince the audience to stop doing an action they were going to do. A message designed to change behavior would require some action on the part of audience members that they would not have taken without the influence of the speaker. In a speech on recycling, a speaker passed out the clear recycling bags from the city and asked the audience to take them home to their apartments and dorm rooms and fill them up with their pop cans. About half of the class reported later in the semester that they had used the bags and several had continued to recycle. Another speaker asked his audience to vote in the upcoming student government election. He gave everyone a mock ballot, a map of all of the polling places, and reminded the class on the day of the election. He even walked some people over to one of the polling places after class. Although this speaker was trying to change the students' attitudes about student elections, he was also trying to change their behaviors by actually trying to get them to participate in the process.

So persuasion is a goal-oriented process in which a person tries to influence other people with a message. Persuasion can create, change, or reinforce attitudes, which are made up of belief/value pairs.

Attitudes and Behavior

In most attempts at persuasion, we want the audience to take some action or to engage in a particular behavior. Those in business want customers to purchase good and services. Politicians want to persuade you to give them your vote (or to contribute money to their campaigns). Special interest groups also want to influence your vote. Graduating college seniors want to persuade interviewers to offer them jobs. Employees want to convince their bosses to adopt their business recommendations – and to give them raises and/or promotions. We often try to convince our friends to go see this movie instead of that one, or to try a new restaurant. At times, behavior is a potential outcome even if we are not personally involved. For example, you may try to persuade my friend that Dave Mathews is a great musician. It probably does not matter to you whether your friend buys a Dave Mathews Band CD, but that could easily be an effect of your enthusiastic endorsement of his music. So, the audience's behavior is often an important desired outcome or effect of persuasive messages.

The fundamental assumption of persuasion is that, if a message changes your attitudes, your new attitudes in turn will influence your behavior. Commercial advertising, for example, clearly makes this assumption. Ads tell us about the wonderful features of a product (or how the product will help us become more attractive, successful, or healthy) because the advertiser wants us to buy this product (and lots of it!). For a time, there was a "crisis" in the literature on persuasion because some scholars raised serious doubts about whether attitudes really had anything to do with behavior (e.g. Wicker 1969). This led to a great deal of research which established that attitudes can be an important influence on behavior (Kim and Hunter 1993a, 1993b). However, our attitudes do not always shape our behavior, so we need to know when attitudes are likely to affect what we do and when they are not likely to affect us.

Chapter 12 will focus on the theory of reasoned action, which makes predictions about behavior (or behavioral intent). Here we will sketch several factors that influence the relationship between attitudes and behavior. First, the way an attitude is formed or created makes a difference. We can learn or develop attitudes through direct or vicarious (indirect) experience (Fazio and Zanna 1981). As you might expect, attitudes formed through direct experience have greater influence on behavior than attitudes we learn "second hand," from the reports or descriptions of others. For example, you can learn how the Mini Cooper handles by driving it yourself, or by reading about it in a car magazine. Or you might meet someone who is homeless and see where and how he or she lives on the street. The attitudes you form about the car or about the homeless from direct experience will probably have a greater effect on your subsequent behavior than if you read about them in the newspaper.

Another important factor in the relationship between attitude and behavior is the audience's level of involvement in the topic. Some topics appear to us to be more relevant or salient. When a topic matters to us, our behavior is more likely to be guided by our attitudes (Thomsen, Borgida, and Lavine 1995). In contrast, when a topic is less important to us, we are more likely to allow our behavior to be guided by other cues (situational norms, expectations).

Attitudes (and behavior) can be thought of at different levels of abstraction. We can talk about attitudes toward soft drinks generally or toward Coca-Cola or Pepsi specifically. We can talk about buying a car or buying a Honda Civic. Behavior will more closely reflect our attitudes when they are considered at the same level of abstraction. That is, Sally's attitude toward Pepsi will predict her drinking Pepsi better than it will predict her drinking soft drinks generally (if she has a negative attitude toward Pepsi that does not necessarily mean she has negative attitudes toward drinking Coke™ or Dr. Pepper). Similarly, Joe's attitude toward buying a new car might not predict whether he is likely to buy a Honda Civic (it is quite possible that he could have a positive attitude toward buying a new car but a negative attitude toward Honda Civics). This idea is often discussed as the relevance of the attitude to the behavior (Kim and Hunter 1993a). The more relevant the attitude appears to the behavior (attitudes toward Pepsi™ are most relevant to the behavior of drinking Pepsi™), the more likely that attitude will influence or predict the behavior.

Human beings are social creatures; few of us want to be hermits. Accordingly, we sometimes care about what others expect us to do. At times our attitudes will encourage us to engage in one kind of behavior but our friends will expect us to do something else. When that kind of conflict occurs, we sometimes ignore our attitudes and conform to social norms or to the expectations of our friends and peers. The theory of reasoned action (chapter 12) discusses the effects of social norms on behavior.

This idea of conforming to social norms is related to the concept of self-monitoring (Snyder 1979). Some people pay close attention to how others react to them and to their behavior. They want to make a good impression on others and are willing (within reason) to mold their behavior to fit with others' expectations. These people are called high self-monitors (although it might be clearer if we call this idea something like "high monitors of others' reactions to self" instead of "self-monitoring"). Another way to describe these people is to say they are highly aware of social norms and believe it is important to comply with them whenever possible. Attitudes are less important in determining the behavior of high self-monitors. On the other hand, some people are what Snyder calls low self-monitors: They do what they want, regardless of what others expect or how they might react. We might call low self-monitors non-conformists. They are less aware or less concerned with social norms and, as a result, their attitudes are more likely to influence their behavior. We list four items from the self-monitoring scale (questionnaire used to measure this variable) in box 1.9, to illustrate this concept.

Box 1.9   Items from the self-monitoring scale

My behavior is usually an expression of my true inner feelings, attitudes, and beliefs.

I have trouble changing my behavior to suit different people and different situations.

When I am uncertain how to act in a social situation, I look to the behavior of others for cues.

I laugh more when I watch a comedy with others than when alone.

Scoring:

Low self-monitors are more likely to agree with the first two than the last two statements.

Source: http://pubpages.unh.edu/~ckb/SELFMON2.html

Another factor that influences the relationship between attitudes and behavior is our ability to engage in certain behaviors. In some cases, our attitudes incline us to do one thing (engage in a particular behavior), but yet we cannot. For example, you may like one candidate for public office (or you may want to buy a particular product), but if you do not have enough money you cannot contribute to that candidates' campaign (or buy that product). Perhaps you really like PT Cruisers, but you cannot afford to buy one right now. Here, your attitude is thwarted by aspects of the situation that you cannot control (lack of money). When circumstances prevent us from doing something we want to, the situation is one of lack of control, or lack of **volitional control** ("volitional" concerns the extent to which a behavior is "voluntary" in the sense of being controlled by one's will). These kinds of situational factors limit the ability of attitudes to influence our behavior.

Thus, research has demonstrated that attitudes do have a significant relationship with, or effect on, our behavior. However, attitudes do not completely determine our behavior: There are limits on their influence. Attitudes formed through direct experience are more likely to shape our behavior than attitudes formed vicariously. The more involved we are in a topic, and the more relevant an attitude is to behavior, the stronger the relationship between attitude and behavior is. Social norms can limit the effectiveness of attitudes in shaping behavior, especially with those who are high self-monitors. Finally, some behaviors are not completely under our volitional control, which limits the effect of attitudes on those behaviors. Attitudes can and do influence behavior, but there are limitations we need to understand.

Overview

This book is divided into four basic parts. First, we discuss several key preliminary matters. Chapter 2 introduces the cognitive approach to persuasion, which, we believe, is a very fundamental concept because persuasion attempts to change the cognitions of the audience (their beliefs, values, attitudes). We discuss how the source is important to the success of persuasive messages in chapter 3. Then chapter 4 introduce the idea of ethics. Because persuasion attempts to change other people, it raises important ethical issues.

The second section of the book is concerned with the mechanics of creating persuasive messages. First we discuss the relationship between the persuader's purpose and the audience (chapter 5). Then, in chapter 6, we explain how the ideas in a speech are organized. Chapter 7 discusses the content of persuasive messages, including evidence and factors of interest. Style (selection and arrangement of the words in a message) comes next, in chapter 8. Chapter 9 explains how to deal with different types of audiences.

The third section of the book introduces attitude change theory. Chapter 10 covers consistency theories, which hold that the amount of persuasion is determined by the extent to which a message disagrees with an audience. Cognitive dissonance is the most widely studied consistency theory. Social judgment/involvement theory (chapter 11) is useful because it focuses our attention on the fact that different audience members can perceive the same message differently. Ultimately, audiences are persuaded (or not persuaded) by the message as they perceive it. The theory of reasoned action, discussed in chapter 12, picks up on the ideas of belief and value introduced in this chapter, adding in the idea of norms or expectation.

The final section of the book discusses persuasion in two particular contexts. Chapter 13 addresses persuasion in advertising. Chapter 14 concerns persuasion in political campaigns.

Glossary

Audience: the target for a persuasive message.

Apathy: not caring enough to work to encourage others to do what you want.

Attitude: a cognition which is developed through experience, is evaluative, and influences behavior.

Belief: a description of the world and of the people, places, things, and relationships in it.

Coercion: using force, violence, or threats to get what you want.

Inoculation theory: theory which explains how to "protect" those who agree with you from messages by those who disagree.

Persuader: the source of a persuasive message.

Persuasion: the process in which a source uses a message to achieve a goal by creating, changing, or reinforcing the attitudes of others.

Resistance: strengthening existing attitudes in order to resist persuasive messages from others.

Values: subjective judgments of worth, which are neither true nor false.

Volitional control: the ability to control our behavior.

Chapter 2

The Cognitive Approach to Persuasion

Chapter Contents

Chapter 1 explained that persuasion is about creating, changing, or reinforcing the audience's attitudes (by changing their beliefs and values). This means that **cognitions**, or thoughts and feelings like beliefs and values, are important to persuasion. Persuasion is successful when the source changes the attitudes of the audience. The elaboration likelihood model (ELM) places the audience's thoughts front and center in the process of persuasion.

As we look back on the traditional approaches to persuasion, scholars often suggest that persuasion was considered to be very much like a hypodermic needle. You put "persuasion stuff" (ideas, evidence, organization) into a message which you inject into the audience. The audience listened and, hopefully, learned what was in your message. If the audience learned the message, this meant that the "persuasion stuff" had moved from being inside your message to being "inside" your audience and would then change the latter's attitudes. Those who accepted this point of view were usually very concerned about whether the audience understood and remembered the content of a message. It is clear that persuasion can occur when we understand the ideas of a persuasive message. On the other hand, if you do not understand the ideas from a message, persuasion is unlikely. So this message learning approach makes some sense, because persuasion can result from learning a message's content.

But learning a message does not necessarily result in persuasion. Sometimes, for example, an advertisement is so annoying that we just cannot forget it (we have learned it very well), but we hate the product or company which sponsored it. Sometimes a commercial is so annoying or so silly that you might vow never to buy that product. A hospital ran a series of advertisements about how they were cutting "red tape": fewer forms to complete for medical treatment. While we do not like red tape, surely the quality of care provided to patients is more important in choosing a hospital than red tape. We learned this message very well – "this hospital reduces needless paperwork" – but it completely failed to make us to want to use that hospital. There can even be a "**boomerang effect**". Instead of liking the product more after the message, the audience likes the product or service less, because the message was so annoying.

Although it may seem unlikely, it is also possible for a message to change our attitudes even though we did not learn much about its content. We might hear or see the beginning of a message and then start thinking about the topic without paying much attention to the message. For example, I see a public service ad about buckling seatbelts, once I recognize the topic, I start thinking about my sister, who was thrown through the windshield of a car and suffered serious cuts to her face. These thoughts renew our determination always to wear seatbelts. But when the commercial is over, we realize we never really paid attention to it. Apart from its general topic, we do not remember what it said: We have no idea what arguments or statistics it might have presented. Still, we were persuaded because our positive attitudes toward seatbelts were reinforced or strengthened as we thought about someone's accident. If the topic of the public service announcement had not prompted us to think about that person, we would not have reinforced our attitude; but still we did not learn anything from the message. Thus, these two possibilities – (1) to understand (or learn) a message but not be persuaded by it and (2) to be persuaded by a message without paying close attention to it (or learning it) – set the stage for introducing the cognitive response model of persuasion.

The Cognitive Response Model

What both of these situations have in common – learning a message but not being persuaded; being persuaded even though we did not learn the message – is that persuasion is related to what we think. In the first example, people might not persuaded by the red tape hospital advertisement because we had thoughts that were unfavorable to the message. We thought that quality of care is so much more important in choosing a hospital than red tape. In the second example, we were persuaded about wearing seat belts because we had thoughts that were favorable to the message topic. I remembered the pain and suffering my sister endured and the plastic surgery she had. Psychologists recognized the general principle that attitude change occurs when we think favorable thoughts about the message and/or its topic, just as they recognized the related principle, that attitude change will not occur when we think unfavorable thoughts about the message and/or its topic. This idea was called the cognitive response model (Greenwald 1968; Perloff and Brock 1980) and it is called that because this model holds that persuasion occurs when the audience has thoughts or cognitions in response to a persuasive message.

The cognitive response approach suggests that receivers, or audience members, can be active participants in the persuasion process. In a very real sense, persuasion is not caused directly by messages; we are only persuaded if we have thoughts which agree with the message. Our thoughts are what directly cause us to be persuaded. So persuasive messages create attitude change indirectly, by encouraging listeners to have favorable thoughts. This means that, if we want to understand persuasion, we have to understand what the receivers are likely to think about a message: (1) the **number** of thoughts they have about a message and (2) the **valence** of those thoughts (whether those thoughts are primarily or exclusively favorable to the message or unfavorable to the message). All or most thoughts being favorable means that persuasion is likely; all or most thoughts being negative means that persuasion is unlikely (and a boomerang effect is possible). The more favorable the thought, the more likely it is for an attitude change to occur; the more unfavorable the thought, the less likely it is that attitude change will happen.

To return to the earlier examples, the thoughts we had in response to the annoying hospital commercial were unfavorable and we were not persuaded by it, even though we learned that silly advertisement by heart. On the other hand, our thoughts in response to the seatbelt commercial were favorable and we were persuaded without paying attention to, or taking in, the details of the message. The cognitive response model states that thoughts about the message topic are what really determine persuasion. The message brings the topic to our attention; it can provide ideas and information in support of its persuasive purpose; but ultimately we are persuaded (or not) by what we think about the message and its topic. The idea that we are persuaded by what we think is quite reasonable.

Of course, there are actually four possibilities here. Besides the first two situations identified above – (1) learning a message and not being persuaded by it and (2) not learning a message but still being persuaded by the topic of the message – it is possible (3) to learn a message and be persuaded and (4) not to learn a message and fail to be persuaded. If a person assimilates, or learns, the information in a persuasive message about why federal taxes should be cut and has favorable thoughts on the topic, the cognitive response model predicts that he or she will probably be persuaded (because there were favorable thoughts as the message was assimilated). On the other hand, if someone does not assimilate a message and does not have favorable thoughts about it, the cognitive response model predicts that there will be no persuasion (because attitude change should not happen without favorable thoughts). For example, if you completely ignore a message about a cell phone that takes pictures, you will not think favorable thoughts about picture phones or be persuaded to buy that phone. Table 2.1 shows how the cognitive response model explains why persuasion occurs, or does not occur, in all four of these possible situations.

Table 2.1   The cognitive response model: learning, thoughts, and persuasion

Case	Learn message?	Thoughts	Outcome
1	yes	unfavorable thoughts	no persuasion
2	no	favorable thoughts	persuasion
3	yes	favorable thoughts	persuasion
4	no	none	no persuasion

The cognitive response model (CRM) is a powerful approach to persuasion, as indicated by the large amount of research support for it. Eagly and Chaiken (1993) explain that there is a great deal of experimental evidence supporting this approach to persuasion (the ELM is one of the most popular versions of the CRM; Eagly and Chaiken's heuristic/systematic model is the other popular version). Although some critics raise questions about the elaboration likelihood model (ELM) (Mongeau and Stiff 1993; Stiff 1986; Stiff and Boster 1987), there is little question that what (or whether) the audience thinks about a persuasive message is important to that message's persuasiveness. Notice that this model focuses attention on the number of thoughts and their valence (favorable or unfavorable). These thoughts concern beliefs and values about the ideas in the message as well as about the topic generally, and even about the source of the message. However, the ELM does not make the distinction between beliefs and values a central concern.

Two "Routes" to Persuasion

Petty and Cacioppo's elaboration likelihood model (ELM) (1981; 1986a, 1986b) is the most influential cognitive response model. The ELM considers receivers or audience members to be active participants, or at least potentially active participants, in the persuasion process. It takes effort on our part to think carefully about a message and the arguments in it, so we do not exert the same amount of time or effort thinking about every message we encounter. Petty and Cacioppo (1986a, 1986b) explain that there are two "routes" to persuasion: central and peripheral. The **central route to persuasion** consists of thoughtful consideration of the arguments (ideas, content) in the message, and occurs when a listener has both the motivation and the ability to think about the message and its topic. The listener or audience member who engages in central processing is an active part of the process of persuasion, thinking carefully about the ideas and arguments in the message. Many thoughts (cognitive responses) are produced during central processing. The key to persuasion in central processing is the strength or quality of the arguments in the message.

The **peripheral route to persuasion,** on the other hand, takes place when the receiver does not expend the effort to think carefully about the ideas in a message. Instead, in peripheral processing the audience member decides whether to agree with the message on the basis of other cues, such as the number (but not the quality) of arguments in the message, its length, or whether the source is credible or attractive. Peripheral processing will occur when the listener lacks the ability or motivation (or both) to engage in much thought on the message. A thought based on a peripheral cue might sound like this: "Hmm. This source seems to know a lot about this topic. I guess I should agree with her because she is an expert." Another example of peripheral processing could be: "Wow, this speaker sure has a lot of reasons for what he believes in. He's probably right." In other words, peripheral cues, like source expertise (credibility) or the use of many arguments in one message, work as a mental short-cut. There are times when we do not want to, or are not able to, think carefully about the ideas in a persuasive message. Still, it makes sense for us to agree with the message if the source appears knowledgeable or if there are many arguments in support of the message. Receivers engaged in peripheral processing are more passive than those doing central processing.

Why does it matter which "route" an audience member takes when hearing or watching or reading a persuasive message? An important prediction of the ELM is that attitudes which are changed through the central route to persuasion will have different effects from attitudes changed through the peripheral route. Petty and Cacioppo (1986a) explain that "[a]ttitude changes that result mostly from processing issue-relevant arguments (central route) will show greater temporal persistence, greater prediction of behavior, and greater resistance to counterpersuasion than attitude changes that result mostly from peripheral cues" (p. 21). It should be obvious that these are important outcomes: Surely, in most cases, persuaders would very much want to know how to make attitude change last longer, have a greater influence on the audience's behavior, and make it more resistant to change from other persuasive messages by competitors or opponents.

Of course, even though central processing has advantages, our audiences do not always oblige us by having the motivation and ability to think about the message. We need to understand both central and peripheral processing, because both of them occur in receivers. During the evaluation section below, we will note that a conceptual weakness in this theory is that it creates the impression that receivers do either central or peripheral processing. But message processing actually exists on a continuum: people can think no thoughts, a few thoughts, a moderate number of thoughts, or many thoughts about a message. So, when people think about persuasive messages, they fall somewhere on the continuum between the two extremes of central and peripheral processing, depending on how many thoughts they have. The choice is not really between only two possibilities, central (many thoughts) or peripheral (few or no thoughts). But because persuasion depends on the thoughts we have about a message, cognitive processing (the central or peripheral route to persuasion) matters. Box 2.1 depicts the central–peripheral continuum of message processing.

Box 2.1   The continuum of message processing

central processing   peripheral processing

many thoughts ————————————————— few thoughts

Two variables determine how many thoughts a member of the audience is likely to have when processing persuasive messages: motivation, which is related to involvement in the message topic; and ability. Next we will discuss each of these factors separately.

Motivation and involvement

Involvement concerns the importance of the topic of a persuasive message to the listener. When a listener cares about a topic, is interested in it or believes that it is relevant or salient, that listener is involved in the topic. The topic matters, and the listener is willing to expend the cognitive effort necessary to think about its message. The more a listener is involved in the topic – the more that topic is relevant or important – the more motivation that listener has to think about the message (Petty and Cacioppo 1979). In other words, the amount of involvement influences the amount of motivation to centrally process a message. On the other hand, when a topic seems irrelevant to us, we are uninvolved and less likely to spend the effort to think about a message on that topic. This makes perfect sense: if a message is about a topic that matters to us or affects us, we have a reason (motivation) to pay attention to that message and reflect on its ideas, evidence, and arguments. On the other hand, the less we care about a given topic, the less motivation we will have to spend time thinking carefully about a message on it. A person who cares about the environment is likely to ponder about a message on saving the rainforests or on the effects of air pollution on the ozone layer. Another person, for whom the environment is not a high priority, will be less involved in those topics and likely to produce fewer thoughts about the same messages. So high involvement makes it more likely that an audience member will engage in central processing; low involvement makes peripheral processing more likely.

Another variable which influences the likelihood of central processing is the **need for cognition** (Cacioppo, Petty, and Kao 1984). This is personality trait which varies from person to person and, essentially, it concerns the extent to which a person is likely to reflect on messages (and other things). Some people enjoy crossword puzzles, brain-teasers, riddles, and the like; others are less interested in these kinds of activity. Box 2.2 offers items from the need-for-cognition scale, to illustrate the

---

Box 2.2   Items from the need-for-cognition scale

I would prefer complex to simple problems.

I prefer my life to be filled with puzzles that I must solve.

I feel relief rather than satisfaction after completing a task that required a lot of mental effort.

Thinking is not my idea of fun.

Scoring: Those highly in need for cognition are more likely to agree with the first two statements than the last two.

Source: Cacioppo, Petty, and Kao (1984: 307)

concept. Audience members who are highly in need of cognition are more likely to process a given message centrally than other listeners, whose need for cognition is low.

Ability

However, motivation is not enough to guarantee that central processing will occur. Receivers must also have the **ability** to think about the message. Ability is more complicated than motivation, because several factors can influence the ability to process a message. If audiences are distracted, or too tired, or under the influence of drugs or alcohol, or ill, they will not be able to think carefully about a message. Research has shown that listeners who are distracted as they listen to, or watch, a message produce fewer thoughts about it than those who are not distracted (Osterhouse and Brock 1970; Petty, Wells, and Brock 1976). Other factors also influence the receiver's ability to process a message. Messages that are more difficult to understand should produce fewer thoughts. Message repetition can increase the audience's ability to process a message, although too much repetition could create boredom or tedium, reducing that message's effectiveness (Cacioppo and Petty 1985; Petty and Cacioppo 1979).

If the listener knows little about a topic, or if a message is difficult to understand (full of unfamiliar terms, confusing, spoken too fast, or with a thick accent), ability is impaired and central processing is unlikely, regardless of how important the topic is to the audience. Some of these factors (an audience that is tired or ill) cannot be controlled by the persuader. However, you can work to make your messages relevant to the audience (chapter 5, on audience analysis, will help here), and you can make them clear and easy to process (chapter 6, on organization, and chapter 7, on factors of interest, will help). So high ability to process a particular messages enables central processing, whereas low ability interferes with thinking about it. If we think only of the extremes (high or low motivation, high or low ability), central processing is only likely to occur when both motivation and ability are high. Table 2.2 shows the relationship between motivation, ability, and type of processing.

You will notice from table 2.2 that only one of these four combinations of motivation and ability leads to central processing. We do not know how often persuaders face each kind of audience (low motivation and high ability, for example, might be much more common than high motivation and low ability). Still, the most common form of processing is probably not central. If true, given the ELM's prediction about the difference between attitude changes reached through these two processes, this means that

Table 2.2 The listener and the type of processing

Listener	Type of processing
low motivation, low ability	peripheral
low motivation, high ability	peripheral
high motivation, low ability	peripheral
high motivation, high ability	central

many attitudes are impermanent (that is, less likely to persist), exert less influence on behavior, and are more vulnerable to change from other persuaders.

However, the variables of motivation and ability also exist on a continuum (i.e. they are not limited either to high or to low levels). This is why processing is best understood as a continuum that ranges from peripheral to central (recall box 2.1). When ability is low, increases in motivation do little to increase the number of thoughts in response to a persuasive message. If a person is distracted or very tired (has low ability), higher levels of motivation may create a few more thoughts, but not many. Similarly, when motivation is low, increases in ability do little to increase the number of thoughts. However, when motivation and ability both increase, the number of thoughts increases slowly at first, but with higher levels of motivation and ability a large number of thoughts is likely to emerge.

Favorable and Unfavorable Thoughts

It is important to realize that simply having thoughts is not enough for persuasion to occur. A receiver's cognitions (thoughts) can be **favorable**, agreeing with the message, or **unfavorable**, disagreeing with the message. Thinking a large number of unfavorable thoughts, or disagreeing with the message, is not likely to cause attitude change. A successful persuader encourages the audience to think favorable thoughts (and lots of them). One way to encourage favorable thoughts is to agree with your audience. If an audience likes a particular product, messages supporting that product are likely to create favorable thoughts. However, persuaders usually cannot switch their topic to match the audience's likes. Your job or goal will almost certainly be to persuade people to buy a particular product, vote for a certain candidate, and engage in a specific action.

One factor that influences the valence of the thoughts receivers have is argument quality or strength. For example, the ideas that a truck has a large cargo capacity, that it has a powerful engine, and that it is reliable are probably seen as strong arguments by most buyers. On the other hand, the argument that it will run in both May and August is a weak argument (every truck can, and should work in every month of the year). It should come as no surprise to learn that strong arguments are more persuasive than weak ones (Benoit 1987; Cacioppo, Petty, and Morris 1983; Petty, Cacioppo, and Goldman 1981). Strong arguments create more favorable thoughts and fewer unfavorable thoughts than weak arguments (Benoit 1987; Petty and Cacioppo 1984). Furthermore, the influence of argument quality is greater on involving than uninvolving topics (Andrews and Shimp 1990; Petty, Cacioppo 1984). So, persuaders can increase the likelihood that an audience will have favorable thoughts by working hard to include strong, high-quality arguments in persuasive messages.

Notice that, as they say about "beauty," the quality or strength of an argument is "in the eye of the beholder." For example, if you are in the market for a truck but you have a very tight budget, arguments about the price of different trucks will be very important to you. On the other hand, if you have a generous budget ("price is no object: I want the best truck money can buy"), then arguments about the cost of a truck will be much less important. Notice that the price of a truck is a fact: An argument about a truck's price can be true but still not be a strong argument. Of course, if you believe an argument is not true ("I don't think this salesperson is telling the truth about maintenance costs"), that argument will not seem strong to you. But arguments can be factually true and yet not seem strong to the audience. Chapter 5 will discuss the importance of audience attitudes in persuasion.

People who see, hear, or read a message containing a large number of arguments (argument quantity) should produce more favorable cognitive responses than those who receive a message with fewer arguments (Calder, Insko, and Yandell 1974). For example, if you are trying to sell new tires to a customer, you might mention multiple ideas: the tread design provides better traction on wet roads, they are guaranteed for 60,000 miles, they provide a smooth ride, free installation is on offer, they are available with whitewalls. It is possible that the sheer number of arguments will favorably impress the buyer in this case. Many studies have found that messages with more arguments create more attitude change than those with fewer arguments (Calder, Insko, and Yandell 1974; Chaiken 1980; Petty and Cacioppo 1984). Argument quantity, unlike quality, is believed to be a peripheral cue. When receivers notice that a message has a large number of arguments, they have some tendency to accept the message. This effect is most likely to occur on uninvolving topics.

Other peripheral cues (which may be thought of as short-cuts) have also been identified besides quantity of arguments. For example, when receivers perceive the source as physically attractive, they may use attractiveness as a peripheral cue (Petty and Cacioppo 1981). An audience member might think, "This is a very attractive source. I think I should agree." Remember that peripheral processing is more likely to occur when motivation and/or ability to think about the message is low, so deferring to an attractive source (instead of expending the effort to think about the ideas and arguments in the message) may make sense to the listener.

When listeners believe that several sources (rather than a single one) endorse a message position, they may be more likely to accept that message. Harkins and Petty (1981) found that more arguments and more sources, each generate more favorable cognitive responses and a greater attitude change than messages with fewer arguments and sources. All things being equal, an idea that many people accept is more likely to be true than one that few people believe.

Furthermore, source credibility, or the extent to which the audience considers the source to be knowledgeable and/or trustworthy, is usually considered a peripheral cue. Chapter 3 will be devoted to exploring source credibility from the cognitive response perspective. Box 2.3 summarizes key elements of the ELM.

Box 2.3   Summary of key ideas in the ELM

1   People are persuaded by their own thoughts; more favorable and fewer unfavorable thoughts mean more attitude change.
2   Message processing runs on a continuum from central to peripheral.
3   Both motivation and ability are needed for central processing to occur.
4   Argument quality is most important for central processing.
5   Argument quantity, source attractiveness, and multiple sources can be peripheral cues.

Evaluation of the ELM

The ELM is a very powerful theory of persuasion. It recognizes that sometimes audiences are active, thinking about messages and the arguments in those messages. However, the ELM also realizes that at other times receivers are passive and let themselves persuaded on the peripheral route. The ELM identifies two readily understandable conditions that determine whether the listener is doing central or peripheral processing: central processing requires that receivers have both the ability and the motivation to think about a message. The ELM identifies several factors that influence the kind of thoughts listeners are likely to have: involvement, argument quality, argument quantity, credibility. Thus, conceptually, this is a very good theory of persuasion.

Research has produced a great deal of experimental support for the ELM. Some of this research was mentioned above. Eagly and Chaiken (1993) provided a more global summary of the research related to the ELM:

> The assumption that systematic or central route processing requires motivation and ability has been documented in many studies, using a variety of motivational and ability variables: Persuasive argumentation is a more important determinant of persuasion when recipients are motivated and able to process attitude-relevant information than when they are not. There is also substantial empirical support for the hypothesis of these models that heuristic or peripheral cues exert a sizable persuasive impact when motivation or ability for argument processing is low, but little impact when motivation and ability are high. (p. 333)

Thus there is a great deal of research supporting the ELM approach to persuasion and attitude change.

One weakness of this theory, oddly enough, is the metaphor it uses. Petty and Cacioppo state that there are two "routes" to persuasion, central and peripheral. If someone says, "There are two routes you can take from Kansas City to Detroit: via Chicago or via Indianapolis," you would take one or the other but not both in the same trip. However, "central" and "peripheral" are not really two choices but the end points of a continuum. As mentioned earlier in this chapter, a listener can think many thoughts (and be closer to the "central" end of the continuum), a moderate number of thoughts (and be in the middle of the continuum), or few thoughts (and be closer to the "peripheral" end). This is not an either/or choice, as the metaphor two "routes" suggests. In fact, even peripheral processing requires some thought. The receiver must notice, for example, "this persuader seems to be an expert" and then think "if an expert says so, it is probably true" for persuasion via the peripheral route to occur. So the metaphor selected by Petty and Cacioppo to represent central and peripheral processing is probably a poor choice, because it could easily create the impression that message processing is an either/or choice, central or peripheral, rather than a continuum.

Using the ELM to Persuade

Effective use of the ELM requires persuaders to begin by thinking about their goals for the persuasive message. Do you want to create (or reinforce, or change) attitudes that are likely to last, influence your audience's behavior, and be resistant to competing persuasive messages from your opponents or competitors? If so, you may wish to try to facilitate central processing. If you want the audience just to agree with you (but not necessarily to behave in a certain way), and if you are not interested in how long that agreement will last, then peripheral processing might be enough.

The persuader who wants to make use of the insights of the ELM should then think about the audience. Is the topic one that the audience will see as relevant to themselves and their lives? If so, they will probably be involved in the topic, and that makes it more likely that they will engage in central processing. If the audience will not think your message topic affects them, can you relate the message to them? The idea here is that you might be able to persuade your audience that your message is relevant to them. That should increase their involvement in your topic and make central processing more likely. Note that you must relate your topic to your audience at the beginning of your message. You want to increase their involvement early, so they will process the entire speech centrally. We have heard speeches where the persuader gave the audience a great reason to listen – at the end of the speech. Of course, it was too late then; the audience had not paid much attention to the speech because they were not involved or motivated to listen until the very end. Chapter 5 will discuss the importance of the audience and how you can analyze your audience so as to adapt your message to your listeners optimally. If you have reason to believe your audience is high (or low) in their need for cognition, that can influence your approach. You should expect to have to work harder to encourage an audience with a low need for cognition to process a message centrally.

You should also think about the audience's ability to engage in central processing. Will they be distracted from listening to you and thinking about your message? If so, can you do anything to lessen the distractions? Make sure your speech is clear. If you are disorganized, vague, or confusing, that will interfere with their ability to do central processing (chapter 6 offers advice about how to organize messages, and chapter 8 will help you express ideas clearly). Receivers must have both the motivation and the ability to process your message centrally (or, to speak most precisely, the greater the receiver's motivation and ability, the more central processing will occur).

Finally, you need to use strong, high quality arguments in your speech. Chapter 5 will provide advice about understanding your particular audience, which can help you select ideas that will appeal to it. Every audience is different, and arguments or ideas that appear strong to one may seem weak to another. If the audience is likely to use central processing when they think about your message, you will be more effective if you can include arguments that your particular audience sees as strong. Chapter 9 will help deal with hostile or multiple audiences, which are particularly challenging. Furthermore, chapter 7 will offer advice on how to strengthen the content (ideas, arguments) of your message.

However, we want to talk about peripheral processing too. Sometimes your persuasive purpose does not require central processing. It is also possible that you do not believe you can motivate your audience and/or overcome factors that impede their ability to engage in central processing. In these situations, you can optimize your message for peripheral processing. Work to ensure that your audience perceives you as an expert (chapter 3 discusses this topic). Take the time to enhance your attractiveness (but always keep your audience in mind; for example, wearing a tuxedo or an expensive gown might favorably impress some people in certain situations; with other people or in other situations formal dress could easily cause your audience to laugh at you). Remember to offer several arguments for those engaged in peripheral processing. If many people agree with you, make sure the audience knows that multiple sources agree. Provide your audience with cues or short-cuts that make them more likely to agree with your message.

The main idea is to keep it in mind that persuasion flows from the audience's thoughts about your message and its topic. Try to understand your audience, so you can anticipate how many thoughts, and of what kind, your message is likely to evoke. Make an effort to encourage more favorable thoughts; try your best to avoid provoking unfavorable thoughts. No theory can guarantee success, but the ELM provides insights into how persuasion works and into what you can do to improve your chances of success.

Glossary

Ability: being able to give full attention to the message.
Boomerang effect: a situation where the audience member becomes less favorable to the persuasive message after hearing it.
Central route to persuasion: a process in which the audience member considers the content of a message carefully.
Cognitions: thoughts and feelings: beliefs, attitudes, and values.
Cognitive response model: model in which persuasion occurs as a result of one's thoughts or cognitions regarding a persuasive message.
Favorable thoughts: thoughts in agreement with one or several ideas in a message.
Involvement: the importance or personal relevance of a topic to a listener.
Need for cognition: a personality trait which indicates the likelihood that an individual will engage in central route processing.
Peripheral route to persuasion: a situation where the audience considers shortcut cues.
Valence: primary characteristic of being favorable or unfavorable to a message.
Unfavorable thoughts: thoughts in disagreement with one or several ideas in a message.

Chapter 3

The Source of Persuasive Messages: Credibility

Credibility refers to the impression produced by the source of a message held by the audience. For over 2,000 years we have recognized that the source of a message can affect persuasion. In the fourth century BC, Aristotle observed: "We believe good men more fully and more readily than others; this is true generally whatever the question is, and absolutely where exact certainty is impossible and opinions divided" (1954: 1356ª6–8). In modern times many would acknowledge that source credibility is an important factor in persuasion (e.g. Benoit 1991; Hass 1981). Petty and Cacioppo (1981) wrote: "The expertise of the source of a message is one of the most important features of the persuasion situation and one of the earliest variables to be investigated" (p. 235). This chapter will explain how, and when, credibility influences persuasion.

Most messages do not stand alone, but they are created and conveyed by sources. When the audience knows the identity of the source of a persuasive message, their beliefs about the source can influence persuasion. For example, when a huckster on late night television offers to sell us a cure for cancer, we should be skeptical. But if the person announcing a cancer treatment is a research scientist at the National Cancer Institute we are more likely to believe this claim. So, one dimension or characteristic of sources is **expertise**: how knowledgeable is the source on the topic of the persuasive message?

Another dimension on which sources vary is **trustworthiness** – or, to phrase it negatively, bias. Consider these two messages:

1   The legal system must show compassion. Sentences are too harsh.
2   Criminal justice is too lenient. It is important to punish law-breakers harshly.

When one audience was told that the first message was from a convicted felon, they were not persuaded. But when another group was told that same message was from a district attorney (a criminal prosecutor), that message was more persuasive. On the other hand, when the audience believed the second message was from a DA, they were not persuaded. When a different audience was told that the second message was from a convict, persuasion occurred (Walster, Aronson, and Abrahams 1966). We assume that a DA, whose job is to punish criminals, will support stricter sentencing, whereas a criminal should be expected to advocate leniency. The assumption is that a source's bias or self-interest (prosecutors want to be tough on crime; criminals want leniency) will color or prejudice their statements. On the other hand, when people make statements that appear to be against their own self-interest (a criminal advocating harsher sentences or a DA speaking for leniency), we are more likely to be persuaded. We might think something like: "If a district attorney thinks sentences are too harsh, they must be too harsh." So the same message coming from different sources can have different effects on the audience. In this case, we are more likely to be persuaded by messages from sources which appear to be objective than by sources we think are biased.

Message sources vary on other dimensions as well. For example, some sources appear to be more **similar** to their audiences than other sources, as when a student speaks to other students or a lawyer addresses a group of attorneys (see e.g. Berscheid 1985). Some sources are perceived to be more physically **attractive** than other sources, which is why many products use beautiful models to sell products (see for instance Berscheid and Walster 1974; Chaiken 1979; Kahle and Homer 1985). Wilson and Sherrell's meta-analysis (1993) (a statistical way to add together the results of many individual studies conducted by different authors) found that the effects of expertise and trustworthiness on persuasion are greater than the effects of attractiveness or similarity. For this reason, expertise and trustworthiness will be the focus of this chapter.

Cognitive Response Analysis of Credibility

How does credibility work? You are probably familiar with the phrase, "Take what he said with a grain of salt." This is a suggestion that, because of who or what "he" is, his comment should be devalued rather than accepted at face value. If Joe said, "Everyone hates that TV show," we should not believe that "everyone" hates it; perhaps we should believe instead that "many" people hate it. Joe is thought to have extreme attitudes or reactions and we need to take his excessive views into account when we think about whether to accept his statement. The statement, "take it with a grain of salt" suggests that our reactions to a message and its source are separate: first, we figure out the meaning of the message; then we consider the source and, if necessary, we devalue the message to reflect the limitations or biases of the source. It is possible that credibility works the way this common phrase suggests: We begin by considering the message itself, and then we devalue that message if the source is biased or not knowledgeable about the topic. On the other hand, if the source is highly credible, perhaps we should begin by considering the message and then "add" something to the impact of the message in order to reflect the special expertise of the source.

However, research shows that credibility does not work this way. The nature of the source affects persuasion by influencing how we think about, or process, the message. Studies have shown that source credibility has effects on persuasion only if the source is identified before the message is heard or read. For example, Ward and McGinnies (1974; see also O'Keefe 1987) found that, as we would expect, when sources were identified (as experts or non-experts) before a message, messages from experts were more persuasive than messages from a non-expert. However, when those sources were identified after the messages had been heard or read, there was no difference in attitude change between high and low credibility sources. Similarly, Greenberg and Miller (1966) reported that low credibility sources hindered persuasion only when they were identified (as not credible) before the message. If an audience is told that a source was unqualified or biased after they had already heard or read the message, this knowledge about the source's defects does not reduce the persuasiveness of the message. Notice that attractive sources, unlike experts, are just as persuasive when identified after a message as before it.

You will recall from chapter 2 that the cognitive response model explains that persuasion occurs when we think about messages. If we think positive or favorable thoughts about a message, we are persuaded; if we think negative or unfavorable thoughts about a message, we are not persuaded. When we are told that a source is credible (expert and/or trustworthy) before we hear the message, that information about the source is likely to incline us to be more accepting of the message. That is, when we know a source is credible from the very start, the fact that we believe the source is credible encourages us to think favorable thoughts (and discourages us from thinking unfavorable thoughts) as we read or listen to the message. Knowing that a source is credible does not guarantee that we will have only favorable thoughts, but it makes them more likely. On the other hand, when we believe that a source is not credible or disreputable before we hear or read the message, our knowledge of the source's defects encourages us to be critical, to think more unfavorable thoughts and fewer favorable thoughts as we listen to, or read, the message. Again, unfavorable thoughts are not guaranteed by a non-credible source, but they are more likely.

But when the source is identified to the audience after the message is over, that message has already been processed. We have already produced our thoughts about the message. If we agreed with the ideas of the message, then we had favorable thoughts; if we disagreed with the message, we had unfavorable thoughts. Our thoughts about the message have already occurred and, once the message is over, it is too late for knowledge that the source is an expert to encourage more favorable thoughts or discourage unfavorable thoughts – or for knowledge that the source is not credible to instigate more unfavorable and fewer favorable thoughts. We must know that a source is credible (or not) before we process the message or the source's credibility cannot possibly affect what we think about the message. So, credibility affects persuasion by influencing how messages attributed to a source are processed. We do not begin by making one judgment of the message (do we agree or disagree with it?) and another judgment of the source (is the source credible or not?) and then combine them together. Our perceptions of the source (if we have any knowledge of who the source is) influence the thoughts we have as we process the message, and the thoughts we have about a message determine whether (and how much) we are persuaded.

Petty and Cacioppo argue that sources can influence persuasion in three ways: "In the ELM, source factors can influence attitude change in three ways: They can serve as arguments, they can serve as cues, and they can affect argument processing" (1986a: 205). It may seem odd that a source can be (or serve as) an argument. However, if Nicole Kidman endorses a beauty product, her personal beauty might be seen as evidence that the cosmetic works effectively. Sources can also serve as peripheral cues, as when an audience member thinks something like: "I'm not excited enough about this topic to analyze all the specifics, but this source seems to know what she is talking about, so I will agree with her." In that example, the source's apparent expertise ("she knows what she is talking about") is a short-cut for deciding whether to agree with the message.

Finally, source characteristics can influence argument processing, or cognitive responses to the ideas in the message. Recall from chapter 2 that there are two important aspects of cognitive responses: their valence (favorable or unfavorable) and their number. Credibility can affect argument processing in two different ways. First, the audience's beliefs about the nature of the source of a persuasive message can cause what is referred to as "**biased scanning**," which means that one kind of thought is more likely than another. In other words, credibility can alter the proportion or ratio of favorable to unfavorable thoughts without changing the total number of thoughts (affecting valence but not the number of thoughts).

This biased scanning effect can be illustrated with a study on trustworthiness. Benoit and Kennedy (1999) investigated the cognitive responses and persuasiveness of three kinds of source testimony: objective, biased, and reluctant. **Objective** testimony has no self-interest in the topic, no reason to favor one side over the other. These are sources we can trust. **Biased** testimony comes from a person who has a reason to take the position he or she does. In the example at the beginning of this chapter, a district attorney, whose job is to punish criminals, can be expected to favor stricter sentencing of criminals. Biased sources are less trustworthy. **Reluctant** testimony occurs when a source advocates a position against his or her own self-interest. The criminal who argues for stricter sentences illustrates reluctant testimony. These sources are considered trustworthy too, because it is clear that their self-interest is not making them shade the truth.

Benoit and Kennedy found that both objective and reluctant testimony produced more favorable and fewer unfavorable thoughts than biased testimony, which of course yielded fewer favorable and more unfavorable thoughts (see table 3.1). In other words,

Table 3.1   Effects of the source on cognitive responses and persuasion: biased scanning

	Cognitive responses		
Source	Favorable	Unfavorable	Persuasive?
Objective	more	fewer	yes
Reluctant	more	fewer	yes
Biased	fewer	more	no

the kind of thoughts produced from messages attributed to objective and reluctant sources was biased toward favorable and away from unfavorable. The kind of thoughts produced from biased testimony was tilted away from favorable and toward unfavorable thoughts. There is no difference in the total number of thoughts produced from these three kinds of sources; the only difference was the proportion of favorable to unfavorable thoughts.

As should be expected from the cognitive responses, both objective and reluctant testimony were more persuasive than biased testimony. These three different kinds of sources did not change the number of thoughts produced in response to a persuasive message; they changed the relative proportion of favorable and unfavorable thoughts. More favorable and fewer favorable thoughts (and more persuasion) from the objective and reluctant sources; fewer favorable and more unfavorable thoughts (and less persuasion) from the biased sources. So, one way that credibility can affect persuasion is to shift the relative proportion of favorable and unfavorable thoughts. The more favorable and the fewer unfavorable thoughts, the more persuasion should occur.

Second, credibility can influence argument processing by altering the total number of thoughts. Believing that a source is credible (either an expert or someone trustworthy, or both) can reduce our motivation to think about a message. In most cases, persuaders are trying to change the attitudes of audience members. Table 3.2 shows the effects of credibility with messages that try to change attitudes (rather than reinforce existing attitudes). These messages are often called counter-attitudinal, because the message runs counter to the audience's attitudes. The most likely kind of thought produced by a counter-message (one that disagrees with the audience) is, of course, unfavorable. Adding a highly credible source to a counter-attitudinal message tends to reassure the audience, making them less likely to question, criticize, or challenge the message. This means they have less motivation to think about the message. Because the audience's natural reaction to a message that disagrees with their own attitudes is to have unfavorable thoughts, a credible source reduces

Table 3.2   Effects of credibility with a counter-attitudinal (disagreeing) message

	Number of unfavorable thoughts	Persuasion
Low credibility source	more	less
High credibility source	fewer	more

motivation to scrutinize the message, reducing the number of thoughts they produce. Because they are prone to think unfavorable thoughts to such messages, the
audience ends up producing fewer unfavorable thoughts. Messages with many unfavorable thoughts are highly unlikely to be very persuasive. Smokers have a reason to
disagree with an anti-smoking message, producing many unfavorable thoughts.
However, when that message is given by an expert, such as the surgeon general, even
smokers might have fewer unfavorable thoughts in response to an anti-smoking
message. If the audience has fewer unfavorable thoughts (because the highly credible
source reduced their motivation to question the message), they should be more persuaded than if they had many negative thoughts. Of course, the greatest amount of
persuasion would arise from messages that produced many favorable thoughts;
however, this explains one way in which credibility helps the persuasion process: it
makes audiences less likely to think unfavorable thoughts about a message.

Table 3.2 shows that low credibility sources are generally less persuasive than
other sources. It is also possible that a disreputable (low credibility) source will provoke suspicion in the audience. Because the audience thinks the source is not knowledgeable about the topic, they may be more critical, thinking more unfavorable
thoughts. So, a highly credible source can reassure the audience, reducing unfavorable thoughts, and a disreputable source can arouse suspicion, increasing unfavorable
thoughts. Again, these two effects are likely to occur with counter-attitudinal messages, to which the likely response is unfavorable.

However, that does not necessarily mean that high credibility sources are always
most effective. Table 3.3 explains a situation which is less common and unexpected.
Moderately credible sources can be more effective than highly credible sources when
the message agrees with the audience. Some persuasive messages agree with the
audience (they are pro-attitudinal). Unlike counter-attitudinal messages, the most
likely response to a message which agrees with the audience is to produce favorable
thoughts. When a highly credible source gives a pro-attitudinal message, effectiveness may decrease. The reason is that if the credibility of the source reduces the
motivation to scrutinize a message, the audience in this case will actually produce
fewer favorable thoughts than if they had no idea who the source is. So, when the
message agrees with the audience, having fewer thoughts (because a highly credible
source reduces the audience's motivation to think about the message) means having
fewer favorable thoughts, and this means being less persuaded (Sternthal, Dholakia,
and Leavitt 1978). We want to make it clear that the comparison we are making is
between a highly credible source and a moderately credible source. We are not suggesting that a disreputable source will be more persuasive than an expert (a disreputable source would probably encourage biased scanning, producing more

Table 3.3   Effects of credibility with a pro-attitudinal (agreeing) message

	Number of favorable thoughts	Persuasion
Moderately credible source	more	more
Highly credible source	fewer	less

unfavorable and less favorable thoughts). However, when the message agrees with the audience, identifying the source as an expert may impede persuasion. Sources who give pro-attitudinal messages should be more effective if they adopt a bit of modesty, so they would appear moderately, but not highly, credible.

In summary, the cognitive response model holds that persuasion occurs when people think about messages. The more the favorable and the fewer the unfavorable thoughts produced in response to a message, the greater the persuasion. Credibility (when sources are identified before the message) can influence the relative proportion of favorable to unfavorable thoughts (biased scanning) and it can influence the total number of thoughts. This section also explained a little-known effect of credibility: when a message is pro-attitudinal, a highly expert source may be less effective than a moderately credible source (because a highly credible source can reduce the total number of thoughts produced, whereas pro-attitudinal messages are likely to produce favorable thoughts).

Involvement and Credibility

Listeners who are highly involved really care about the topic of the persuasive message; the subject is very important to them. Therefore highly involved receivers are likely to be motivated (by their level of involvement) to think carefully about the message, regardless of who it is from. This means that knowing that the source is an expert is unlikely to decrease the motivation of a highly involved listener. Thus, like other peripheral cues, source expertise is likely to have more influence on uninvolved than on involved receivers. Research shows that credibility appeals, which are often peripheral rather than central cues, are more likely to influence attitude change on uninvolving than involving topics (Petty, Cacioppo, and Schumann 1983). In other words, if your audience is involved in your topic, do not expect that credibility appeals will be likely to sway them very much. They will be more concerned with, and more influenced by, the content of the message than the nature of the source.

Intrinsic and Extrinsic Credibility

As we indicated at the beginning of this chapter, credibility refers to perceptions of the source held by the audience. In cases where the audience believes that the source is an expert and/or trustworthy, the source has high credibility for the audience. This section raises the question of exactly when those audience perceptions of the source arise. The audience can come to the message with an impression of the source – the source's prior reputation – and the audience can form an impression of the source based on the message itself. If the message sounds reasonable to the audience, they are likely to develop a favorable impression of the source; if the message sounds extreme, ridiculous, silly, or stupid, the audience will probably develop an unfavorable impression of the source. The first kind of credibility, prior reputation, is considered **extrinsic** because it is external to the message. The second form of credibility, formed as the audience processes the message, is considered **intrinsic** because it arises from the audience's reactions to the message itself (credibility created by the message).

Although this distinction between extrinsic and intrinsic credibility is rarely discussed, the two towering rhetoricians of the ancient world, Aristotle and Isocrates, had indeed different ideas about credibility. For Isocrates, credibility referred to the speaker's prior reputation (extrinsic credibility):

> The man who wishes to persuade people will not be negligent as to the matter of character; no, on the contrary, he will apply himself above all to establish a most honourable name among his fellow-citizens; for who does not know that words carry a greater conviction when spoken by men of good repute than when spoken by men who live under a cloud, and that the argument which is made by a man's life is of more weight than that which is furnished by words? (1976: 278)

Isocrates' references to "men of good repute" and "men who live under a cloud" indicate that he was concerned with prior reputation. He even explicitly juxtaposes the "argument which is made by a man's life" (extrinsic credibility) with "that which is furnished by words" in the speech itself (intrinsic credibility). Clearly, for Isocrates, credibility was extrinsic to the speech, consisting in the speaker's prior reputation.

By contrast, Aristotle's conception of credibility (he called it "ethos") was intrinsic, consisting in the impression of the speaker created by the speech itself: ethos "should be achieved by what the speaker says, not by what people think of him before he begins to speak" (1954: 1356^{a}8–10). Aristotle clearly rejects the idea that "ethos" concerns the speaker's prior reputation ("not by what people think of him before he begins to speak"); for him, credibility is developed in the speech ("achieved by what the speaker says"). This is an intrinsic conception of credibility.

This distinction between the two ways of creating credibility is important for two reasons. First, extrinsic credibility is a more reliable influence on persuasion. Benoit (1991a) reviewed a number of experimental studies which varied depending on whether or not the audience was told the speaker was credible before the speech (extrinsic credibility or prior reputation) and studies which attempted to create credibility from the speech itself (intrinsic credibility; for example by including more evidence or stronger arguments in one speech than another). When credibility was created via the speaker's prior reputation, there was a consistent increase in the persuasion instilled by high credibility sources. However, when credibility was created in the speech itself (and the speakers had no prior reputation for the audience), credibility did not have a consistent effect on persuasion. Some speakers with no prior reputation were seen as more credible after the speech and were more persuasive; in other cases speakers were perceived as more credible after the speech but were not more persuasive. Intrinsic credibility does not work as consistently as extrinsic credibility, which underscores how important the message can be in persuasion.

Benoit explains these results through the cognitive response model. You will recall that sources must be identified as credible before the speech in order to influence the way the audience processes a message. With extrinsic credibility, the audience believes the speaker is credible before the speaker begins the message (because it is the speaker's prior reputation that created high credibility). This means that the speaker's credibility can influence the way the audience processes the entire message. However, with intrinsic credibility, created by the message itself, the audience's processing of the message cannot be influenced by their perception that the speaker is credible until after the point in the speech when the audience decides that the speaker is credible. Suppose the audience does not decide that the speaker is highly credible until at, or near, the end of a persuasive speech. That would mean that any unfavorable thoughts to the message would already have been experienced by the audience by the time they finally decided he or she was credible. It would be no different from identifying the speaker as an expert after the speech was finished, which, as we know, does not have an effect on persuasion. So, if the message creates the impression that the speaker is credible early enough to alter the processing of a substantial portion of the message – early enough to reduce the number of unfavorable thoughts noticeably – intrinsic credibility can help persuasion. But if the message does not convince the audience that the speaker is credible until the end of the message, intrinsic credibility will not be helpful.

The fact that extrinsic credibility is more consistently effective than intrinsic credibility means, of course, that persuaders are better advised to rely on extrinsic credibility (prior reputation) to enhance their persuasiveness. Sources who have a positive prior reputation should know how to make use of it in their persuasive messages. However, the second reason why this distinction between extrinsic and intrinsic credibility is important is that some sources cannot use extrinsic credibility. Students, newly hired employees, parents trying to influence others at Parents and Teachers Association (PTA) meetings, and others may simply not appear credible to the audience. Some people are not experts on the topic of their messages and some people are (or appear to be) biased. Those speakers do not have a positive prior reputation; they cannot use extrinsic credibility. They must rely on intrinsic credibility instead; they must use the words of the speech to try to enhance their credibility with the audience.

Finally, it is important to realize that credibility exists in the minds of the audience. It does not matter that you truly are an expert, or trustworthy, if your audience believes otherwise. If, for some reason, an audience believes that the attorney general is not an expert on the law, she will lack credibility with this audience regardless of how well she actually knows the law. Of course, if you are qualified to speak on the topic, if you really are objective, that should make it easier to convince your audience that they should consider you to be credible. The attorney general may find it easy to convince this audience that she is knowledgeable about the law, but she must make the effort, or her credibility will be low for this group. Nor does it matter what other groups of people might think: a speaker is credible only if the audience addressed believes he or she is credible.

Using Credibility in Persuasion

This understanding of the role of credibility in persuasion can be helpful to persuaders. First, take steps to help your audience come to the conclusion that you are an expert on your topic (except remember that moderately credible sources are more persuasive on pro-attitudinal topics). Audience analysis (chapter 5) can help you determine whether your audience perceives you as credible. If necessary, take steps to ensure that your audience knows your qualifications. When speaking in person, it is often possible to have someone to introduce you to the audience. Make sure they know that you are knowledgeable and unbiased on your topic (unless you are giving a pro-attitudinal speech; then appearing moderately credible, rather than highly credible, would be better). One of the authors of this book (Bill) once spoke to a group of alumni from his university. He sent an email to the moderator explaining why he was qualified to speak on the topic; however, she said nothing about his background when she introduced him to the group. It is likely that the audience would have been more receptive to his message if they had known his qualifications to talk on the topic. If an introduction is not an option, you can mention your expertise near the beginning of your presentation (however, you should try to avoid sounding like a braggart). If the message is written, it can be useful to include the qualifications of the source in the message.

Keep in mind that you want to appear trustworthy to your audience as well as knowledgeable on your topic. Without dwelling on the point (you want to focus most of your message on your topic rather than yourself), let your audience know that you are independent and objective. If they believe you are self-interested or biased, your message will probably be less effective.

Those speakers who do not have clear qualifications as experts on the topic must rely on intrinsic credibility, using the words and ideas of the speech to establish their credibility with the audience. Those who may appear untrustworthy to the audience should attempt to display their objectivity in the speech. You may be able to explain that you are not self-interested in the topic (or that you are providing reluctant testimony, arguing against your own self interests).

Several chapters in this book will be useful in developing your messages in ways to enhance your intrinsic credibility with the audience. First, credibility exists in the mind of your audience. Avoid making statements that your audience is likely to consider unreasonable; take their views into account as you develop your message (chapter 5). Make certain that your persuasive message is well organized, so that your points will appear clear and logical (chapter 6). Make sure that you offer strong arguments and appropriate evidence to support those ideas (chapter 7). Finally, it is important to keep in mind that, for credibility to be effective, the audience must believe the source is credible at (or near) the beginning of the message. For example, some magazine articles provide an author identification note at the end of the article. This is, of course, too late for the author's credentials to enhance the credibility of the source. If the audience learns that you are knowledgeable and trustworthy at the end of your message, it will be too late to help. The audience may have already had too many unfavorable thoughts for your message to persuade them. Try to establish your credibility at the very beginning of the message.

Of course, if your audience is highly involved in your topic, their perceptions of your credibility may not influence their reactions to your message. We recommend that you focus most of your effort on providing strong arguments for involved audiences. Still, you might want to make sure that they are aware of your qualifications to speak on the topic, so there would be no risk that perceptions of low credibility will impair your persuasiveness.

The source of a persuasive message matters in persuasion. Expertise and trustworthiness are the two most influential aspects of sources. A person's credibility exists in the audience's perceptions of the speaker. When you have a positive prior reputation, this can enhance your persuasiveness. However, if you do not have special qualifications, you can enhance your (intrinsic) credibility by taking special pains to show that you are knowledgeable and reasonable are in your speech.

Glossary

Attractiveness: property of being physically, visually appealing.

Biased: a source with self-interest in the topic; not neutral or objective.

Biased scanning: a situation where favorable or unfavorable thoughts are more likely to occur when processing a message.

Credibility: impression of the source held by the audience.

Expertise: the amount of knowledge, experience, or training a source has on a topic.

Extrinsic credibility: credibility which is external to the message; prior reputation of the source.

Intrinsic credibility: credibility created by the message.

Objective: a source without self-interest in a topic; unbiased.

Reluctance: advocating a message against the source's own self-interest.

Similarity: extent to which an audience is like the audience.

Trustworthiness: audience perception that they can believe the source.

Chapter 4

Ethical Concerns

Chapter Contents

Fourteen UCLA football players submitted applications for handicapped parking tags. Although the applications required a signature from a physician, they had been allegedly submitted with the signatures and medical identification numbers of non-existent doctors. The players were charged with misdemeanors for illegally possessing the handicapped tags when they were not disabled ("Athletes claimed," 2000). Their actions were illegal. Were they also unethical?

A *New York Times* Pulitzer Prize-winning reporter resigned after being suspended for filing a story with his byline, which was in fact researched in large part by a freelance reporter. This followed another resignation at the *Times*, when the newspaper investigated another reporter for fraud, plagiarism, and inaccuracies in 36 out of 73 recent articles, including some high-profile stories on sniper shootings (Burghart 2003). Were these reporters unethical?

Ethical concerns have been highlighted in the news. Eighty percent believe that leaders do not deserve to be trusted as much as in the past and 61 percent believe that there is evidence of a moral collapse (German, Gronbeck, Ehninger, and Monroe 2000). In a survey of college students, many admitted to behaviors that could be classified as unethical: 87 percent had cheated on written work and 70 percent cheated on a test at least one time; 49 percent had collaborated with others on an assignment that was supposed to have been done independently while 52 percent had copied from someone else; 26 percent had plagiarized (Bramucci 2003). A survey of high school students suggests that 74 percent cheated on exams, 86 percent lied to teachers, and 39 percent lied in job interviews (Alm 2002). There is a sense that many people have lost their way and are finding it more difficult to make ethical decisions.

Ethical Issues and Defining Ethics

A persuader must be particularly concerned about ethical decisions. Persuasive messages often attempt to change the behavior of audiences. Unethical behaviors by a persuasive speaker can mislead an audience and change the way the audience believes or behaves. This possibility is why persuasion inherently involves **ethical issues**, situations in which an ethical question about what ought to be done will occur. Johannesen (1996) has outlined three conditions when ethical issues arise:

1   The behavior has a significant impact on others.
2   The behavior involves a conscious choice of means and ends.
3   The behavior can be judged by standards of right and wrong.

If persuaders are successful, they can create, reinforce, or change an audience's attitudes or behaviors. Because a persuader can potentially have a significant impact on another person, ethical issues must be weighed carefully. Ethical issues are brought into play when persuaders have a conscious choice of means and ends. Persuaders choose from the available strategies (i.e. means) to accomplish their purposes (i.e. ends). The reporter in the example we started with might argue that his end was to write a story by a deadline and his means to accomplish that goal consisted in using the freelancer's notes. In this case, we might argue that the "ends did not justify the means." His deadline does not justify passing off another's work as his own. An issue is also an ethical one when standards of rightness or wrongness can be applied to the behavior. These standards are based on particular ethical perspectives. When we judge the UCLA football players' alleged faking of physician signatures to get a handicapped tag to be wrong because this abused a system intended to help those who were truly disabled, we have used a utilitarian ethics standard (we assessed the effects of their actions and who was affected) to make an ethical judgment.

Johannesen defined **ethics** as "the general and systematic study of what ought to be the grounds and principles for right and wrong human behavior" (1996: 1–2). According to the *Internet Encyclopedia of Philosophy*, "The field of ethics, also called moral philosophy, involves systematizing, defending, and recommending concepts of right and wrong behavior" (Fieser and Dowden 2001). Ethics provides a guide for making decisions about what is and is not acceptable behavior.

This chapter will underscore some important ethical issues for the persuader and the audience of persuasion. The chapter describes six ethical perspectives that establish grounds and principles for assessing the rightness and wrongness of behavior and then takes up the issue of the ethical responsibilities of audiences.

Ethical Perspectives

Ethical perspectives offer different lenses for viewing the rightness or wrongness of human behavior. Each perspective will lead you to ask a different set of questions to evaluate your own and others' behaviors in order to make an ethical decision or judgment. It is not our intention to impose an ethical standard but instead to encourage you strongly to think about your decisions consciously and find an ethical perspective or a combination of perspectives to ground your own ethical decision-making. Whether you are an audience member who might be persuaded to do something unethical or you are a persuader who might (purposely or accidentally) persuade others to behave unethically, you need to understand ethical issues in persuasion. Although there are many ethical perspectives, we have chosen six that we think are most relevant for persuasion: the human nature, the dialogical, the utilitarian, the situational, the legal, and the feminist perspectives on ethics. No single approach is acceptable to everyone, so we will describe criticisms of each to help you choose the perspective that best suits your value system.

The human nature perspective on ethics

The **human nature perspective on ethics** assesses behavior as ethical when the essence of human nature is preserved. It places great value on the characteristics that make human beings distinctive. Actions taken by a persuader which diminish these qualities are considered unethical, whereas actions which enhance them are judged as ethical. Aristotle believed that the ability to make rational choices was a distinctive characteristic of human nature. Thus, persuaders who restrict their audience's abilities to make reasoned choices would be acting unethically from this perspective. They might do this by altering or withholding information. Using the human nature perspective, we would ask the questions given in box 4.1.

Consider the example of a speaker who was doing research for a persuasive speech on the effectiveness of diet drugs. She found excellent evidence in medical journals that endorsed many of these prescription drugs, but also found an article that explained

Box 4.1   Questions about the human nature perspective

Did the persuader insure that the audience could make a rational choice?

Did the persuader preserve the essence of the humanness of the audience?

that the authors had been paid to publish these favorable articles ("Diet drug," 1999). As a result of that money, the articles downplayed the negative effects of the drugs. The speaker decided to use the evidence from the medical journals anyway, because it supported her point that the drugs in question were a safe way to lose weight. But the human nature perspective would indicate that the audience was not given the information they needed to make a rational choice about these drugs. They were misled about the risks of these drugs on the basis of evidence which the speaker knew to be biased (but did not reveal this fact). From the human nature perspective, one would argue that the behavior of this persuasive speaker was unethical. What do you think?

Critics of the human nature perspective on ethics argue that there are two problems with using this approach. The first problem is that there is little agreement on the essence of being human. The human nature perspective depends on identifying these characteristics before judging that persuaders have restricted the essentially human attributes. Even if Aristotle's criterion of rational choice is accepted as unique to human nature, a second problem emerges. In practice, it is often very difficult to determine how much information an audience must be provided to insure that their rational choices have not been impeded. For example, does this mean that all persuasion must include both sides of an argument on an issue? How does a persuader do this when they are working within a time limit? It can be difficult to do justice to an issue and provide the necessary information if there is a limited amount of time to speak. How can a persuader be sure to treat both sides of an issue fairly?

The dialogical perspective on ethics

The **dialogical perspective on ethics** asserts that behavior is ethical when it promotes active interaction that will allow people to achieve their potential. This perspective has three basic assumptions. The first assumption is that ethical situations involve mutual control. Mutual control means that the persuasion process is not a passive one, where a persuader influences an audience. Instead, the persuader is also willing to be persuaded and engages in an interaction in which this can take place. The second assumption is that individuals treat others in ways that will allow them to realize their potential. Third, participants should seek a dialogue rather than a monologue in their interactions with others.

Dialogues can be contrasted with monologues on several dimensions. These **ideal dialogues** are authentic in displaying honesty and sincerity; monologues can be deceptive and manipulative. Dialogues are inclusive because they require perspective-taking and accepting others, while monologues can be dogmatic and restrictive. Ideal dialogues are confirming, supporting, and empathic; monologues are self-centered, contrary, and rigid. Dialogues require the full concentration of the participants and equality, whereas monologues often involve a sense of superiority by one party. In other words, engaging in a dialogue commits an individual to a full-fledged "cards on the table" discussion with an equal where it is quite possible that the outcome will be mutual persuasion. The questions posed when you assess whether a message is ethical according to a dialogical perspective on ethics are given in box 4.2. If a persuader can answer these questions affirmatively, the behavior can be judged as ethical.

Box 4.2 Questions about the dialogical perspective

Did the persuader allow mutual influence to occur in the process?
Did the persuader respect the potential of the audience?
Did real dialogue occur with the audience?

For example, one person wants to convince her best friend to start an exercise program five times a week; so she develops a persuasive message to convince him that this is a good idea. If she is using a dialogic ethic, she must use a dialogue and she must also be willing to be persuaded. It is not enough that she wants what is best for her friend. She makes the arguments that exercising will improve her friend's health; that he will actually notice how much better he feels; that it does not take that much time to do it. He is reluctant to do it even though he agrees with all of the reasons she has given. Instead, he challenges her to exercise with him and to compromise on a more moderate program of three times a week. This perspective would also require that we assess the nature of the interaction between the participants to determine whether the persuader respected the potential of the friend in making her arguments for exercising, and to confirm that the characteristics of a real dialogue occurred during the interaction (i.e. empathy, honesty, support). If the advocate attempted to coerce the friend into exercising, an ideal dialogue would not have taken place.

The dialogical perspective has been criticized for being idealistic and time-consuming. Those who see it as idealistic complain that the real world is aggressive and that "putting your cards on the table" and being empathic, equal, supportive, honest, sincere, and inclusive can be disadvantageous in some highly competitive settings. Others have argued that dialogue requires considerably more time and effort than monologue (this is true!) and the urgency of some situations does not permit a lengthy discussion. In response, advocates of this perspective would ask you to think whether the ends of being more aggressive justify the actions that are often taken in the name of competition. Advocates would also argue that dialogue is worth the time invested in it. The dialogical perspective is designed for situations in which mutual influence is possible and thus mass mediated persuasion, which is typically one way, would be considered a monologue and viewed negatively. According to this perspective, ethical advocates need to seek more opportunities for dialogue with their audiences.

The utilitarian perspective on ethics

A **utilitarian perspective on ethics** assesses the rightness or wrongness of an action by examining the consequences of the behavior. So, it would determine whether the effects of a persuasive message were predominantly positive or negative for a larger number of people. In many ways, a utilitarian perspective is considered very practical because it does not require a consideration of intentions or abstract concepts like the essence of human nature. On the utilitarian perspective, the questions to ask in order to apply the standards of right and wrong are given in box 4.3.

> **Box 4.3**   Questions about the utilitarian perspective
>
> What are the effects of this action?
> Who is affected by this action?
> Are more people affected positively or negatively by this action?

We could apply this perspective to evaluate a persuasive speech in which the speaker said that a message would be about general issues regarding human sexuality and drew a large audience, but actually gave a speech on sexually transmitted diseases. The speaker presented graphic details of the effects of these diseases and the number of college students who are infected each year. These intense fear appeals made some members of the audience extremely anxious, while others vowed to change their sexual practices. The utilitarian perspective would determine the effects of the action (anxiety and safer practices) and who is affected by the action (audience members), and would assess whether more people were affected positively or negatively by the action. This procedure would establish whether the positive results (safer practices) outweighed the deception and the anxiety, which were both negative effects.

Critics of the utilitarian perspective on ethics argue that it can be difficult to assess the consequences of actions. As a case in point, a persuader often needs guidance as to whether to use particular message strategies with an audience. In these cases, the consequences of choices are often unknown. One can make educated guesses about the likely effects, but unintended consequences are always a possibility. In our example of the fear appeals, the advocate may not have predicted that some audience members would become very anxious. Detractors offer a second criticism when they suggest that minority interests are not appreciated in such an approach. The outcomes for the majority are valued in making the assessment. When the negative consequences affect you in the minority group, this is not a particularly appealing approach. For example, if you were among those who experienced great anxiety after hearing the persuasive speech but only a few individuals experienced anxiety, you may still feel that the speaker acted unethically to mislead you into thinking the speech would be about a different topic than the one you actually heard. This perspective does not attempt to minimize the harm to those who are not in the majority.

The situational perspective on ethics

The **situational perspective on ethics** directs our attention toward the context of an action in order to judge whether it is right or wrong. This approach is also known as relativism, because whether an action is ethical is relative, differing according to aspects of the situation. In other words, the judgment of whether an action is ethical is made on a case-by-case basis.

Situations vary dramatically but five factors are commonly described that influence ethical judgments: (1) role of the communicator; (2) audience standards for ethical communication; (3) degree of audience awareness; (4) degree of urgency; (5) audience goals and values (Johannesen 1996; see also box 4.4).

The **role of the communicator** is the part or character assumed by the communicator. We hold some people to higher ethical standards because of the roles they play (e.g. doctors, teachers). For example, lying would seem more unethical if performed by a priest than by a con artist.

The **audience standards** for ethical communication sets out the expectations or norms that govern a particular situation. For example, the norms for the sale of a car may legitimize some hard sell techniques that would be entirely inappropriate for convincing someone to become romantically involved.

The **degree of audience awareness** recognizes that audiences vary in the extent of their knowledge about persuasive strategies and about the topic. Exaggeration in advertising aimed at adults may be considered ethical, but is viewed as unethical when children are targeted.

The **degree of urgency** may alter an ethical judgment. In order to get quick action on a proposal to install security cameras after an assault, a speaker inflates the number of assaults on campus. The speaker argues that it is important to get the cameras installed promptly, and the importance of the matter justifies the slight exaggeration in numbers. The matter is urgent, because taking immediate action can prevent another assault.

The **audience's goals and values** will influence its judgment concerning the ethical nature of particular actions. For example, if an audience values order, civility, and decorum, individuals will probably judge agitation actions taken by social protest groups as unethical. In contrast, audiences who value civil disobedience are much more likely to see these actions as ethical choices.

Box 4.4 Questions about the situational perspective

Does the role of the communicator establish a higher ethical standard?
Does the audience in this situation expect this behavior?
Is the audience fully aware of the persuasive strategies?
Does urgency justify the means used by the persuader?
What are the audience's goals and values and how are these influencing their judgment of the ethics of the persuader?

A few years ago there was a lot of hype about an 18-year-old writer, Riley Weston, who wrote for the television show "Felicity." She was heralded as a rising star and had secured a $500,000 writing and production contract because producers believed she identified with the main character of the television show, a beautiful 18-year-old college freshman. Then a news story revealed that this supposedly 18-year-old writer was actually 32. She responded that the deception never had the purpose to advance her career as a writer, that she had adopted an age that was appropriate to her physical appearance in order to find work as an actress, and that she needed to do this to succeed as an actress because the entertainment business discriminates on the basis of age (Tourtelotte 1998). According to the situational perspective, did she act ethically by changing her age?

You could argue that Riley's actions were ethical because this behavior is expected in the entertainment industry. It is commonplace for actresses to change their ages. Riley Weston was both an actress and a writer, and her audience could have expected that her résumé age was not an accurate indicator of her true age. Riley argued that a sense of urgency compelled her to change her age. She needed the work and felt that the age discrimination justified her actions. These two aspects of the situation could be used to argue that her behavior was ethical. Do you agree?

A persuasive speaker might feel justified in modifying her background to improve credibility with a particular audience. For example, a speaker who was running for school board suggested she had been a member of the Parents and Teachers Association (PTA) for fifteen years. She had not actually been a member although she had attended meetings sporadically. She exaggerated her level of involvement to enhance her résumé for the job, and acted unethically.

One of the most compelling criticisms of the situational perspective on ethics is that it endorses an individualized ethics, that "I'll determine what's right for me, and you can decide what's right for you. Carried to its outer limits, relativism can lead to moral anarchy in which individuals lay claim to no ethical standards at all" (Day 1991: 52). Advocates have rejected this criticism and argued that situational ethics does not abandon standards entirely, but does allow for consideration of situational variations.

The legal perspective on ethics

The **legal perspective on ethics** equates ethics with legality. The behaviors which have been stipulated in rules and laws and interpreted by authorities are also judged as unethical. This perspective appears to be straightforward: a persuader needs only to make sure that the message strategies stayed within the rules or laws. And this ethical standard appears to be easy to apply to others, because the legality of the behaviors can be assessed to determine the rightness or wrongness of the act. The questions that would be asked from the legal perspective are given in box 4.5.

> **Box 4.5** Questions about the legal perspective
>
> What is the relevant law or rule in this instance?
> Have the persuader's behaviors or actions violated this law or rule?

For example, there are ethical rules within a classroom. A speaker must give an original speech. A persuasive speaker who gives a speech that has been given by a previous speaker violates these ethical rules. When a student turned in an outline of a speech with another student's name on it, it was clear that an ethical violation had taken place. He had violated the ethical rules in place for that class and therefore was unethical.

Contrary to appearances, the legal perspective is actually difficult to apply in many cases. First, the law and its interpretations are often convoluted and unintelligible to those who are not trained in the legal profession. To adopt their rules as standards for everyday practice is not practical. Second, there are many instances in which "there ought to be a law" but there is not one. Just because the behavior is not considered illegal, it does not follow that the behavior is ethical.

The feminist perspective on ethics

Although it is important to acknowledge that there are multiple feminist perspectives on ethics, our purpose is to introduce the feminist perspective generally. For that purpose, we have chosen the ethics of care. The **feminist perspective on ethics** suggests that there are two different and valuable voices in the moral development of adults in our society. The male voice is that of an ethics of justice. It emphasizes individual autonomy and independence. Individuals must balance the competing needs of self and others. This system of ethics is rule-centered and uses standards of equality and fairness. Rationality is highly valued. By contrast, the female voice carries an ethics of care. Relationships and the interdependence of self and others are stressed. The standards for assessing rightness and wrongness are compassion and sense of nurture, even as the needs of self and others are taken into account to resolve ethical dilemmas. The ethics of care recognizes the influence of situation on ethical judgments (Gilligan 1982). Feminists argue that, although the male voice is valuable, the dominant role it has played in our culture has minimized the worth of the alternative ethical perspective offered by the feminist ethics of care.

A male voice and **ethics of justice** determines whether each person has been treated equally and fairly. It assesses whether there has been a compelling reason for the action. This ethical perspective also determines whether the relevant rules have been followed. In following a female voice and an **ethics of care**, a different set of issues are important (see box 4.6).

Box 4.6   Questions about the feminist perspective

Have individuals been treated with compassion and respect?
Have situational factors been considered?
Has the interdependence between individuals been accounted for?

A persuasive speaker has completed an audience analysis and realized that a large percentage of his audience smokes and has no intention of quitting. He decides that the best approach is to use fear appeals, and works hard to coerce his audience into giving up. According to the ethics of justice, the speaker has treated all smokers the same. He believed that he was saving lives through his use of fear appeals and coercion. According to an ethics of care, audience members were not treated with compassion and respect. Attempts to coerce behavior were not appreciated. The speaker had not taken into account differences between the smoking members of the audience or between their individual needs. The message also failed to recognize that there would be an effect on others in the smoker's life if the smoker attempted to quit. The message was unlikely to be persuasive; it was also likely to be judged unethical according to the feminist perspective.

Although feminists argue that both voices can be complementary, they recognize that the two may be difficult to reconcile in some situations. This example makes that difficulty apparent. Critics have also argued that the feminist perspective works best in the private sphere, but is less adaptable to the public sphere. The private sphere is the place of family relationships, while the public sphere is the place of business and politics. Feminists respond that both an ethics of care and an ethics of justice are needed to address public issues, and that the public arena can be enriched by incorporating the ethics of care within its ethical perspectives (Tronto 1993).

Ethical Responsibilities of Audiences of Persuasion

So far, we have discussed ethics from the standpoint of the persuader. However, an audience also has an ethical responsibility to be mindful about processing persuasive messages that influence one's core attitudes and behaviors. As audience members, we are exposed to so many persuasive messages that we cannot hope to spend the same amount of time and effort thinking about every message. At the same time, consistent with the elaboration likelihood model that we discussed in chapter 2, audiences should be giving thoughtful consideration to the message when they are motivated and have the ability to think about it. The audience member who is engaging in central processing is not a passive receiver of information but an active part of the persuasive process. Consistent with the human nature perspective on ethics, they should be using their unique capacities as human beings to evaluate arguments and argument quality rationally. For example, messages about whether smoking is harmful are more involving than messages about what brand of catsup to buy. The former message has more ethical implications for the audience than the latter.

In the dialogical perspective on ethics, one of the assumptions is that mutual persuasion is possible. Thus, from this perspective, an ethical responsibility of an audience member would be to participate in the dialogue and to attempt to engage the persuader, with the purpose of winning that person over to his or her view on the issue. This perspective requires others to engage others actively. There is no avoiding, thinking about the issue later, or zoning out in this kind of persuasion.

Audiences have an ethical responsibility to be informed about persuasive strategies. A critical awareness of persuasive strategies and tests of evidence is part of the ethical responsibility of audience members. Within days of the terrible events at the World Trade Center and at the Pentagon, an article appeared in the local newspaper carrying warnings from the State Attorney General that consumers should be wary of the persuasive techniques of scam artists who would use this tragedy to line their own pockets. He urged contributors to avoid groups pushing for immediate or cash donations, and reminded consumers that scam artists often use names that closely resemble a respected charity, to fool those willing to donate ("Disaster Notes," 2001). It is unfortunate that audiences need to be suspicious, but, in being so, audiences help to insure that persuaders do not manipulate a trusting populace. This does not mean that persuaders are any less responsible for their behaviors.

Although audiences have a responsibility to be critical of persuasive strategies, they must temper this with an open-mindedness and readiness to consider issues brought before them by persuaders. Audiences have an ethical responsibility to listen before rejecting ideas. For example, my brother has a very different attitude toward guns from the one we hold. We do not like guns and do not believe that individuals should have guns in their homes. My brother, on the other hand, was a military guard and worked as a policeman for several years. He owns several guns. After discussions with him, we have come to believe that some people who have adequate training can have guns in their homes in a safe way. We would still never want a gun in our house. Audiences who are intolerant of the expression of other ideas allow no room for mutual persuasion.

An audience has an ethical responsibility to allow a speaker to be heard even when its members disagree with the speaker's views. Our democratic principles safeguard the right to free speech. We value the ability to discuss ideas and to engage in political discourse. The opposition also has the same right to use speech to express disagreement, but not in a way that prevents a speaker from being heard. But in the next example the audience failed to be open-minded and to allow mutual influence to occur. They acted unethically by preventing the speaker from expressing her beliefs.

During the 2000 Presidential election, Karenna Gore Schiff, the daughter of Al Gore, visited our campus. She tried to speak but a group of activists protesting the actions of Occidental Petroleum, which displaced a South American tribe, shouted her down. Schiff "tried several times to engage the protesters, but they rejected her request to talk about the issue after her speech" (Rose 2000). The protesters asserted that the Gore family were partial owners of Occidental Petroleum. The campus police did not intervene. The opposition prevented the speaker from being heard.

Audiences have an ethical responsibility to provide accurate feedback to a persuader. Persuaders depend on this feedback to adapt their messages and, when this feedback is absent or erroneous, it is of little value. We once heard a presentation by a colleague advocating a new program. The audience smiled, laughed, and clapped. They nodded in the appropriate places and told the speaker how much they enjoyed his presentation. When there was an opportunity for questions, none was asked. On the basis of this feedback, the colleague believed he had given a successful presentation and had received the backing he needed to move forward on the program. When he began to call on these individuals to get the specific support he needed, he was surprised when he could not get any commitments to his programs. The absence of questions from the audience about the program and their negative reactions to the program had not provided any form of feedback during his earlier presentation. If the speaker had been given some feedback, he might have been able to adapt the presentation so as to respond earlier to some of these concerns. The audience had an ethical obligation to give him accurate feedback.

Using Ethics in Persuasion

Ethics is the responsibility both of the persuader and of the audience. Although this chapter has concentrated on ethics from the perspective of the persuader, we have also recognized that you are probably more often in the position of being an audience member. Audiences also face ethical issues and have ethical responsibilities.

Six ethical perspectives have been described: that of the human nature, the dialogical, the situational, the utilitarian, the legal, and the feminist. Each of these perspectives offers a different lens for viewing ethical issues. We have described the basic assumptions of the ethical perspective, provided an example to illustrate that perspective, discussed a set of questions to assist in applying this perspective to ethical situations, and described the evaluation of the perspective. You need to find the perspective that is most consistent with your own value system. It is important to have a perspective to use when you face an ethical issue, so that you can ask yourself the proper questions and come to an appropriate decision about the behavior. Over time, you may find that your values change and your perspective changes, but you do not want to adopt a different perspective for each situation you face. An ethical perspective can be most valuable in guiding your behavior if you use it consistently and it is in harmony with your own values.

In the examples, we have illustrated ethical issues faced by persuasive speakers, but we can be more explicit by suggesting a partial set of guidelines that are commonly accepted (Woodward and Denton 1996):

1   Accurately represent your personal background and knowledge.
2   Be honest about your intentions, thoughts, and feelings.
3   Advocate positions you believe in.
4   Allow others to be persuaded by your arguments rather than coerced or manipulated.
5   Make arguments that you can support and use relevant and logical reasoning.
6   Use language that is clear and truthful.
7   Use timely, relevant, and accurate information.
8   Make complex issues easier for an audience to understand, without oversimplifying the ideas.
9   Attribute the sources of information accurately and use qualified and unbiased sources to support your arguments.
10 Provide quoted material in context, so that the original meaning is retained.
11 Include the essential information that audiences must have in order to make an informed decision.
12 Treat with respect those you disagree with.

Glossary

Audience standards: a situational factor which influences ethical judgments about the context by assessing the expectations or norms which govern a particular situation.

Audience's goals and values: in the situational perspective, this is an aspect of the situation which describes the important objectives and ideals in making ethical judgments.

Degree of audience awareness: an aspect of the situation which can influence ethical judgments and describes an audience's knowledge of persuasive strategies and of the topic.

Degree of urgency: in the situational perspective, a sense of the immediacy for action is an aspect of the context that can influence ethical judgments.

Dialogical perspective on ethics: an ethical perspective which indicates that decisions or actions should involve the characteristics of a dialogue, for instance mutual control and allowing the participants to realize their potential.

Ethical issues: situations in which an ethical question about what ought to be done will occur.

Ethics of justice: the position that ethics is determined by equality and fairness.

Ethics of care: the position that ethics is determined by compassion, situation, and interdependence of individuals.

Ethics: the study of laws, rules, and guidelines that establish right and wrong human behavior.

Human nature perspective on ethics: an ethical perspective which indicates that decisions or actions that enhance the essence of being human are ethical.

Ideal dialogue: an honest, confirming, supportive, and empathetic active interaction with another person.

Legal perspective on ethics: an ethical perspective which determines whether a given action or decision is ethical by assessing whether it meets legal rules and principles.

Role of the communicator: in the situational perspective, this is a situational factor which can influence ethical judgments and describes the part or character assumed by the communicator.

Situational perspective on ethics: an ethical perspective which indicates that an action or decision is ethical by considering the relevant aspects of the situation.

Utilitarian perspective on ethics: an ethical perspective which assesses the rightness or wrongness of an action by examining the consequences of the behavior.

Part II

Preparing Persuasive Communication

Chapter 5

Purpose and Audience

Chapter Contents

When persuasive messages are unsuccessful, it is often because the speaker did not adequately analyze the audience. When Martha Stewart was indicted for securities fraud, she immediately published an open letter in *USA Today* and established a personal website to present her case to the public which received 1.7 million hits within the first 17 hours (Horowitz 2003). Even critics were impressed by the persuasive messages designed to influence public opinion about Martha Stewart's innocence. In contrast, when Gary Condit gave his interview about Chandra Levy's disappearance with Connie Chung on "Prime Time," it was an opportunity for the Representative to change the audience's increasingly negative attitudes toward him. We believe Condit's audience wanted to see a remorseful and cooperative person, but he continued to rely on evasive maneuvers to avoid answering questions. With very few exceptions, his behavior was criticized and his attempts to persuade his audience to change their attitudes failed miserably.

We begin this chapter by examining how important it is to refine the purpose of a persuasive message so that it is adapted to an audience. Then the characteristics of an audience, what you need to know about your audience, and how to gather information about your audience will be discussed.

Refining the Purpose of Persuasive Messages

First, it is important to select a clear and specific purpose for your persuasive message. For example, consider the following potential purposes:

- to discuss diseases;
- to discuss AIDS;
- to encourage audience to be more tolerant of those with AIDS;
- to recommend more federal funding for AIDS research;
- to recommend more US funding for AIDS treatment in developing countries;
- to recommend needle and condom distribution on campus;
- to encourage audience to volunteer to help AIDS patients.

The first purpose is more general than the rest because it does not address a particular disease. Without a specific focus, it might be difficult to decide what to include and how to tie together information about different diseases. The first two purposes are very vague and do not necessarily appear to be persuasive. Every other topic clearly can be persuasive because those purposes encourage a change ("more" tolerant, "more" funding). The fourth and fifth purposes are more specific because they recommend a particular action (being more tolerant is relatively vague). The sixth purpose is more limited in scope because it pertains to local action. The last purpose asks the audience to take a specific action (presumably, your audience would not have the power to change federal funding levels, for example).

We do not suggest that the last purpose is necessarily the best, although we do believe that the first two purposes are too vague to help guide your research and the development of your outline. You may want to take a broader perspective (funding for AIDS research or treatment), or you might prefer to recommend something your audience can do themselves. But, regardless of which of the more specific purposes you choose, they will help you decide what information and ideas are relevant to your persuasive message. Having a specific, focused purpose will help design a coherent message.

Second, you need to select a realistic purpose. The question here is what you can reasonably expect to accomplish with your audience. If your audience is the campus Young Republicans, you might be wasting your time (and theirs) if you adopt as your purpose to persuade them to vote for the Green Party nominee. However, you might be able to convince them that it is important to support candidates who will protect our environment. On the other hand, if you are addressing that same group, it might be a waste of time to persuade them that the Republican Party has better answers to most issues – they would not belong to this group if they did not already believe this. But you might try to persuade them to canvas door-to-door, to hand out campaign literature for Republican candidates. The point here is that you need to understand your audience in order to select a purpose that is realistic and worth persuading about.

Audience Characteristics

What are the important **characteristics of an audience**? You have probably noticed, as you have been part of various audiences, that each one has its own unique nature. What are the factors that influence this character? We identify four such elements: size, history, homogeneity, and demeanor.

Size

Small audiences are often intimate and speakers can develop more rapport with them. In large audiences, individual members tend to feel anonymous and the speaker must work very hard to connect to the individuals within this large group. Of course, the larger the audience, the more potential there is influence from an effective message.

History

If the speaker knows members of this audience or has addressed it in the past, that prior **history** will influence the speaking situation. It may make the speaker feel more comfortable because this audience is a "known" quantity – there is a number of expectations that are likely to be fulfilled. Prior history could also make the audience more receptive. This assumes, of course, that the prior history between the speaker and the audience has been positive. If the speaker must address credibility issues with the audience to repair a negative prior encounter, that will change the dynamics of the situation.

Homogeneity

Audiences vary in the diversity of demographic characteristics represented among members. An audience of which 95 percent is made up of 18–20-year-olds, Protestants, and middle-class people would be a homogenous audience. This is in contrast to a heterogeneous audience composed of individuals in which 10 percent are 18–20, 30 percent are 20–30, 30 percent are 30–40, and 30 percent are 40+; 20 percent are Protestants, 40 percent are Catholics, 20 percent are Jewish, 20 percent are Other; and 10 percent are lower class, 50 percent are middle class, and 40 percent are upper class. Audiences with **homogeneity** (less diversity) in demographic characteristics are more likely to have similar knowledge, interests, and attitudes toward a topic a speaker will introduce than audiences with heterogeneity (greater diversity). When an audience is heterogeneous (diverse), the speaker faces the more difficult task of persuading people who would probably respond to a message in different ways.

Demeanor

An audience's **demeanor** toward the speaker and the topic can reveal their positive or negative attitudes: Audiences can be motivated or hostile toward speakers and particular issues. Speakers need to be very aware of an audience's demeanor and sensitive to shifts in attitudes that may occur during a speech. Motivated audiences will often provide positive feedback and be ready to be inspired and further motivated by a speaker. On the other hand, hostile audiences may not want to listen and could even heckle the speaker. This can present the speaker with a particularly difficult situation, although the speaker can ask the audience for a fair hearing. This involves asking the audience to allow the speaker to have the opportunity to express his/her ideas and to respond to questions. It suggests that dialogue is a more productive way to resolve disagreement than simply refusing to allow another person to speak. An audience's demeanor may be demonstrated through their behaviors while a speaker is talking. Some audiences are attentive while others show their lack of interest by talking to others, reading a newspaper, or even sleeping! The audience is giving cues about their level of interest in the speaker and the topic. Chapter 9 will discuss these cues and the strategies for responding to these kinds of audiences.

Knowing your Audience

Audiences differ from one another. This is a vital assumption for persuaders. A message that works well for one audience could fail or even backfire with another audience. This is why it is so important for persuaders to know their audiences.

Knowledge about your topic

You need to learn what your audience knows about your topic. For some audiences and some topics, it may be nothing at all. For others, you may have expert audiences. You will need to consider whether your audience will be familiar with the terms, abbreviations, and special vocabulary you may use. Will they know the basic concepts and ideas? Will they agree with what you think are generally accepted facts, or will you need to make persuasive arguments in your speech? It is important to consider what your audience already knows so that you can determine what to include into, and what to exclude from, your speech. Nothing is quite as boring as listening to a speech with no new information to offer, and speeches which leave out key ideas are bound to fail.

A biochemistry major in an introductory speech class decided to give a persuasive oration on genetically enhanced foods. After completing an audience analysis, he knew his audience had little knowledge on the topic. They knew about a possible ban of these foods because some people thought they were dangerous. As a biochemistry major, he knew all the right jargon ("transgenic nutraceuticals" and the like) but realized that using such expressions in his speech was a good way to lose his audience. Instead, he began with a familiar example, corn, and explained how it was an example of a genetically enhanced food.

Consider these questions: When you think about what your audience knows on your topic:

1 Is your language appropriate for the knowledge level of your audience? Are you speaking above their heads (e.g. transgenic nutraceuticals)? Are you speaking down to them (e.g. a circle is a round object)?
2 Will you give your audience new information, facts that they did not already know?
3 Will you explain concepts or ideas that are unfamiliar to your audience?

Interest in your topic

If your audience believes your topic is interesting, your task is simply to sustain that interest during your presentation. But if your audience is neutral or not interested, your task will be to convince them that the topic is relevant and important to them. You must give them a reason to listen, and this must be done very early in the speech. If you wait too long you will not be able to secure the audience's attention and they may ignore your message.

Julia's university was considering adopting a policy requiring that all freshmen purchase laptop computers. Julia thought this was a bad idea and began to prepare a persuasive speech against the policy. As she began her audience analysis she discovered that her class-mates, who were mostly sophomores, had little interest in the topic because the policy would not require them to purchase laptops. Should Julia have abandoned the topic because her audience had little interest in the topic?

How could Julia give her audience a reason to listen? One possibility was to argue that they should care about freshmen because these sophomores were once in their place. However, because that part of their education is over, she decided to try something else. Instead, she made the argument that, because freshmen were required to have laptops, there would be a reduction in computer lab services on campus and her audience of sophomores would have fewer services available to them if this policy was adopted. This means they had a clear reason to listen to her speech, because she showed them how her topic directly affected them.

As you consider whether you have generated enough interest in your topic, ask yourself these questions:

1 Does your introduction generate interest in your topic – for instance by using stories, personal examples, humor? (Chapter 6 describes attention-getting devices that can be used in introductions.)
2 Does your introduction make it clear why the topic is important to the audience?
3 Does the body of the speech continue to generate interest in your topic? (Chapter 7 illustrates the factors of interest.)
4 Does your conclusion remind the audience why the topic is important to them?

Attitudes toward your topic

If you are going to persuade your audience to have a favorable attitude toward your topic, you need to know something about what your audience thinks about it before you even begin to prepare your presentation. You should consider the audience's beliefs and values related to your topic. A presentation designed to strengthen an audience's attitudes and get them to take action should be quite different from one that attempts to create an attitude by convincing an apathetic audience that their neutral attitudes should actually be favorable. Each of these speeches should be quite different from one given to a hostile audience with a negative attitude toward your topic. You will need to make choices about the arguments that will be most persuasive with this audience. Many arguments can be made to support your position, but some will be more likely to convince your particular audience. Some of your arguments will require more support than others, and you should also give some thought to the kind of support to use that will be most persuasive with your audience. As a persuader, you can also adapt the structure of the message to your audience. If you know that your audience believes that there is a problem and needs to be persuaded about the most appropriate solution, an organizational pattern that focuses on solutions (i.e. the two-sided pattern that we discuss in chapter 6) is likely to be most appropriate.

1 What are your audience's attitudes toward your topic?
2 What arguments will be most persuasive with your audience?
3 Which of your arguments will require the most support?
4 What support will your audience consider to be more persuasive?
5 How can you structure the message to be most persuasive?

Kim's university, like several others, was considering parental notification policies for students between the ages of 18 and 21 who violate drug and alcohol policies in the residence halls. She decided this would be a good topic for her next persuasive speech because her audience would be interested in it; she also had a strong favorable opinion about it on account of her job as a residential advisor. Her audience analysis revealed that most of her audience lived in the residence hall and strongly opposed the policy because: (1) they were adults; (2) they believed other forms of discipline for drug and alcohol violations had been effective.

Kim has probably chosen one of the most difficult persuasive situations. The audience is highly involved in the topic – it has direct personal relevance to them. If this policy is adopted, audience members could potentially be reported to their parents and would have to provide an account for their behavior. Kim knows that her audience opposes her position on the topic. Should she change topics? Should she expect radical changes in her audience's attitudes? The answer to both questions is "no." It is an unrealistic goal to expect that a single message on this topic will convert Kim's audience to become advocates for the parental notification policy. A more practical purpose would be simply to get the audience to reassess their position on the topic. She does not want to argue that the members of her audience are not really adults, but she can provide some information about whether the current policies are being effective. She can also suggest that this policy is aimed at the 1 percent who have repeatedly violated the rules – those who are difficult to tolerate. This policy is for those who have a serious problem that cannot be taken care of with a simple slap on the wrist. This dissociates the policy from those in class and makes it less personally threatening.

If Kim were giving this presentation to a parents' group, would she use the same message? No. This is why audience analysis is so important. A parents' group would have a very different attitude toward this topic from that of the students, and Kim's arguments would have to be very different. Kim would argue that parents should support the new policy because they want to be informed about what their sons and daughters are doing at university. She would suggest that the present policy does not keep parents informed when problems with alcohol and drugs do occur, and parents are not able to help their children get the help they need. Obviously, this is not an argument that Kim would make to students who are enjoying their new independence.

Attitudes toward you

An audience also makes judgments about you that can influence whether your persuasive message will be successful. If an audience has a negative attitude toward the speaker, they may be less receptive to a persuasive message even if they agree. And audiences are quick to make judgments about a speaker's character. It is important to establish a positive first impression, because this judgment is difficult to change once it has been formed.

But there are ways to address negative feelings or expectations that an audience might have about a speaker (extrinsic credibility from chapter 3). If this is your first interaction with the people in your audience, how can you make a positive impression (intrinsic credibility from chapter 3)? If your audience knows you, what are their attitudes toward you? Do they have certain expectations that will influence the way they receive your next message? You can speak to concerns about your expertness by researching the topic thoroughly, so that you are knowledgeable about it and you identify the sources of information you are using to support your arguments. You can address audience concerns about your trustworthiness by speaking frankly and sincerely and by being responsive to the audience's beliefs.

The infamous basketball coach, Bobby Knight, provides a great example of the effects of reputation. Bobby Knight coached Indiana University's basketball team from 1971–2000 with eleven Big 10 titles and three national championships to his credit. But he also had a fiery reputation, based on several antics which included throwing a chair across the court, choking players during practice, and throwing a potted plant against a wall to intimidate an athletic department secretary. His behavior finally culminated in an investigation by the board of trustees, which confirmed many of the allegations, and on May 15, 2000 the university announced it was going to fine Bobby Knight and adopt a "zero tolerance policy" for future misbehavior (Suggs 2000). Shortly after this announcement, Bobby Knight had an interview with Entertainment and Sports Programming Network (ESPN) ("Knight speaks," 2000). His audience had knowledge about Bobby Knight's behavior. It is interesting to consider how he tried to influence the audience's impressions of him during this interview. He used the following strategies to address his credibility:

Acknowledge past mistakes:
"I think that I've obviously made a mistake here and a mistake there. But I don't think those mistakes define the person."

Knight creates some sincerity by owning up to his mistakes in the past while arguing that his mistakes do not define his character.

Minimize past mistakes:
"I think that in many, many cases I've conquered it (my temper), and in some cases I haven't."
"There's nobody on Earth that occasionally hasn't had a problem with overreaction."

In these two excerpts, Knight indicates that he has often managed his temper and that everyone has difficulty with overreacting, so his situation is not unique. He is telling the audience about his difficulties in an honest and straightforward way.

Project future success:
"To me, it is kind of a simple equation: I have to be able to do all the time basically what I've done most of the time now" (control my temper in order to comply with the zero-tolerance policy).

Finally, Knight contends that he can be trusted to keep his temper in the future and that he has been able to do that most of the time anyway. By September, Knight had violated the zero tolerance policy and was fired. He was later hired to coach for Texas Tech University.

If this is your first appearance before an audience, think about how you can improve your credibility with your audience:

1 Are you knowledgeable about your topic?
2 Are you identifying your information sources?
3 Are you using "straight talk" and recognizing some objections to your position?
4 Are you speaking with sincerity?
5 Are you interested in listening to what your audience wants to tell you?

These questions are designed to get you thinking about how you might build your intrinsic credibility with your audience (chapter 3). Your audience is more likely to be persuaded if your message creates the impression that you are well informed on the topic and you can be trusted.

If your audience has a negative attitude toward you before you begin to speak, you'll need to do some repair work. First, you need to know more about their negative attitudes toward you. What is the basis for their negative attitude? Do they think you are insincere? Uninformed? Biased? Why do they believe this? Is this based on some past experience with you? Your past history? Bobby Knight needed to convince his audience that he could be trusted to keep his temper after he had lost it several times. The audience's knowledge of his prior behavior needed to be addressed. Once you understand what the issues are, you will need to address the audience's concerns in your presentation.

Jack has a natural gift for charm and can talk about anything. He does not usually end up saying much but he can always get the audience to laugh. Do you know the type? When he enrolled in the persuasion course, he did not take it very seriously and the first couple of speeches he prepared on the way to class. But he decided that he was going to do the next speech on lung cancer. He recently learned that his favorite uncle has lung cancer and he was only 45. He recognizes that his audience expects him to do another speech off the cuff and are unlikely to take him seriously. He needs to convince his audience that he is sincere early in the presentation. To do this, he can:

- acknowledge his past reputation;
- demonstrate his sincerity by explaining the personal significance of this topic.

Here is an introduction to that speech:

> If you'd asked me a week ago what the "Big C" was I'd have said it was the grade I got on my Accounting midterm and I was very lucky to get it. I didn't spend a lot of time studying for it and it isn't the kind of the thing you can just talk your way around. But that was before I got the news about my Uncle George. George is my dad's brother and he's like having a second dad. He never missed one of my high school football games, he's the one who encouraged me to come to school here, and he's the one who understood even when my own dad got stubborn. And now George has the "Big C." Cancer. It's not a topic I can b.s. about for 10 minutes.

Jack acknowledged his past reputation for glib talk and minimal preparation. He explained to his audience that this presentation would be different because he had a personal investment in the topic. He made an argument early in the speech that he should be given the chance to show that his own personal experience had transformed his behavior and the presentation would be different from the audience's negative expectations. The credibility of a speaker affects how audiences think about messages, so it is important for speakers to deal with this issue early in the presentation.

Gathering Information About Audiences

The more you know about your audience, the easier it is to adapt your message and be more persuasive in accomplishing your purpose. You need to know what your audience knows about your topic, their interest level in your topic, their attitudes toward it, and their attitudes toward you as a speaker. We begin by describing two kinds of information that can be gathered to make inferences about knowledge, interests, and attitudes, and then we detail three methods of collecting this kind of information from audiences.

There are two primary types of information that can be collected and analyzed about audiences: demographic information and audience opinions.

Demographic information

Demographic information categorizes audience members into social groups. Although there is a wide range of demographic variables, common variables include gender, political orientation, religious preference, and age. The demographic variables questionnaire suggests how you might collect information on these kinds of variables (see box 5.1). Relevant demographic variables will vary according to a particular audience and according to the topic. For a college audience, for example, year in school could be a relevant variable. A speaker who was persuading her audience that the career center should provide more job placement services would want to know how many seniors were in her audience. On the other hand, a speaker who wants his college-aged audience to sign a petition against tuition increases will not find demographic information about year in school to be particularly relevant because tuition increases affect all students (except graduating seniors), regardless of year in school. Speakers should collect demographic information about audiences to make inferences about their knowledge, interests, and attitudes.

It is important to realize that demographic information is only useful if it helps the speaker make an inference about the audience's knowledge about the topic, interest in the topic, attitudes toward the topic, or attitudes toward the speaker. Some demographic information will be relevant for particular topics; other demographic information will not. You will need to select the demographic characteristics that allow you to make inferences which are useful for your topic. Men and women are charged the same tuition and increases would affect both groups equally, so gender might not be important demographic information on this topic.

Suppose, for example, that you plan to give a speech on retirement. Age is a relevant demographic variable. If your audience is primarily over 50 years of age, they are more likely to be interested in this topic than an audience with an average age of 20. Or suppose that you are interested in giving a speech on new legislation that raises the minimum wage. Demographic variables that are relevant are age and whether your audience works part-time or full-time. If your audience is primarily young and working part-time, they are more likely to have positive attitudes toward legislation that would raise the minimum wage, because they will benefit from this action. You use the demographic variables to make inferences (i.e. educated guesses about

Box 5.1   Demographic variables for audience analysis questionnaire

1   Gender:_____Male_____Female

2   Age: _____Under 18_____18–22_____23–29_____30+

3   Student status:_____Full-time_____Part-time

4   Greek membership:_____Greek_____Independent

5   Political orientation: Far Left _____ Liberal_____ Middle of the road_____ Conservative_____ Far right_____

6   Political action/Interest in political issues: Very active_____Somewhat active_____ Not very active _____

7   Religious preference:
Protestant_____Catholic_____Jewish_____Hindu_____Bhuddist_____ Confucian_____Islamic_____Muslim_____Agnostic/Atheist_____ Other_____ No religious preference_____

8   Religiosity: Very active_____Somewhat active_____Not very active_____

9   Employment: Work part time_____Work full time_____No employment at this time_____

10 Racial and Ethnic Background: Caucasian_____African American_____Asian _____Mexican–Amercian/Chicano_____American Indian/Alaska Native_____ Other_____

11 Year in School: Freshman_____Sophomore_____Junior_____Senior_____ Other_____

12 Primary Residence: Rural_____Urban_____Suburban_____

13 Number of siblings (not counting yourself): 0_____1–2_____3–4_____5+_____

14 Your birth order: Oldest_____Middle_____Youngest_____I am the only child _____

15 To how many countries have you traveled to outside the US? 0_____1–2_____ 3–5_____6+_____

16 Languages spoken fluently: 1_____2_____3+_____

17 Marital status: Single_____Married_____Divorced_____Other_____

18 Educational goal: Bachelor's degree_____Master's degree_____Doctoral degree_____Other_____

19 College Major:
Business_____Engineering_____Science_____Journalism_____Humanities (English, Philosophy, Classics, etc.) _____Social Science/Behavioral Science (Psychology, Sociology, Political Science, Anthropology, etc.) _____Arts (Theater, Music, Art, etc.)_____Other_____

20 Current residence while attending the university: Residence hall/dormitory_____ Fraternity or sorority house_____Apartment_____Parents' residence_____ Other_____

attitudes, interests, or knowledge). By contrast, an older, middle-class audience who is working full-time may be more likely to oppose such a measure because they are worried about the tax implications of such legislation. They are not making minimum wage and are less likely to benefit directly. So, demographic information can be very useful when it relates to your topic.

Audience opinions

In addition to demographic information, it is useful to collect information about the audience's opinions on issues. Pollsters routinely collect this kind of data and a speaker can also collect them: namely, how a particular audience feels about the specific topic the speaker plans to speak about for an upcoming presentation. When this kind of information is sought, audience members are often asked to react to statements by indicating whether, and how much, they agree or disagree with such statements as the one shown in box 5.2.

Box 5.2   People have a right to know about the personal lives of public figures

Strongly agree	Agree	Neutral	Disagree	Strongly disagree

Or they are asked to circle a number that indicates where their opinion falls on a continuum with two opposing adjectives anchoring the ends (see, for example, box 5.3).

Box 5.3   Technology use in the classroom at this institution

Frequent	1	2	3	4	5	6	7	Infrequent
Effective	1	2	3	4	5	6	7	Ineffective

This kind of information is compiled in order to assess an audience's opinions on an issue. Sometimes an audience's opinion on one issue can be used to make an inference about their opinion on a related issue.

   You can also ask audience members open-ended questions to solicit their opinions on issues. For example, you might ask: "What kinds of experience have you had with the technology being used in the classroom? Have these been positive or negative experiences? Why?" If members of your audience are willing to talk with you for a more extended period of time, you may gain some rich information that can inform your analysis.

Collecting Information From Audiences

You know that you need information about your audience's knowledge on the topic, interest in the topic, attitudes toward the topic, and attitudes toward you; but now you need to find this information. There are three primary methods for collecting this kind of information: observation, interaction, and summary data.

Observation

Observation of an audience involves careful listening and scrutiny of audience behaviors and characteristics. Observation requires that a speaker may have access to an audience in situations where information is likely to be shared. For example, in most speech classes, students give introduction speeches and learn a great deal about each other at the beginning of the term. This information can be useful in determining class-mates' attitudes toward a number of topics. In other situations where a speaker has a prior history with an audience, there have been many opportunities for observation that have provided rich opportunities to gather data for audience analysis, which can be used to assess the audience's knowledge, interest, and attitudes.

Interaction

Interaction involves talking with one or more members of the audience as a sample that would, hopefully, represent the entire audience. The more homogenous the audience is, the fewer people you will need to talk to in order to get a sense of the audience's attitudes. If the audience is diverse, you will need to interact with more people to get a better sense of the diversity of your audience. You interview these individuals about their knowledge, interest, and attitudes in order to develop an analysis of your audience and adapt your speech. A sample interview for a speech on whether employers should be allowed to require drug-testing for employers is presented in box 5.4. The interview asks questions so as to determine what these individuals know about the topic (question 1), what their potential interest in it is (questions 2, 3, 6), and what their attitudes are (4, 5).

Box 5.4 Drug-testing questionnaire

1　Can employers legally require drug-testing of employees?
2　Have you ever worked in a job where you were drug-tested by an employer?
3　Do you have friends who have worked in jobs where they were drug-tested?
4　Do you think employers should have the right to require drug-testing of employees? Why or why not?

Summary data

Summary data refers to information collected about a group of individuals like the audience. These data may have been collected at a prior time, and an assumption is made that this particular audience is similar to the audience at hand. For example, in the fall of 2003, the *Chronicle of Higher Education* reported the results of a study of the attitudes and demographic characteristics of the freshmen class. The report showed that 51 percent described themselves as middle of the road politically, 32 percent agreed strongly (or somewhat) that the death penalty should be abolished, and 64 percent believed that there is too much concern in the courts for the rights of criminals (Freshman survey, 2003). A speaker might speculate that these data would fit an audience of freshmen to whom the author was about to give a speech to on the death penalty. If you want to know more about the results of this survey, check out box 5.5. This summary data, collected for others, who are similar to the audience, could be useful in making an inference about this audience's attitudes.

Box 5.5   Freshmen survey results

Racial and ethnic background:

Caucasian	76%
African American	10%
Asian	7%
Other	7%

Summary data can also be collected for the specific audience the speaker is trying to persuade. This provides the best insight into an audience. Demographic information as well as information about your audience's attitudes can be collected and used for your audience analysis. Questionnaires can be designed so as to be filled out quickly. The example given in the next section was meant for a persuasive speech on why college students should get the experience of studying abroad (see box 5.6). These questionnaires can be filled out in just a few minutes, collected, and then the speaker can compile the results and use them to develop the presentation.

Using Audience Analysis in Persuasion

The questionnaire on study abroad was filled out in a class of 25 students and the results were tallied. The next step is to make decisions about how to use this audience analysis information to adapt the persuasive speech to it. The questionnaire results suggest that most of the audience are sophomores or freshmen, but they are worried that studying abroad will delay their graduation. On the basis of this information, one of the main arguments the persuasive speaker should make is that most study abroad programs offer a variety of general education courses that will transfer back to degree programs. Freshmen and sophomores are in a particularly good position to take advantage of study abroad programs because they have not completed all of their general education requirements. Second, you will notice that the open-ended questions (6, 8) as well as question 9, indicate that this audience is concerned about the cost of study abroad. This indicates that this issue must be addressed in some detail. It would be useful to compare the cost of a semester on campus with a semester abroad. It would also be useful to research into the cost of different programs, so that some cheaper programs could be suggested for the cost-conscious student. Most of this audience has not traveled outside of the country and does not have strong language skills, so an argument should be made that there are many opportunities in English-speaking countries, as well as English programs in other countries. Language need not be an obstacle that stops someone from enjoying the experience of studying abroad. The largely female audience is also concerned about leaving behind a social life, but this can be addressed by describing the vibrant social life in exotic locations in other countries. Two people in this class have studied abroad, and it would be useful to interview them and use their experiences as supporting material in the speech. With this audience, testimonials and examples from students will make important support toward overcoming resistance to studying abroad and toward making a case for a worthwhile experience.

In this example, we have shown how the demographic information and the information about the audience's attitudes have been used to select the main arguments and the type of supporting material for the persuasive speech. If the audience analysis had shown that the audience consisted primarily of seniors, well traveled, and concerned mostly about their safety, this would have been a very different speech.

Box 5.6   Questionnaire for studying abroad

1   Gender:
    Male _____Female_____

2   Year in School:
    Freshman_____Sophomore_____Junior_____Senior_____Other_____

3   How many countries have you traveled to outside the US?
    0_____1–2_____3–5_____6+_____

4   Have you studied abroad?
    Yes_____No_____

5   If you answered no to question 1, have you ever considered doing a Study Abroad Experience?
    Yes_____No_____

6   If no, why not?

7   Do you have friends who have studied abroad?
    Yes_____No_____

8   If yes, what would be the biggest obstacle to actually studying abroad?

Please indicate whether how strongly you agree with the following statements by circling the descriptor that best fits your attitude, where SA = strongly agree, A = agree, N = neutral, D = disagree, and SD = strongly disagree.

9   I don't have enough money to study abroad.
    SA   A   N   D   SD

10   Studying abroad will delay when I can graduate.
    SA   A   N   D   SD

11   My foreign language skills are not strong enough to study abroad.
    SA   A   N   D   SD

12   I am not sure I could adjust to living and going to school in another country.
    SA   A   N   D   SD

13   I would miss my social life here too much if I studied abroad.
    SA   A   N   D   SD

This speech would have focused on where it is still safe to travel and how to fit a "study abroad experience" in to your senior year. Audiences differ from one another. A message that works well for one audience will not be effective with another.

Audiences can be described by their size, history, homogeneity, and demeanor. These audience characteristics influence the speaking situation. A speaker needs to know what the audience knows about the topic and what are their interests in the topic, their attitudes to it, and their attitudes toward the speaker. Demographic information and audience opinions are gathered about audiences. This information is accessed through observations, interactions, and summary data and then used to adapt the persuasive message to the audience.

In summary, what, in your message, can be changed on the basis of your audience analysis? Everything: your purpose, your organization (chapter 6), your main points and arguments, your supporting material (chapter 7), your factors of interest (chapter 7), your stylistic choices (chapter 8). No principle of persuasion is more fundamental than this one: Audiences can vary greatly, and a message that works well with one audience can fail completely with another.

Glossary

Audience characteristics: the unique nature of the audience.

Demeanor: positive or negative attitudes towards the speaker or topic.

Demographic information: characterization of audience members into social groups.

History: prior speaking experience with a given audience.

Homogeneity: less diversity in the demographic make-up of an audience.

Interaction: talking to one or more members of the audience as a sample of the entire audience.

Observation: the careful listening and scrutiny of audience behaviors and characteristics.

Summary data: information collected about a group of individuals who are similar to the audience.

Chapter 6

Organization: Structuring the Message

Every May and December, like clockwork, you will find us attending the graduation ceremony for our college and congratulating the graduating seniors in our department. There is something very special about the mingling of faculty and students in academic regalia and the playing of Pomp and Circumstances. At the most recent graduation, the graduation speaker chose to address the audience on the topic of a famous historical figure. We could not tell you the main points of the speech, although we think the thesis had something to do with not giving up in the face of many obstacles. The speaker rambled from point to point. The audience grew restless. The simple fact is, anyone who has more than one idea or thought to express must put one idea first, then a second, and so on until the end. We cannot speak (or absorb as listeners) more than one idea at a time. Through organization, the speaker arranges these ideas in a systematic way, so that all of a speaker's ideas fit together into a clear whole.

There is nothing worse than having to listen to a disorganized speech. Most of us have had this experience and would rather avoid it. When you are the speaker, you don't want your audience wondering what your point is. Instead, you want to organize your speech clearly, so your audience can understand its main ideas. This chapter describes organizational plans for structuring persuasive messages and the process of outlining your speech to insure that your organization is clear.

Organizational Plans for Structuring Persuasive Messages

Although there are many types of organizational plans that can be used for speeches, we will focus on those that are most common in persuasive messages. This chapter describes three organizational plans for structuring persuasive messages: introduction–body–conclusion, AIDA, and the motivated sequence.

Introduction–body–conclusion

The introduction–body–conclusion organizational plan divides a persuasive message into three essential parts. First, the speaker must introduce the topic. Next, the speaker must describe the main points in the body. Finally, the speaker must give a conclusion to the speech. Within each part of the speech, there are five important functions to be accomplished and the speaker makes choices about how this will be done.

Introduction

An **introduction** is the preliminary part of a speech and has five important functions: Gaining attention, establishing rapport, giving the audience a reason to listen, stating the purpose, and previewing the main points of the speech.

The introduction should get the audience to stop reading their newspapers, talking to their neighbors, or daydreaming. Some audiences are interested to hear what you have to say and you do not have to work to get their attention. But other audiences may not think that you have anything useful, relevant, or important to say to them. For these audiences, it is particularly important to convince them otherwise. And it must be done immediately! So a speaker needs to give some thought to gaining the audience's attention in the introduction. You know from reading the last chapter that using what you know about the audience will be helpful in deciding what might get your audience's interest. Should you use an analogy? Will a compelling story be more effective? See box 6.1 for a list of common attention-getters and examples to remind you of the kinds of choices you can make to accomplish this function.

You may also need to establish rapport with your audience in the introduction if you think they are hostile toward you or your position. If they are unwilling to listen to you with an open mind, your introduction must convince them to give you a fair hearing. Hostile audiences will be discussed in more detail in chapter 9.

Giving the audience a reason to listen is another important function of an introduction, because this shows the audience that the topic is significant and worthy of their attention. Some speakers mistakenly wait until the end of their speeches to explain why their speech topic should matter to the audience. However, if this is not done early in the speech, the audience will almost certainly have missed important information. A speaker can give the audience a reason to listen by demonstrating how the problem affects them (Clark 1984). Audiences are most interested when they can see that a problem has some connection to their own lives. For example, statistics indicate that 16 million Americans have diabetes, although 5 million do not know it. This means that each person has a 1 in 17 chance of developing this disease. In a class of 25, this means that at least one person is likely to suffer from diabetes at some time in their lifetime. It also means that, in your circle of friends and family, there is a very high probability that you know someone who has diabetes (American Diabetes Association, n.d.). It is much easier to get an audience to listen if they think the topic has some relevance to them. Ask yourself: Why should my audience care about my topic? If you cannot think of any reason, you need to reconsider your topic. When you figure out some reasons why they should care, make sure you tell them these reasons in the introduction.

Introductions also need to state the purpose of the speech and preview the main points of the body of the speech. On the whole, audiences like to know what is coming and will track a speech better if they have some idea of its structure. The preview is the first of many efforts a speaker should use to signal the structure of the speech clearly. When you are considering the purpose of your speech, you need to give careful consideration to your goals. A persuasive speech must do more than simply discuss an issue. As chapter 1 indicated, the purpose of a persuasive message should be to create, reinforce, or change the attitudes or behaviors of individuals in an audience. A speaker should have a clear purpose in mind. A preview of the main points of the body of the speech will briefly state the primary arguments in the persuasive message.

Body

The **body of the speech** contains the main ideas of the speech. In other words, the body constitutes the substance of your speech and is the place where your arguments and support (evidence) are developed to support the purpose statement or thesis. While there are numerous organizational patterns that can be used in other kinds of speeches (e.g. chronological, or spatial), the most common organizational patterns for persuasive speeches that use the introduction–body–conclusion organizational plan are described in box 6.1.

The cause–effect pattern. The cause–effect pattern is used when a speaker is focusing on the nature of a problem. The first point describes factors that influence, while the second point follows with the results. For instance, in a persuasive speech convincing an audience not to download music, a speaker explained that the primary cause for the increase in downloads is the belief that compact discs are overpriced, but the result is that legal action is being taken by the recording industry and by universities when students download music. Another student gave a persuasive speech designed to get the others involved in fighting tuition increases. A cause of increasing tuition is decreasing state expenditure on higher education, and one result has been an increase in student loans. Of course a fully developed speech would describe all the important causes and effects.

Box 6.1   Types of attention-getters

Reporting a startling statement or statistics: Sharing unexpected information or data that makes the audience curious about what else the speaker may have to say on this topic

EXAMPLE: Businesses plan to hire 19 percent more new college graduates this year than last according to a survey of 229 employers conducted by the National Association of Colleges and Employers. Those of you who are graduating need to make sure you are prepared to compete for those jobs.

Asking a question: Posing a provocative question to the audience to generate interest in the topic

EXAMPLE: Should human cloning be banned? Some argue there could be enormous medical benefits while others counter that we have only begun to explore the ethical consequences.

Using a quotation: Using the eloquent or vivid words of another person to capture an important idea or feeling

EXAMPLE: "Our greatest concern is that we'll turn the war against terrorism into a war against immigrants." This concern was expressed by Anthony Romero, the Executive Director for the American Civil Liberties Union after September 11. And he has cause to be concerned.

Referring to the audience or the speaking situation: Using the context as a way to establish a connection with the audience or the situation

EXAMPLE: "This is truly a celebration–a celebration on the contributions women make in every aspect of life: in the home, on the job, in their communities, as mothers, wives, sisters, daughters, learners, workers, citizens and leaders. It is also a coming together, much the way women come together every day in every country. We come together in fields and in factories. In village markets and supermarkets. In living rooms and board rooms." Hillary Rodham Clinton addresses the fourth UN World Conference on Women, Beijing, China, September 5, 1993.

Using an analogy: Explaining something by comparing it to something similar

EXAMPLE: Life is a lot like a chess game. You need to have goals and plan ahead. You need to be strategic and consider each move carefully if you are going to be successful. Most people don't like to think about life insurance. But it's an important part of thinking strategically – of making sure that you've planned far enough ahead in the game of life.

Telling a story: Relating a sequence of events to evoke interest

EXAMPLE: Tom Gadowski spends over a thousand dollars a month for seven medications to treat manic depression. He says "I've been on everything, and what I'm on right now seems to have me most stable." Currently, he's unemployed and half the costs of his drugs are picked up by Medicaid. But all that is about to change because of a new trend to try to control the cost of drugs.

Talking about a personal experience: Relating one's own events or episodes to generate interest

EXAMPLE: I spent my junior year abroad in France. It was a terrific experience because it gave me a chance to live in a completely different culture and experience a different way of life. I visited 11 countries and got to see the world! I feel like I'm a different person as a result of my experience.

The sequential pattern. The sequential pattern is adopted when the speaker is presenting one solution to a problem in great detail. The main points of the speech are the steps of the plan and the subpoints justify each step. This pattern would be used when the audience is in agreement that a problem exists and the speaker has decided to focus on persuading the audience that a particular solution should be adopted, without explicitly considering other possible alternatives. In a persuasive speech on alternatives to the university bookstore, a persuasive speaker provided a detailed plan for establishing a student-run bookstore. The speech was a set of steps for accomplishing this goal (e.g. obtaining the necessary funding, finding a central location, convincing professors to order books, and so on). The speaker knew that his audience was dissatisfied with the prices of the university bookstore and wanted an alternative, so the speech focused on presenting that alternative.

The two-sided pattern. The two-sided pattern can be used when a speaker focuses on two solutions. Some beginning speakers present the alternatives to the audience without advocating either of them, but this is not a persuasive speech. The two-sided approach considers the pros of the best solution and refutes the cons of that solution. It advocates the best solution to a problem. The speaker does not stand on the sidelines. A persuasive speaker might evaluate two possible solutions to the problem of second-hand smoke in residential halls on campus: Designating some residential halls as smoke free or designate some floors as smoke-free. For each of these solutions, the pros and cons could be evaluated. For example, making the some residential halls smoke free has the greatest chance of actually reducing the harmful effects of second hand smoke but has the negative effect of segregating smokers and non-smokers. The pros and cons of each of the alternatives would be considered, but the speaker should clearly propose one of the solutions over the other as the better of the two.

There has been some controversy over whether a speaker should tell an audience about other possible solutions or should only speak about the solution that she wants adopted. Early research suggested that two-sided messages were more effective with more educated audiences. On the other hand, one-sided messages were more effective when the audience already agreed with the speaker (Hovland, Lumsdaine, and Sheffeld 1949).

More recent research suggests that there are different kinds of two-sided messages: non-refutational and refutational. Non-refutational messages simply describe the opposing arguments. Refutational messages argue against the opposing arguments. Prior research indicated that refutational two-sided messages are most persuasive, but non-refutational two-sided messages are even less persuasive than one-sided messages (Allen 1991, 1993). This research also concluded that speakers who use refutational two-sided messages are perceived as more credible (e.g. honest, trustworthy) than speakers who use one-sided or non-refutational two-sided messages. This is consistent with the idea of intrinsic credibility from chapter 3. Speakers opting for non-refutational two-sided messages were least persuasive.

So what does this mean for a speaker choosing the two-sided organizational pattern? It means that you need to consider the pros and cons of each of the alternative solutions, but you need to make it clear to your audience which solution you favor.

Arguments that have been made against your solution should be refuted. Weaknesses in alternative proposals that you do not favor should be explained.

The problem–solution pattern. The problem–solution pattern is used when a speaker establishes that there is a problem and argues that a particular solution would solve it (see box 6.2). A speaker who argues that the number of stray dogs and cats is a serious problem and then explains that the audience should support a local animal rescue service has chosen a problem–solution organization. Another speaker argues that students have a responsibility to become involved in student government to improve the campus. The problem is the apathy of students who form the belief that no individual can make a difference. This speaker calls for a solution in the form of student involvement.

Box 6.2   Problem–solution outline

I Introduction
  A Attention-getter
  B Establish rapport
  C Give audience a reason to listen
  D State purpose
  E Preview of main points

II Body
  A Main point (statement of the problem)
    1 Subpoint (cause of the problem)
    2 Subpoint (effect of the problem)
    3 Subpoint (problem will continue)
  B Main point (statement of the solution)
    1 Subpoint (solution will address the cause of the problem)
    2 Subpoint (solution will work)
    3 Subpoint (solution is the best of all the possible options)

III Conclusion
  A Summary
  B Connection
  C Cohesive element
  D Appropriate frame of mind
  E Final appeal

Topical organization. The topical organizational pattern is a set of coherent arguments about a topic. For instance, a speaker gives a persuasive speech encouraging the audience to complete an internship before graduating. The speech is organized by reasons why students should do internships (e.g. they provide valuable experience, they can help you find a job). These reasons do not fit any of the previous patterns but do fit a topical organization one because they form a set of logical topics organized around the purpose statement.

In the topical organizational pattern, you have more choice about the order of the main points. In the example about why students should do an internship, the speaker knows that some arguments are stronger than others because there is better evidence for them or better possible reasoning. The research suggests that you should put your strongest arguments either first or last, but not in the middle (Igou and Bless 2003).

Conclusion

The **conclusion** is the final part of a persuasive speech and has four functions: Summarize the main points; to create a sense of connection; to inspire an appropriate frame of mind; and to make a final appeal.

By summarizing the main points in the conclusion, the speaker takes advantage of another opportunity to make the major ideas of the speech clear to the audience. Research suggests that speeches which include explicit conclusions are easily understood, but are also more persuasive than those do not include these conclusions (O'Keefe 1987). A summary also conveys a clear sense of finality to the audience, a signal that the speech is moving toward the end.

The parts of a speech should be connected to each other, and the conclusion is a place where all of these parts should be woven together. This can be accomplished by referring back to an example, a narrative, or a statistics introduced earlier in the message. Some speakers like to return to an idea from the introduction by way of putting the finishing touch on the speech.

Another function of the conclusion is to inspire an appropriate frame of mind in the audience. At this point, the speaker wants the audience to be the most moved, motivated, and persuaded at its most. The speaker may be trying to maintain a particular attitude by instilling a positive mood and by creating inspiration through vivid imagery and eloquent quotations.

Finally, the last function of the conclusion is to make a final appeal to the audience. The speaker may ask the audience to reconsider their attitude to an issue. Or the speaker may ask the audience to take an action and provide motivation by issuing a challenge, and then to provide the information and resources they need to act (e.g. pre-addressed post cards to Congresspersons). The conclusion is the speaker's last opportunity to influence the audience. This last message needs to be a powerful inducement to turn a favorable attitude into a behavior.

AIDA

AIDA, which stands for attention, interest, desire, and action, is an acronym describing an organizational plan that is often taught to salespeople (see box 6.3). It can provide a useful way of selling ideas as well as products or services. A speaker begins by getting the audience's attention, generates interest in the topic, builds desire for what is being proposed, and closes by asking for an action.

It is easy to see how a salesperson would use this organization to pitch a product to a customer. In looking for a new car, a car salesperson approaches a potential

Box 6.3   AIDA outline

The AIDA outline would have four parts and would fill in the following headings:
I   Main point (attention)
   A   Subpoint (attention-getting device)
   B   Subpoint (preview of purpose and main points)
II   Main point (interest)
   A   Subpoint (state why the problem is important)
   B   Subpoint (demonstrate who is affected by the problem)
   C   Subpoint (explain why the audience should care about the problem)
III   Main point (desire)
   A   Subpoint (develop a reason for the audience to want to change the situation)
   B   Subpoint (give the audience a solution that will allow them to change the situation)
IV   Main point (action)
   A   Subpoint (indicate how the action will satisfy the desire)
   B   Subpoint (show how the action will be effective)
   C   Subpoint (tell how the audience can accomplish the action)

customer on the lot and notices that she is looking at a silver PT Cruiser. He gains her *attention* by telling her that the PT Cruiser is the fastest selling model this year. Then he builds *interest* by describing the current sale and the safety ratings on the car. He encourages her to take a test drive to stimulate *desire*. He wants her to visualize herself in this car. Most importantly, he tries to make the close and get *action* by asking her to step inside his office to discuss an offer for the car.

Now let's see how this organizational plan can be used for other kinds of persuasive speeches. Jan decides to give a speech persuading her audience to volunteer with the local Big Brother/Big Sister organization. She builds *attention* by using a personal story about her own experience with her "little sister." She explains why she became involved and how important this experience has been to herself and her little sister. Jan develops *interest* in her topic by citing some statistics about the number of children waiting for a Big Brother or Big Sister. This evidence shows that there is a critical need. She inspires her audience's *desire* to help others by sharing several stories about the importance of this program in the lives of these children. Finally, she passes out a brochure about the program that includes the telephone number of the program and she asks each audience member to take *action* by calling the number and by volunteering their time to become a Big Brother or Big Sister.

Motivated sequence

The **motivated sequence** is an organizational plan that gets its name from the idea that individuals go through a normal sequence of steps as they are motivated to respond to the speaker's purpose (German, Gronbeck, Ehninger, and Monroe 2000). This sequence has five steps: attention, need, satisfaction, visualization, and action. It is very similar to the AIDA organization.

The attention step gets the audience to notice the speaker. This is accomplished through any of the attention-getting devices we described earlier (see box 6.4). Speakers who assume they have the audience's attention will often fail, because they have not established early in the speech that there is a reason to listen.

Box 6.4   Motivated sequence outline

The motivated sequence outlines should be divided into the five primary parts. The following outline makes clear which are main points and which are subpoints:

I   Main point (get attention)
   A   Subpoint (attention-getting device)
   B   Subpoint (preview the purpose and the main points of the speech)

II Main point (state the need for action)
   A   Subpoint (demonstrate the severity of the problem)
   B   Subpoint (show the extensiveness of the problem)
   C   Subpoint (relate the problem to the audience)

III Main point (state the solution that will satisfy the need)
   A   Subpoint (show how the solution will respond to the need)
   B   Subpoint (show how the solution works)

IV Main point (visualize the solution)
   A   Subpoint (describe the positive consequences of acting)
   B   Subpoint (describe the negative consequences of inaction)

V   Main point (state the action you are asking your audience to take)
   A   Subpoint (step 1 of the action)
   B   Subpoint (step 2 of the action)

The need step establishes that there is a serious problem that needs to be changed. A persuader should clearly state the problem and address the extensiveness and severity of the problem. To show that a problem is extensive, a speaker needs to be able to demonstrate that large numbers are affected. For example, Mary Fisher, an AIDS activist who tested positive for HIV, spoke eloquently about the enormous problem presented by AIDS in the introduction of her speech to the Republican National Convention in 1992: "The reality of AIDS is brutally clear. Two hundred thousand Americans are dead or dying; a million more are infected. Worldwide, forty million, sixty million, or a hundred million infections will be counted in the coming few years" (Fisher 1992). Another way to demonstrate need is by illustrating that the problem is severe or has had serious implications for those who have been affected. A story about the negative consequences for an individual would be useful in establishing the need to address such a problem. In a speech on crime on campus, a speaker began with a recent incident on campus:

> At 1:00 in the afternoon on a sunny day, Susan walked to her car after class. She was approached by a man who said he had a gun and forced her into her car. He made her drive to an ATM and withdraw cash from her account. Then he made her drive him to

another bank machine before releasing her. We think college campuses are safe – particularly in the middle of the afternoon. But a student was kidnapped in broad daylight.

It is particularly important for the speaker to show how the problem directly affects the audience. If the speaker has been successful in establishing a need, the audience will be prepared for the next step.

The satisfaction step presents a solution to the problem established in the need step. The solution needs to be specific, so the audience can see how it will address the problem that has been outlined. Evidence from experts and statistics about the solution should be used to support a speaker's claims about its efficacy.

The visualization step extends the audience's thinking about the solution by asking them to imagine how the solution will affect them. This is done by drawing a vivid picture of the positive consequences of adopting the proposed solution and/or the negative consequences of not implementing it. This is an opportunity to project your audience into the future and motivate them to take action – the next step.

The action step moves the audience to do something that will bring about the solution. You need to give the audience a specific action and make the action as easy as possible for them actually to do it. For example, if you want them to write to their representatives in Congress, give them a pre-addressed postcard. If you want them to participate in a random act of kindness, give them a list of possibilities and ask them to circle the one they plan to do that day. You could even get your audience to visualize when they might do this during their day, or whom they might choose for their kindness.

Michael decided to give his persuasive speech on racial profiling. He began with a story about how Aaron Campbell, a Metro-Dade police officer, was stopped on the Florida turnpike by the Orange County sheriff's deputies. Despite the fact that he had identified himself, he was wrestled to the ground, sprayed with pepper spray, and arrested. The records show he was targeted to be pulled over because of an illegal lane change and a covered license plate. Aaron Campbell believed that it was because he was black. Michael used this narrative to get his audience's attention. Next, he established the need for a change by describing the practice of racial profiling by law enforcement officers. He quoted experts who suggested that law enforcement officers stop and search the cars of minorities in disproportionate numbers, even when they do not have evidence to do so. He described the results from the Fourth Monitoring Report that was conducted in Philadelphia. This study found that 86 percent of the traffic stops in a one week period represented minorities, while minorities are only 46 percent of the population (American Civil Liberties Union (ACLU), n.d.). Michael described additional examples that have happened close to home. In the satisfaction step, he described the Traffic Stops Statistics Study Act that has been proposed in Congress. This act requires law enforcement officers to collect information on every traffic stop, including the race of the driver and whether a search was conducted. As Michael asked his audience to visualize the future, he asked them to put themselves in the driver's seat. He had them imagine what the future would be like if racial profiling continued and law enforcement officers were allowed to pull people over simply because a person fits a profile or looked suspicious. Michael pointed out that several classmates looked pretty suspicious to him. Finally, he asked them to take action by writing to their Congressional representatives to urge them to pass the Traffic Stops Statistics Study Act. If this law passed, additional evidence could be collected to document the extent of racial profiling. He passed out pre-addressed stamped envelopes and a fact-sheet about the issue, to make it easier for his audience to write a letter. He finished by relating his own racial profiling experience.

Outlining

Reasons to outline

The top ten reasons to outline your speech can be summarized to explain the importance of outlining. Outlining a speech is like building a house. It provides the essential structure and support. If the structure is strong, the building is sound; if it is not, the building will collapse. And now for the top ten!

1   *Outlines help you think through your ideas carefully and organize them logically.* Outlines lay out your ideas in a skeletal structure. This allows you to organize and evaluate your thinking easily.
2   *Outlines make it easier to see if you are missing some important information you need in order to establish your purpose statement.* As you construct an outline, you can more easily see when you are missing an important idea or piece of supporting material. You can correct this before you give your speech.
3   *Outlines help you determine whether information is relevant to your purpose.* Sometimes we include information which is interesting but not really relevant to the purpose of the speech. By constructing a good outline, you should see that this information does not fit your organizational pattern when you have trouble figuring out where it belongs in the outline.
4   *Outlines are a good way for you to keep a record of your speech.* Unlike papers, once speeches are given there are often no records of them if you want to consult them later. But, if you have done an outline, you have a written record of your organization and information.
5   *Outlines help your audience remember your main ideas.* Outlines help your audience remember because they help you become more organized. Audiences will remember a clear speech, which they can follow as they listen to it. This is why it is particularly important to have a clear structure, which an outline can help you to achieve, and then to mark that structure clearly as you deliver your speech.
6   *Outlines help you to remember your main ideas and become familiar with the points you want to make to your audience.* When an outline has helped you to organize your main ideas, they are easier for you to remember as a speaker, as you practice the speech. Disorganized ideas have no pattern and are difficult for a speaker to recall.

7 *Outlines build confidence, because you are putting together a well-organized speech to use when persuading your audience.* Having a well-constructed outline goes a long way toward giving a good speech. A speaker knows when the information is well-organized and the arguments are well-supported. This should build confidence for giving the speech.

8 *Outlines help you figure out the logical relationship between each idea and the others in the speech.* In deciding where ideas belong in an outline, you should consider the relationship between them. For example, in preparing a speech on crime, Julie gathered statistics about the effectiveness of video camera systems. As she was working on her outline, she had to decide whether this information belonged in a section on the causes of crime, the effects of crime, or the solutions. She decided that the information belonged in the solutions section but it also needed to be logically related to one of the causes of crime presented in her speech (i.e. inadequate security). By outlining, Julie was able to see how this solution should be logically connected to a cause of crime as well.

9 *Outlines are often useful to your instructor because they can be used to provide feedback about the structure of your speech.* This is particularly true when there may be a difference between what you were attempting to do and what you actually did during the speech. It is also useful if there were places where you were not particularly clear about your structure. Your instructor may be able to offer advice about how to make your structure more apparent to your audience.

10 *Outlines are often required by your instructor for all of the above reasons.* In the classroom, we sometimes do things because we are required to do them as part of an assignment. Many instructors require that you turn in an outline before you speak. But, as you can see from out list of the top ten reasons for outlining, there are many reasons why they should ask you to do this (they might even add to the list we have generated).

Types of outline

Two types of outlines are the planning outline and the speaking outline. The **planning outline** is the detailed outline you will make as you prepare to give your speech. You will probably turn in the planning outline to your instructor. The **speaking outline** is a very abbreviated outline that you speak from; it uses the planning outline as the model.

The planning outline

The planning outline is written in full sentences. This forces you to think through your ideas and be precise about what you intend to say. It also makes it easier for your instructor to see what you intended. The supporting material is inserted in the outline where it is relevant. A bibliography is a part of the planning outline.

The form of the planning outline varies depending on the organizational plan you have chosen. The introduction–body–conclusion organizational plan would divide the speech into the three parts to create an outline like the one created in box. 6.5. There are many choices of organizational patterns for the body and we have used the problem–solution pattern for this example.

Box 6.5   Sample of a problem–solution outline on college student smoking

I Introduction
  A "Kissing a smoker is a lot like liking an ashtray." [attention-getter]
  B Many of us care about our health and our bodies. [establishing rapport]
  C Are you one of those people who only smoke when you drink? You don't buy your own cigarettes but borrow them off of others? [giving the audience a reason to listen]
  D I will persuade you not to start smoking in college. [statement of purpose]
  E I will explain the problems of "casual" smoking, discussing both the causes and effects, and then offer a solution. [preview of main points]

II Body
  A Smoking among college students is a serious problem. [statement of the problem]
  B There are several causes of smoking among college students. [statement of causes]
    1 Cigarette companies promote smoking to college students. [cause 1]
    2 Smoking is common in settings in which college students socialize. [cause 2]
  C There are multiple effects of smoking among college students. [statement of effects]
    1 Casual smokers become regular users of nicotine. [effect 1]
    2 Smoking is expensive for college students. [effect 2]
    3 Smoking causes death and disease. [effect 3]
  D We must reduce college student smoking by targeting anti-smoking ad campaigns toward college students. [statement of the solution]
    1 These ad campaigns can counter the promotions by cigarette companies. [solution will address the cause of the problem]
    2 Ad campaigns can be effective in changing attitudes. [solution will work]

III Conclusion
  A College students smoke because they have been primed to do so by cigarette companies and their social settings while the effects are addiction, costs, and health issues. Anti-smoking campaigns are a solution that should be considered. [summary of main points]
  B No one wants to kiss an ashtray. [creating a sense of connection with introduction]
  C We can fight back. We are smart – much smarter than the cigarette companies and we can win this battle. And it is a battle – for our lives. [inspiring an appropriate frame of mind]
  D Write your state congresspersons and encourage them to use the tobacco settlement funds to underwrite anti-smoking ad campaigns targeted toward college students. [call for action]

The speaking outline

The speaking outline consists of key words that will remind you of the structure of the speech, statistics, quotations, and so on. Some speakers like to include notations on their speaking outline regarding delivery if they want to remember a particularly important cue or are working on correcting a problem. (One of your authors writes SLOW DOWN in capital letters at the top of every speaking outline, because of a tendency to speak too quickly when nervous!) We recommend writing your speaking outline on a note-card: they are less flimsy than a piece of paper. A note-card can be cupped in your hand so it is less noticeable, it makes less noise, and it does not shake as much when you get nervous. If you use more than one note-card, be sure to number them, just in case you drop them and need to reconstruct their order in a hurry.

Principles of outlining

There are six principles of outlining, to follow as you construct an outline for a speech: division, symbolization, coordination, subordination, progression, and completeness. These principles work together to insure that the outline accomplishes the many reasons we outlined earlier for outlining.

Division

The **division** principle states that an idea must be subdivided into at least two parts in an outline. Although there may be more than two parts, the point is that there is no reason to subdivide an idea if there are not at least two parts of it to indicate in the outline. In other words, if there is a I in an outline, there must be a II; if there is an A there must be a B, if there is a 1 there must be a 2, and so on.

Symbolization

The most common form of outlining uses the following set of symbols to indicate the most general to the most specific ideas:

I   The first level heading uses a roman numeral.
   A   The second level heading uses a capital letter and is indented.
      1   The third level heading uses an arabic number and is further indented.
         (a) The fourth level heading uses a bracketed and is indented again.
         (b) This would be another example of a fourth level heading.
      2   This heading returns to the third level.
   B   This heading returns to the second level.
II This heading is at the first level.

The principle of **symbolization** indicates that ideas at the same level of abstraction should use the same symbols and the same kind of indentation.

Coordination

If all of the ideas at the same level in the outline are at the same level of generality, then the outline has satisfied the principle of **coordination**. In other words, if all of the ideas using first level headings share the same degree of generality, they are coordinated. This principle should apply equally to all levels of heading used in the outline. An example may help to clarify this principle. A speaker's first point is that college students are pressured to drink alcohol, and the second point is that 40 percent of academic problems in college are caused by excessive alcohol consumption. We can tell that this speaker has chosen a cause–effect organizational pattern, but has violated the coordination principle. The first point is general and will be developed with several subpoints and supporting material. The second point is very specific and acts as supporting material for a more general idea about the effects of excessive alcohol consumption. The two points are not at the same level of generality.

Subordination

The principle of **subordination** states that secondary ideas which are at lower levels in the outline must be more specific than ideas at higher levels. So: I should be more general than IA, IB, and IC. These ideas should be subpoints of a heading rather than being placed at the higher level, if they are actually subordinate to a more general idea. Again, an example will make this abstract idea more understandable. John decides to give a speech on crime about campus and he begins his planning outline with the following main ideas:

  I Crime on campus has increased in the last two years.
  II Within the last two years, burglaries have increased by 15 percent.
  III Assaults have increased by 5 percent in the same time period.
  IV A crime prevention program would be effective in reducing crime.

The problem with John's outline is that the ideas in II and III are subpoints supporting the first point. This could confuse listeners. They are more specific types of crimes that have increased on campus. John's outline should be revised to reflect the following:

  I Crime on campus has increased in the last two years.
    A Within the last two years, burglaries have increased by 15 percent
    B Assaults have increased by 5 percent in the same time period.
  II A crime prevention program would be effective in reducing crime.

Now John's outline does not violate the principle of subordination because those points that are more specific (IA, IB) are positioned in the outline to indicate their appropriate place.

Progression

Are the ideas arranged in a logical order in the outline? The principle of **progression** assesses whether the ideas make sense in the sequence in which they are organized. For example, causes usually precede effects; south usually follows north. The speaker can help the audience see this logic by making reference to these relationships in transitions between points in the speech.

Completeness

The principle of **completeness** assesses whether the speaker has omitted important ideas from the outline. There may be ideas that the speaker is leaving out. Or there may be critical ideas that the speaker should include that are absent. Has the speaker considered the causes of the problem? Who is affected by it? has he visualized the results? Demonstrated that the solution will work?

Using Organization in Persuasion

The graduation speaker we referred to at the beginning of this chapter had not outlined her speech. Her ideas were a jumble that her audience found difficult to sort out. They became increasingly restless as she continued to speak and her attempts to persuade them were not effective. They had stopped listening. Audiences need organization and structure to comprehend and be persuaded by your message. This chapter has given you the tools to organize your messages by describing three common organizational plans in persuasive messages: introduction–body–conclusion, AIDA, and motivated sequence. In addition, we have considered the importance of outlining, the difference between a planning and a speaking outline, and the principles of outlining that will help you to construct a good outline, so that you can feel confident that this outline will be the underpinning of a great speech.

But how do you choose which of these organizational plans and patterns to use in your persuasive speech? Is one clearly better than another? We propose that you keep in mind the PAR principle when you make your choice of organizational plan and pattern: purpose, audience, research.

In considering purpose, you need to consider what you are trying to accomplish by giving your persuasive speech. In a public speaking or persuasive speaking course, your instructor may assign a general purpose to give you practice with a particular kind of speech. An assignment may require that you describe both the problem and a solution. In this case, a pro–con organizational pattern will not be adequate to the task. In actual speaking situations, your own goals will influence your choice. Are you attempting to convince your audience that a particular solution is the best option or do you want to convince them that a problem exists? Do you want to heighten the audience's awareness of the problem or move them to take action? These goals would require different organizational plans and patterns.

Your choice may also be influenced by your assessment of your audience. If your audience is already convinced that a problem exists, you may choose to focus on the solution to the problem. On the other hand, if the audience knows little about the problem or if aspects of it are controversial, the cause–effect pattern may be more appropriate. President Bush did not need to convince Americans that terrorism was a problem that could affect them after September 11, but there was far less agreement about what steps should be taken to fight global terrorism and whether these steps were infringing on human rights. President Bush and his advisors focused their persuasive messages on convincing Americans that the appropriate and necessary steps were being taken. You may want your audience to concentrate on visualizing the solution; the motivated sequence would be the most appropriate choice in this case.

The organizational plan and pattern that you choose is often influenced by what you find when you do your research for the speech. You will need solid supporting material to back up your main points. As you begin to investigate your topic, you may find that there is considerably more information about particular aspects of your topic than about others. As you gather this material, you'll need to assess which organizational pattern you have the supporting material to argue persuasively. What information you have (what you can prove) could influence your choice.

Organization and outlining are important tools for the persuader because they are essential for effectively communicating the persuasive message.

Glossary

AIDA: an organizational plan that involves attention, interest, desire and action.

Body of speech: main part of the speech; contains major ideas.

Completeness: a principle of outlining which states that all important information on the message topic should be included.

Conclusion: the final part of a speech.

Coordination: all ideas at the same level of the outline should have the same degree of generality.

Division: a principle of outlining, which states that every idea which is divided should have at least two parts.

Introduction: the beginning of a speech.

Motivated sequence: an organizational plan which has five steps: attention, need, satisfaction, visualization, and action.

Planning outline: detailed outline used for preparing a speech.

Progression: a principle of outlining which assesses the logical sequence of ideas.

Speaking outline: abbreviated outline used when presenting a speech.

Subordination: a principle of outlining which states that secondary ideas should be lower (more specific) than primary ideas.

Symbolization: a principle of outlining that uses symbols and indentation to indicate levels of abstraction of every point in the outline.

Chapter 7

Substance: Support for Your Ideas

Chapter 6 introduced the idea that a persuasive message is like building a house. The organization of ideas (chapter 6) can be considered the framework of the building (girders or supports). The evidence and arguments are the floors, walls, ceilings windows, and doors that are attached to the framework (outline) and turn it into a house. The outline, using principles of outlining like subordination and coordination, arranges your specific ideas or points in an order from first to last (humans can only speak one idea at a time; the outline represents the persuader's decisions about which idea comes first, which is next, and so on, through to the end of the message). An effective outline arranges those ideas in an order that makes sense to the audience. But the outline is just a list of ideas: Those ideas must be conveyed to the audience; your points must be explained or proven to your audience. The support you offer for those ideas (included in your planning outline) turns the outline into a speech.

Supporting Materials

Evidence is information or proof provided by a speaker to convince the audience of the truth, or acceptability, of the claims (statements, ideas, assertions) made in a persuasive message. Specifically, evidence consists of factual information (statistics, dates, examples or descriptions of people, events, things, and ideas) and statements of opinion from those who ought to be believed (experts or eyewitnesses). Closely related to evidence are other forms of support (like comparison), discussed below.

An audience can react to the claims (ideas, outline points) of your persuasive message in three ways. First, some statements that you make in a persuasive message seem plausible, true, or reasonable to your audience. For example, most people would probably agree that heroin is a dangerous drug. Second, your audience can be uncertain about whether to accept something you say. For instance, an audience might not know whether the percentage of twelfth-graders who have used heroin is about 2 percent (according to Black (1998), in 1996 the percentage was 1.8 – but few people probably know this fact). Third, an audience can reject some claims as unreasonable or false. For example, the assertion that "heroin is the most serious problem facing America today" might well be rejected by audience members who think that terrorism, or abortion, or the environment, or some other problem is really the most serious problem.

Statements or claims that your audience already accepts do not require evidence. You may wish to provide a little evidence to support some claims the audience already accepts, to reassure them or to enhance your intrinsic credibility (use of evidence might make you appear knowledgeable, as suggested in chapter 3), but it is not necessary to provide evidence for the claims that appear reasonable to your audience. We would not advise persuaders to load up speeches with lots of evidence proving ideas the audience accepts (the audience could easily become bored). However, statements that your audience rejects, or that your audience is unsure about, require evidence in order to be persuasive. So, evidence can encourage your audience to accept claims when they are uncertain, and it can increase the likelihood that they will even accept claims which seem unreasonable without evidence. This underscores the importance of audience analysis (chapter 5): Only if you understand your audience's attitudes can you decide which ideas in the outline require support.

Note that, when a persuader uses evidence, there are, in an important way, two different sources involved: the speaker, who is the source of the persuasive message in its entirety (this is you, when you create a persuasive message), and the author of the evidence, who is the source of the information used as evidence by the speaker (this is the source of the evidence which you include in your speech). Just as the speaker has credibility, as discussed in chapter 3 (some speakers are perceived by the audience to be more believable than others), so can the author of evidence, too, have credibility (be perceived as an expert or as a reliable eyewitness).

Reinard (1988) reviewed fifty years of experimental research on the persuasive effects of evidence. He concluded that speeches giving evidence are more persuasive than those without evidence. Also, persuasiveness is increased when the speaker identifies the source of evidence (as being an expert). On the other hand, when the speaker simply says something like "a study found" or "the newspaper said," without more information about the evidence source, that does not improve the message's persuasiveness. Persuaders should specifically identify the authors of the study or the newspaper. Reinard also noted that it was difficult to define or distinguish clearly high and low quality evidence (but see the discussion below on tests for the evidence). Nevertheless, he concluded that high quality evidence is probably more persuasive than low quality evidence. Many people now believe that the quality of evidence (intelligence) used by President Bush and examined by members of Congress about weapons of mass destruction in Iraq was weak; of course, we cannot know whether criticism of that evidence could have led to different decisions in the past. So your messages will be more persuasive if you use strong evidence and identify your sources as experts when you quote them.

Sometimes persuaders have competitors (rivals who sell competing goods or services) or opponents (particularly in political campaigns), who will try to change the attitudes of the consumers or voters who like your product or your candidate. When your audience may be exposed to persuasive messages that attempt to change their attitudes (away from the attitudes you want them to have), it is better if they can be made resistant to those contrary persuasive messages. McCroskey (1970) found that including evidence in a persuasive message creates resistance to counterpersuasion (the audience is less likely to switch opinions when another persuader, such as a competitor or opponent, tries to change their minds). For example, consumers who were persuaded by an advertisement from Coke will be more less susceptible to an ad from competitor Pepsi if Coke's ad included evidence.

The elaboration likelihood model (ELM) (chapter 2) would explain that this probably occurs because evidence is likely to be processed centrally, and that attitudes changed via the central route are more resistant to change. If evidence is processed centrally, that could also explain why high quality evidence is more persuasive than low quality evidence (just as strong or high quality arguments are more persuasive in central processing than weak arguments). Only if an audience is actively thinking about the content of your message, doing central processing, would they notice whether evidence is of high or low quality and react accordingly.

Types of support

Supporting materials actually have two basic purposes. As noted above, evidence can be used to prove claims that the audience is unlikely to accept. Supporting materials can also be used to explain ideas that might not be clear to the audience. You have to decide whether a given point in your outline needs explaining or proving (or both) in order to determine whether you should use supporting materials and which supporting materials you should use for that particular idea. Because audience members are different (people with different knowledge and attitudes), this situation highlights once again the importance of audience analysis (chapter 5). You must understand your audience if you want to know which ideas might be unclear – needing further explanation – and which claims the audience probably would not accept – needing evidence. Furthermore, as we will explain later, an audience may reject evidence if it is from a source which appears (to the audience) to be biased or a unqualified. So you need to understand your particular audience in order to know which sources of evidence are likely to be persuasive for it.

There are six different forms of supporting materials. The concept of supporting materials refers to the factual items we call "evidence" – for instance examples, statistics, and expert testimony. However, supporting materials also include other options that do not really fit the label of evidence. Although some supporting materials can help to explain and prove, it might be useful to think that some forms of support are best at explaining and others are most appropriate for proving. Table 7.1 displays the forms of evidence and their primary use. It is also possible to use physical objects, like "exhibits" in criminal trials. We focus on verbal evidence.

Explanation and description

Persuasive messages often need to provide background information, **describing** or explaining people, places, events, and ideas. If you want to persuade an audience that the Internet is changing the way people work, shop, and play, you might want briefly to explain when the Internet was created and how it has exploded – both the number of users, or access to the Internet, has grown and what is available to users on the world wide web has greatly increased. Ideas can be relatively vague ("The Internet has changed our lives") until they are described or explained.

Comparison and contrast

Comparison and contrast help explain ideas by showing similarities (comparison) and differences (contrast) between what you want to explain and something else, which the audience already understands. We opened this chapter with a comparison

Table 7.1   Forms of supporting material

Supporting material	Primary purpose
explanation/description	explain
compare and contrast	explain
hypothetical example	explain
specific example	prove
statistics	prove
expert testimony	prove

between speeches and building houses, assuming that readers understand the basics of buildings (e.g. framework, floors, walls) and hoping that this comparison will help you grasp the relationship between organization and supporting materials. Another example can be found in references to drug abuse as an "epidemic." The word "epidemic" refers to a disease which spreads by infecting healthy people who become sick. The idea is that drug abuse is "contagious" or can be spread from one person to another. Persuaders who compare drug abuse to epidemics may also be trying to suggest that, just as some diseases spread rapidly and threaten life and health, so does drug abuse. Comparison and contrast function by pointing similarities and differences between something the audience already understands well and the new idea you want to explain.

Sopory and Dillard (2002) conducted a meta-analysis of metaphors, which are a common form of comparison used in persuasive messages. "My job is a death-sentence" is a metaphor that uses comparison (a person's job, death) to convey the idea that the speaker's job is extremely unpleasant. Sopory and Dillard found that metaphors have a small but consistent effect on persuasion. Messages with novel (new, unfamiliar) metaphors are more persuasive than messages using old metaphors. It is also better to use a few metaphors (perhaps only a single one) rather than several different metaphors. Metaphors usually are more persuasive when used in the introduction than in the body or the conclusion of a speech.

Hypothetical example

A **hypothetical example** is a fictional instance, usually employed to help the audience understand the nature of a problem. Hypothetical examples illustrate the nature of a problem (or, on occasion, a hypothetical example could show what a solution would look like). If you wanted your audience better to understand the problem of homelessness, you might give them a hypothetical example of a day in the life of someone who is homeless.

> Imagine waking up outside on a dreary wet and cold day, sleeping on the ground. Other people, most of them complete strangers, walk past you as you try to sleep. They look disgusted, pity you, or try to ignore you, none of which are good for your self-esteem. You can't take a shower. You have to go to a bus station to go to the bathroom. You can't go into the kitchen for breakfast because you don't have a kitchen either. You don't change clothes when you wake up because you don't sleep in pajamas when you are outdoors! You can't turn on the heat or the air conditioning or come in out of the rain or snow. You don't have much "stuff," because there are no shelves for books, CDS, DVDs, or other things. Being homeless is physically, psychologically, and emotionally draining.

Because this form of support is hypothetical (made up), these examples are not well-suited for proving that a problem exists, but they can help an audience understand the nature of the problem.

Specific example

A **specific example** (sometimes called a "concrete example" because it is real) is like a hypothetical example, except that a specific instance is something real (not hypothetical). Usually specific examples are not as detailed as the hypothetical examples, but this is not always true. Like a hypothetical example, a specific example can help the audience understand a problem (or a solution). However, because it is real, a specific example also helps to prove that the problem really exists. A persuasive message about the problem of homelessness might mention a homeless person. Specific examples are not well-suited to showing that a problem is widespread or extensive (statistics do that), but they do show that a problem exists and they help the audience understand that problem.

Statistics

Statistics describes things numerically, in three ways. First, it can count or summarize. The statement (in 2003) that there have been 43 presidents of the United States so far is a convenient summary for the specific examples that begin with George Washington, John Adams, Thomas Jefferson and finish with George H. W. Bush, Bill Clinton, and George W. Bush. Second, statistics can compare things. According to US Census Bureau data (2003), in 1995 Alabama had about seven times the population of Alaska (4,253,000 to 604,000). Percentages are a common form of comparative statistics. Finally, statistics can be used to measure (e.g. a table is 4 feet long, a bottle holds 1 liter, or a class is 50 minutes long). It should be obvious that statistics can be useful in proving that a problem is extensive or increasing, or in documenting that a particular solution will noticeably decrease the extent of a problem.

Expert testimony

This form of support can help establish a problem in a variety of ways. **Expert testimony** can explain the causes of the problem, offer predictions about whether it will become worse in the future, conclude that it is serious or widespread, or offer predictions about the benefits (and costs) of possible solutions. As indicated earlier, the audience is more likely to be persuaded by evidence if you make clear to them that each source you use is an expert on the topic. It is probably not necessary to provide a great deal of information about your sources. Noting that a source testifying about the problems of urban sprawl is a Professor of Urban Studies at the University of Chicago is probably sufficient; there is no need to list all of his degrees or publications. Just provide enough information to insure that your audience is likely to agree that your source is an expert on the topic of his or her testimony.

Tests for support

Recall that Reinard (1988) found that high quality evidence is more persuasive than low quality evidence. So, as a persuader, you should use the best quality evidence you can find, not just the first evidence you happen to come across. When you are an audience member, you should evaluate the evidence used to persuade you, so that you are not unduly influenced by weak or poor quality evidence. The tests for supporting material are displayed in table 7.2.

Tests for support which explains (explanatory)

There are two tests for supporting materials of the kind that explains (such as explanation/description, comparison/contrast, and hypothetical examples): relevance and clarity. Supporting materials should have *relevance* to the ideas they explain. Obviously, your support cannot explain an idea if it is irrelevant to it. For example, suppose you want to explain what it is like to have cataracts. Consider these two possibilities.

1 Having cataracts is like looking through dirty glasses. The world is neither bright nor clear; instead, things look blurry and dim.
2 Cataracts form when the lens of the eye becomes discolored. This occurs as part of the natural aging process. Just as elastic loses the ability to stretch as it ages, so too the eyes' lenses gradually lose the ability to pass light effectively.

Both these examples use comparison to explain. However, the first comparison is relevant because it explains the idea (what it is like to experience cataracts). In contrast, the second comparison is irrelevant, explaining a different idea (how cataracts occur).

Second, supporting materials should have *clarity*, or be easy for the audience to understand. Again, it should be easy to see why material that is supposed to explain should be clear to the audience. Consider these two possible supporting materials:

1 Gambling is a real problem today. I had a cousin who gambled all the time. He was a hard-worker, but needed to blow off some steam, if you know what I mean. He really liked to make bets: He bet on the horses, bet on sports, and he liked casinos too. He loved the excitement of thinking he could win big.
2 Gambling is a real problem today. I had a cousin who gambled all the time. He really like to make bets: He bet on the horses, bet on sports, and he like casinos too. But, like most people, he lost most of the time (race tracks, bookies, and casinos stay in business because people lose more than they win). Bets weren't

Table 7.2   Tests for support

Support that explains	relevance
	clarity
Support that proves (demonstrative)	relevance
	recency
	source qualification
	source bias

the only thing my cousin lost: He didn't concentrate on his work and he lost his job; he couldn't keep up the mortgage payments so he lost his house, and he lost his family too. All because of gambling.

Both these excerpts use specific instances about the speaker's cousin. However, it is not clear how the first specific instance shows that gambling is a problem. We do not hear what the consequences were that make gambling a problem. But the second instance clearly explains the problem: He lost most of his bets and this led to losing his job, his home, and his family. The second instance makes it clear why the speaker thinks gambling is a problem.

Tests for support which proves (demonstrative)

The quality of evidence, or the supporting materials used to prove (specific example, statistics, expert testimony) can be evaluated on the basis of four key criteria: relevance, recency, source qualifications (expertise), and source bias (trustworthiness). We will examine each test separately. It is important to understand the tests for the evidence, because our audience may apply such tests as they hear or read our persuasive message. They may not use these terms, but they can use the ideas. We should select the strongest evidence we can find, so that our messages have the highest chance of persuading. The tests can help us weed out evidence which might not be effective with our audience. Furthermore, it is useful for audience members to understand these tests. Although you may use some of the methods of testing when you are yourself an audience member, as just suggested, you may not know all of the tests (and every test of evidence is important).

Relevance.   To be effective, evidence should be **relevant** to the claim being advanced in a persuasive message. The closer a piece of evidence is to the claim being advanced, the stronger the support. For example, this evidence does not support the claim being advanced, that sexually transmitted diseases are increasing: "We must work to reduce sexually transmitted disease because this problem is increasing every year. The Alan Guttmacher Institute reported that 'Every year 3 million teens – about 1 in 4 sexually experienced teens – acquire an STD' (1999)."

This evidence does not prove that the problem is increasing; in fact, the phrase "every year" suggests that teen STDs may be the same every year, not increasing. The evidence provided is relevant to the topic (teen sexually transmitted diseases) but not to the specific claim being made here (that teen STDs are increasing). However, this piece of evidence is relevant to a different claim about the severity of the problem: "Sexually transmitted disease is a serious problem because it affects so many teen-agers. The Alan Guttmacher Institute reported that 'Every year 3 million teens – about 1 in 4 sexually experienced teens – acquire an STD' (1999)."

So, to pass the test of relevance, evidence should relate to the argument being made in a persuasive message. When the evidence is relevant, the message is more likely to be persuasive, but irrelevant evidence cannot be expected to increase a speech's effectiveness.

Recency.   A second standard in evaluating the quality of evidence is recency. The test for *recency* asks if the situation described or discussed in the piece of evidence has changed since that piece was published. Generally, the more recent a piece of evidence is, the more likely is it that it is still true. However, there are exceptions to this rule. For example, any evidence stating that Bin Laden and al Queda did not pose an immediate or serious threat which was published on September 10, 2001 became outdated the very next day, with the tragic events of 9/11. On the other hand, evidence about the date when President Lincoln was shot – April 14, 1865 – which was published, say, in 1870 is still accurate, even though that evidence is now over 130 years old. The key is that the situation involving Bin Laden and al Qaeda changed after the evidence on September 10, 2001; the date of Lincoln's assassination has not changed after 130 years. So evidence becomes outdated, violating the test of recency, when the situation it describes has changed since the evidence in question was published.

If we know that the situation has changed in an important way after some evidence we have found was published, we should not use that evidence (to do so would probably be an ethical violation; see chapter 4). Of course, in practice we do not always know the "facts" behind a piece of evidence independently of that evidence itself. In most cases, we should use the evidence from the most recent sources available, as long as those sources do not violate other tests for the evidence.

Source qualification.   The question of whether a source of evidence is qualified to talk or write about a subject is basically the same as we encountered it in discussing the concept of source expertise (chapter 3). When the source of evidence is *qualified* to comment on a topic, an audience should be more likely to accept that evidence. On the other hand, when a source appears to have no special knowledge of the topic, the audience is probably less persuaded by that evidence (as they should be). The key here is audience perception (as noted earlier, selection of the most persuasive evidence depends on understanding the audience). This is why, if your source might not be known to your audience, you should mention in your message that your source is an expert. Expertise can be established by the source's education, position (job), or past experience in relation to the topic of evidence. The Surgeon General of the United States is likely to be considered an expert on health-related topics, but probably not on sports or economy. If a source is testifying about an event (eyewitness), expertise can be established if the source was present at the event and capable of observing and reporting on it (awake, sober, not too far away to see, and so on). You should identify each source before you present the evidence emanating from it. You want your audience to accept the evidence as you present it: If you identify the source after the evidence, the audience might have dismissed the evidence while they heard it, because they did not realize it was from an expert.

Source bias.   This standard for evaluating the quality of evidence is related to the dimension of source credibility or trustworthiness discussed in chapter 3. A *biased* source is someone who is self-interested in a topic. You would expect a Chief Executive Officer (CEO) making millions of dollars a year in salary and stock options to defend lavish compensation for CEOs. Accordingly, when a highly-paid CEO is used as a source in a persuasive message to prove that CEOs are not overpaid, most audiences will not be very persuaded. Similarly, evidence establishing the dangers of child-birth from pro-choice groups, or evidence stressing the risks of abortion from pro-life groups, might be considered to be from biased sources. Our audiences should be more likely to accept evidence from unbiased (trustworthy) sources than from biased ones. If the audience considers the sources biased, evidence from them will be less persuasive. Persuaders should try to use unbiased sources and they should make it clear to the audience that their sources are objective. This means that it is necessary to learn something about your sources: who they are, where they work, anything relevant to the question of their objectivity.

Notice that source bias is not necessarily a matter of truth. Biased sources may tell the truth. Pro-choice groups might be telling the truth about the dangers of child-birth, and pro-life groups could be accurately reporting on the risks of abortion. However, regardless of whether a biased source is telling the truth, if the audiences views it as biased, that piece of evidence is unlikely to be persuasive. Again, we want to stress that source bias is a perception of the audience, and a persuader must understand his or her audience to know which sources are likely to appear biased (or objective) to it.

Research on the persuasiveness of evidence

Each of the three forms of support that are best suited for proving – expert testimony, specific example, and statistics – has been studied to determine whether they actually increase the persuasiveness of a message. Reinard (1998) has conducted a meta-analysis (a method of combining the results from many individual studies) of the effects of testimony by experts. He found that there is very good reason to conclude that testimony can enhance the persuasiveness of a message.

The other two kinds of evidence are compared quite frequently in research: specific example and statistics. Allen and Preiss (1997) conducted a meta-analysis of research carried on the effects of these kinds of evidence. They concluded that (1) both forms of evidence increase the persuasiveness of a message and (2) statistical evidence tends to be even more persuasive than examples. They also noted that research has not yet tested messages which include both kinds of evidence: It is distinctly possible that the most persuasive approach is the one that uses both statistics and examples. The examples can make the claim seem real, while the statistics can make the it seem more significant.

Reasoning with Evidence

When you need to prove a point in your persuasive message, there are three basic options available to you. For example, suppose you wanted to show, in the summer of 2007, that unemployment is a problem in the United States. The easiest (and arguably the best) way to support this claim is, quite simply, to find evidence about unemployment in America. This could be expert testimony, for example, or a statistics like this: "The unemployment rate was 4.5 percent in May of 2007 in the US" (US Bureau of Labor Statistics, 2007a). This evidence would be easy to use in a speech to support your point: "Unemployment is a problem today in America. According to the US Bureau of Labor Statistics (2007), the US unemployment rate was 4.5 percent in May of 2007. Clearly, four and a half unemployment is a problem." Assuming your audience would agree that 6.1 percent unemployment is undesirable, this evidence proves your claim.

However, it is possible that your research might not find this statistic. Suppose you found these statistics instead: "Unemployment in May 2007 was 3.5 percent in Alabama, 5.2 percent in California, 5.7 percent in Ohio, and 3.8 percent in Vermont" (US Bureau of Labor Statistics, 2007b). Could you somehow use this evidence to support your claim? The difficulty is that you want to show that joblessness is a problem in the United States, but you only have evidence about four states. Still, you could say something like this: "Unemployment in the US is a problem because, according to the US Bureau of Labor Statistics, in April of 2007 the jobless rate was 3.5 percent in Alabama, 5.2 percent in California, 5.7 percent in Ohio, and 3.8 percent in Vermont. So, if the unemployment rate around the country, South, West, East, and Midwest ranges from 3.5 percent to 5.7 percent, the US unemployment rate is probably around 4 percent."

This second option is probably less effective than the first, because your audience might wonder if unemployment in these four states are typical of all fifty states. For all they know, the rate in these four states could be higher or lower than the US unemployment rate. Still, if you cannot find evidence about the US jobless rate, these examples could probably help prove your point.

However, you might not find evidence about unemployment in several states. Perhaps you would find this evidence instead: "Unemployment is increasing everywhere, and international growth is stagnating" (quotation from a business journal, 2007). Again, this evidence does not support your point (unemployment in the US), but it is better than nothing. You could say something like this in your speech: "According to *Business Week*, "[u]nemployment is increasing everywhere, and international growth is stagnating." If unemployment is increasing everywhere, that includes the US. So unemployment is a problem here in America."

As with the previous example, this is not the strongest support for your claim. Your audience may think, for instance, that the US is one of the strongest economies in the world and that, therefore, what is true of other countries might not be true of America. However, if this is the only evidence you can find about unemployment, it is again better than offering no support for your claim.

These examples illustrate an important idea about proving the points in your persuasive message. The evidence you happen to find in your research, if relevant to your point, will be (1) like the point you want to prove, (2) more specific than your point, or (3) more general than your point. The piece of evidence in the first example was just like your point. You wanted to prove that unemployment is a problem in the US, and the evidence you found is a statistics reporting the extent of US unemployment.

The second piece of evidence does not directly support your point because it does not report on US unemployment. The examples given there (of the unemployment rate in Alabama, California, Ohio, and Vermont) are more specific than your point (the entire US). So you need to add something to this evidence, namely a piece of **inductive reasoning** arguing that we can reasonably infer the general (US) unemployment rate from several specifics (the unemployment rates of several states). Inductive reasoning is not certain; as suggested above, if these states are not typical or representative of all states, their jobless rate might be higher, or lower, than in the entire country. We used this kind of reasoning to support an idea when the evidence is relevant to that point, but more specific than the idea.

The third piece of evidence does not directly support your point either; again, it does not tell US joblessness. The evidence there is more general, saying that unemployment is increasing everywhere (in every country in the world). To move from this evidence to your claim, you need to use **deductive reasoning**, which moves from a general statement to something more specific. In this case, if it really is true that unemployment is increasing everywhere (which is what the evidence states), then we can deduce that joblessness must be increasing in America too. So, again, we use reasoning, but one of a deductive nature, to support an idea when the evidence is relevant but more general than the idea.

Hence there are three ways of supporting an idea with evidence (the evidence, of course, must be relevant to the idea; we could not support the claim about US unemployment with statistics about taxes or inflation). If the evidence is just like the idea, we can offer the evidence, and it should support our idea all by itself. However, we can use reasoning to support our idea when the evidence we find is either more general or more specific than our point. The first option is easiest, but we may not always find evidence in the same form as our point. The first option is also less risky, because the audience may be skeptical about the reasoning, be it the movement from specific examples to a general claim or from a more general statement to our point. But when we cannot find evidence that supports our claims directly, we have no choice but to use reasoning.

Tests for reasoning

Both inductive and deductive reasoning involve inferences; the conclusions they support are probable but not certain. Each form of reasoning admits of tests (like the tests for the evidence) that can help you separate weak and strong arguments (so that you can rely on strong ones in your message). The tests for these two forms of reasoning are different.

Tests for inductive reasoning

There are three tests for inductive reasoning, or arguments that move from specific examples to more general claims. Remember the argument that began with the unemployment rates for four states (Alabama, California, Ohio, and Vermont) and drew a conclusion about US unemployment. First, the examples selected for your argument must be *typical*, or just like any other examples you might select. For example, unemployment is 3.1 percent in South Dakota and 3.4 percent in North Dakota. However, these states are in the upper Midwest and less industrialized than many other states, so their unemployment rate may not be typical of the entire country. On the other hand, joblessness was 8 percent in Oregon and 7.3 percent in Washington. But these two states are both in the Pacific Northwest. The four states we selected in the example above (Alabama, California, Ohio, and Vermont) showed more geographic diversity. Of course, you cannot always know whether your examples are typical or not. However, you should try to use examples that are typical whenever possible. This is important, both to be ethical and because you can lose credibility if the audience decides you picked atypical examples.

A second test of inductive reasoning is *sufficiency*, a principle which questions whether or not you have examined a large enough number of examples. It should be clear that the more examples you provide, the more likely your conclusion is to be true. There is no universal answer to the question, how many examples are enough. Three examples are better than one or two. The audience will probably be bored if you give them too many examples. We think that giving unemployment rates for four states was probably sufficient to support our claim. This means that the sufficiency test for inductive reasoning depends on the audience: Is it likely that the audience will think you have given enough examples?

The third test is whether negative instances (exceptions, examples that are inconsistent with your claim) can be explained. It has been said that every rule has an exception (except this rule itself!). If you look at the jobless rate in every individual state, there will of course be differences. A few states have very high unemployment rates, whereas in others rates will be quite low. If you are trying to conclude that unemployment is about 6 percent, you need to be prepared to answer questions that the audience might have about exceptions: Unemployment was only 3.1 percent in South Dakota and it was 7.2 percent in Alaska. Most people realize that unemployment varies somewhat from state to state, and these two states are exceptions (they had, in fact, the lowest and highest rates of unemployment in April 2003; US Bureau of Labor Statistics, 2003b). However, if you cannot explain instances that contradict your conclusion, the audience is unlikely to agree with your point.

Tests for deductive reasoning

There are two important tests for deductive reasoning. First, is the specific instance included in the generalization? This form of reasoning applies a generalization (unemployment in the world) to a specific instance (unemployment in the US). In this example, the United States is clearly a part of the world. So, when you have a generalization like "unemployment is increasing everywhere [= internationally]," it is reasonable to assume that this generalization includes the US. However, if the generalization had been different ("unemployment is increasing across Europe," or "unemployment is rising in the third world"), the US would have been excluded from the generalization. Clearly, one cannot reasonably infer that, because unemployment is increasing in Europe, it is also increasing in America. It might be increasing in both places, but then again it might not. So, when you apply a generalization to an instance, that instance must be included in the generalization.

Second, is the specific instance an exception to the rule? As noted above in the tests for an inductive argument, most rules have exceptions. When we say something like "unemployment is increasing around the world," that may not necessarily mean "in every single country in the world." Perhaps the US, because it is such a large industrialized country, is one of a few exceptions to the generalization. The US is still a country in the world (so it is not excluded from the generalization, as the US would be excluded from generalizations about European countries). However, it might still be an exception. When you apply a generalization to a specific instance, you need to make sure your instance is not an exception, but is just like most (or all) of the other instances in the generalization.

Fear Appeals

A persuader can base an argument on appealing to the audience on different emotions. However, one emotional appeal is used extensively in persuasion and has been the subject of both theory and research: fear appeals. The basic idea is that you can change a person's behavior by engaging their fear. An example of a fear appeal is a doctor who tells a patient that he has diabetes, and that diabetes can cause blindness (and other health problems) unless the patient reduces his blood sugar level. When and how should you use fear appeals in your persuasive messages?

Early work on fear appeals asserted a curvilinear, inverted U relationship between fear and persuasion (Janis 1967): moderate amounts of fear were more effective than small or large amounts of fear. However, meta-analysis (research that statistically combines the results of many earlier studies) has shown that the relationship between fear and attitude change is direct and linear: High levels of fear can be very persuasive (Mongeau 1998).

Research has clearly established that persuasive messages designed to evoke fear (e.g. describing the terrible consequences of some danger) usually increase the perceived fear (ibid.). However, reactions to that fear can vary (Leventhal 1970). Persuaders want their audiences to use their fear as motivation to comply with recommendations in the message. This reaction is called **danger control** – the attempt to alleviate fear by taking action to reduce the feared risk. However, an audience may become so anxious from the fear appeal that they engage instead in **fear control**, ignoring the message or denying the risk, trying to reduce the fear without taking constructive action to cope with the danger.

Witte (1994) elaborated Leventhal's perspective into the extended parallel processing model (EPPM) of fear appeals. A fear appeal message can contain two elements: the **threat**, which arouses fear by describing the consequences of a particular danger, and the **recommendation**, which allows the audience to reduce the danger by averting the threat. O'Keefe (2002) notes that a fear appeal message is similar to a problem-solution organizational pattern (chapter 6). The problem part identifies the danger which arouses fear, and the solution part offers recommendations to reduce that danger. Each of these two general elements, in turn, has two other specific components. Threat is made up of **severity**, which concerns how serious the effects of the danger are, and **susceptibility**, which concerns the likelihood of the danger's afflicting the audience. A doctor who says "diabetes can cause blindness" is stressing severity. By contrast, a doctor who says "a man of your age, weight, and blood sugar level is in much greater risk of losing his eyesight from diabetes" is emphasizing susceptibility. It makes sense that an audience would be likely to experience fear from a threat that is (1) severe and (2) represents a danger they are likely to experience.

The recommendation is another important component of a successful fear appeal. In fact, it seems likely that the fear control response, in which the audience does not do anything constructive about the danger, is much more likely to occur when they do not know what to do to prevent that danger. The first component of the recommendation is **response efficacy**, which measures the extent to which the solution is likely to prevent the danger. **Self-efficacy**, which is the extent to which the audience believes they are capable of implementing the solution, is the second element of the recommendation. A doctor who recommends a low carbohydrate diet because "this diet has been proven to reduce weight and to bring blood sugar levels down to a normal level" is discussing response efficacy. The question of whether the patient believes he can stick to that diet is self-efficacy. Again, this theory makes sense: For a recommendation to be seen as desirable, the audience must believe that (1) the solution will work (prevent the danger) and that (2) they are capable of putting the solution into effect. These concepts are displayed in table 7.3.

Several recommendations arise from this understanding of fear appeals in persuasive messages. The persuader should address both the threat and the recommendation. The threat should be described as severe and as a risk that could afflict the audience. The recommended solution should be portrayed as effective and as something the audience can do. Messages that lack one or more of these elements may fail, either because they do not evoke fear or because the audience reacts with fear control rather than danger control.

Factors of Interest

Another important part of the substance of your speech are the *factors of interest*, which are strategies to help you gain the attention of your audience in the introduction and then maintain their interest throughout the remainder of your message. Factors of interest can also be important if you are trying to increase your audience's

Table 7.3 Elements of the extended parallel processing model (Witte)

Threat	*Recommendation*
severity	response efficacy
susceptibility	self-efficacy

Source: Witte 1994

involvement in your topic, so that they will be more likely to engage in central processing. As with supporting materials, you need to understand your audience in order to know which ideas or topics will be interesting or boring to them.

Reality

Persons, things, and events that are real (true, not hypothetical or imaginary) have the quality of *reality*. Things that are real tend to attract our attention more than hypothetical or abstract ideas. Surely interest in things that are real explains part of the appeal of the current wave of reality television. A persuasive message about a problem can make the problem seem more real by referring to real events and victims. "Car-jacking is, unfortunately, a fact of life. Sheri Newman had her car stolen at a stop light in Indianapolis." This factor of interest can be useful throughout a persuasive message.

Conflict

Writers of fiction know that *conflict*, or clash between people and groups, tends to catch our attention: We want to know who will win or lose, what the outcome will be. The existence of conflict in a topic area shows that the situation is not a one-sided one and suggests that we might want to learn more about it to make up our minds. Conflict is probably best used as an attention-getting device in a persuasive message. Consider a dialogue between an environmental advocate and a logger:

> FIRST SPEAKER: You greedy loggers are destroying our forests! Don't ruin another wild-life habitat.
> SECOND SPEAKER: Stupid tree-hugger! We bought these trees and we're gonna cut them down.

This brief confrontation between logging and environmental concerns should help create interest in a speech on this topic.

Novelty

Products are often advertised as "new" and "improved" because things that are *new* (novel) are often interesting. Some things we know well still interest us, but as a general rule things which are new are interesting simply because we do not know about them. Knowing that something is new can spark our interest in it. This factor of interest is another one that is probably best suited for catching our attention in the introduction. A message about a new product could stress: "Have you seen the latest in urban transportation? It is small, motorized, and you need to buy one today." The fact that a product or topic is new to your audience can lead them to pay attention to your message.

Curiosity

Human beings are often inquisitive, or *curious*. Sometimes we can ask a question or make a statement that arouses our audience's curiosity. If so, they are more likely to pay attention to our message. This factor of interest is also, probably, most useful in the introduction. "It's a rush! It will spike your adrenaline! The view is amazing! What is it? You have to try skydiving." The first three statements and the question are designed to pique your curiosity and attract your interest in a message which attempts to persuade you to try skydiving.

Proximity

People, places, and events that occur near to us in space or time (in proximity) are more likely to affect us personally, and thus they tend to catch our attention. Therefore specific instances might be more effective when they concern things that the audience experiences in daily life. A message which recommends obtaining inoculations for a disease could start this way: "Hepatitis B is a serious disease. There are cases every year right here on our campus." *Proximity* is a factor of interest that can be used throughout a message both to gain and to maintain audience interest.

Humor

We like to be amused, so humor has the potential to put an audience into a more receptive mood. Using *humor* can be risky, because some people do not have the personality (or the timing) to pull it off effectively. Audience analysis is very important, because what seems funny to you may not sound funny to your audience! Furthermore, building persuasion often revolves around serious topics, and humor can be inappropriate in such situations. Still, humor is a potential method of stimulating your audience's interest. We believe humor is best used in the attention-getting portion of the introduction.

Vital factors

Vital factors refer to life, health, economic security, and other things that affect our well-being. It should be obvious that we have good reason to pay close attention to topics that can affect ourselves (or our family and friends) in important ways. A message advocating a home alarm system might begin this way: "Home security is important to your peace of mind. Thieves can break into your house, steal your property, and threaten you and your loved ones." Vital factors can be particularly useful in providing the audience with a reason to listen and in establishing the severity of a problem.

Familiarity

Although things that are new can attract our attention, we care about things and understand them when we are *familiar* with them. A speaker might hold up an automobile safety belt: "See this? You probably see one of these every day when you ride to school or work. In fact, some people are so used to this sight that they take their seat belts for granted." Familiarity can encourage the audience to care about the topic. It can increase their sense of involvement in the topic.

Activity or movement

Advertisers have long known that things (and people) which show *activity* or *movement* tend to stand out from the background. Persuaders can use this factor of interest when giving a presentation, using physical movement to add interest to the message. We do not recommend incessant movement, which appears to be aimless or nervous. However, using gestures from time to time and taking a step or two between main ideas can make your message visually more interesting. Judicious use of visual aids can also provide some purposeful activity to a message.

Notice that some of these factors of interest appear to be contradictory. Novelty and familiarity are clearly quite different ideas. However, both factors can increase the audience's attention, but for different reasons. People are complex. That which is novel can command our attention because it can satisfy our curiosity. That which is familiar can be interesting too, because it may be something that actually affects our lives. Understanding different ways to capture and maintain an audience's interest gives you more options to increase the effectiveness of your persuasive message.

Using Supporting Materials and Factors of Interest in a Persuasive Message

Theoretically, once you have organized the ideas in your message (chapter 6), you need to have support for them. This suggests that the outline comes first and, after the outline is completed, you develop the support for your idea. Often, however, the process of developing a persuasive message does not actually work this way. For example, when you are preparing a persuasive message on a topic that is new to you, you may not have many ideas about what to say until after you have done research – and found evidence – on your topic. When you find evidence to prove an idea, you learn about the idea itself. On the other hand, if you understand a topic well at the beginning of your message preparation, you might know that your problem has, say, three causes and two effects. You can decide to use a cause–effect outline and then, after you have sketched it out, you can go on to look for the best evidence to prove each of the three causes and both of the effects. So sometimes your outline will come first, and only after the outline is complete can you look for evidence to support the various ideas in it.

It is important to realize that you do not necessarily have to find evidence for every point in your speech. The only "rule" that matters is to provide evidence (support) for any point your audience might not already believe or be willing to accept. If much of what you plan to say are ideas your audience already accepts, then you may need relatively little evidence. Some evidence might reassure them, or enhance your credibility as a knowledgeable speaker on the topic, but there is no need to go overboard with evidence if the audience is generally in agreement with you. If you are planning to say many things your audience will probably reject, you will need more (and high quality) evidence. Even then, success is not guaranteed, but evidence will increase the likelihood that your message will be persuasive. If your purpose is to reinforce your audience's existing attitudes, you may not need as much evidence.

A second suggestion is that you should design the claims in your message carefully. For example, if you are trying to persuade an employer to offer you a job, you might want to argue that you have the highest grade point average compared to any applicant. However, this claim would be difficult to establish (unless you knew every applicant's grade point average), and in fact it might not be true. It would be much easier to prove that you had high grades, and that could well be enough to get you the job. You should develop claims or arguments or points that (1) will help achieve your goal and (2) your audience will probably be willing to accept.

This distinction between "highest grades" and "high grades" may sound trivial, but it is not. First, a persuader should not invite disagreement. If you think you can persuade a company to offer you a job by claiming that you have high grades, it would be a mistake to take the risk of possibly making your audience reject your message by making a stronger and unnecessary claim ("my grades are the highest among those of any applicant"). Second, the more reasonable claim ("I have high grades") might not even require evidence if it is plausible to your audience (of course, your transcript might reassure or reinforce your audience). If you choose to advance the more extreme claim ("highest grades"), you will need more evidence than your transcript, and, even then, your audience might not agree. Of course, if you are convinced that your speech will not be effective if you make the weaker claim, you should try to prove the stronger one.

Third, we urge persuaders to collect more evidence than they could include in a persuasive message. Having too much evidence allows you to select the pieces which will be most effective (on the basis of tests for evidence): evidence that is most relevant to the claims your audience might not accept, evidence that is recent enough, evidence from sources your audience will perceive as both expert and unbiased. Only if you have more evidence than you need can you choose the one that will be most persuasive for your audience.

A fourth suggestion concerns the use of inductive and deductive reasoning. Reasoning should be used when a piece of evidence is either more general than the claim you need to support (which calls for deductive reasoning) or more specific than the claim you need to support (which calls for inductive reasoning). Keep the tests for reasoning in mind, so as to avoid relying on an argument that the audience might reject.

Fear appeals can be a useful means of motivating your audience – a fifth suggestion. Your message is more likely to arouse fear if you demonstrate both (1) the severity of the threat and (2) the audience's susceptibility to that threat. Your audience is more likely to adopt your recommendations to reduce the fear (danger control) when you persuade them both (1) that the recommendations will effectively deal with the threat and (2) that they have the ability to implement those recommendations successfully.

Factors of interest should be used throughout your speech. You should gain your audience's attention in the introduction and then try to maintain interest throughout your message. There are two places in the introduction where factors of interest are particularly important. Recall that introductions usually have five parts. Two of these parts, namely the attention-getting device and the reason to listen, should make use of the factors of interest. Another way to attract the audience's attention is to gain their interest. It is human nature to pay attention to things that are interesting; we are more likely to ignore things that do not interest us. So, understanding the factors of interest can give you ideas about how to attract the audience's attention.

Furthermore (unless you want the audience to engage in peripheral processing), the part of an introduction which deals with the reason to listen can increase involvement in your message and its topic. Knowing the various factors of interest (and knowing your audience, as explained in chapter 5) can help you relate your topic to the needs and interests of your particular audience. This can increase the likelihood that they will pay attention to (and centrally process) the rest of your persuasive message. For instance, a speech on alcohol abuse to a group of college students could use proximity and mention instances of alcohol abuse at their university. Or that speech could use vital factors and remind them that the potential victims of this problem include themselves, their friends, and their brothers and sisters.

Finally, it is a good idea to make an effort to maintain the audience's interest throughout the entire message. You can use the factors of interest to help you make points or select supporting materials that will be more interesting to the audience during the body of the message. For example, if you are developing a persuasive message about bankruptcy for an audience in St Louis Missouri, you might have found two examples of businesses that recently went bankrupt. If one of these companies is located in St Louis and the other in Albuquerque, you might select the St Louis company to include in your message, because proximity (to your audience) might make this example more interesting. This reinforces the idea that you should collect more evidence than you can use in your message, so that you can choose the best (most persuasive) support for your message.

Glossary

Comparison and contrast: (demonstrating) similarities and differences between what a speaker wants to explain and what the audience already understands.

Danger control: attempting to alleviate fear by taking action to reduce risk.

Deductive reasoning: inferring specifics from generalities.

Evidence: information provided by a speaker to explain or prove ideas.

Expert testimony: a credible source (quotation) that provides information.

Explanation/description: (providing) background information on a topic.

Fear control: ignoring the message or denying the risk without taking constructive action to cope with danger. Hypothetical example: fictional instance that helps the audience understand the nature of a problem. Likely to be extended rather than a brief mention.

Inductive reasoning: inferring a general principle from specific examples.

Recommendation: a suggestion for reducing the risk of danger.

Response efficacy: the extent to which the solution advocated in a persuasive message will probably prevent danger.

Self-efficacy: the extent to which an audience member believes that he or she is capable of implementing a recommendation.

Severity: the degree of seriousness of the danger.

Specific example: a real instance, usually brief, that helps explain the nature of the problem.

Susceptibility: the likelihood that danger will afflict the audience.

Statistics: numerical descriptions of information (counting, measurement, comparison).

Threat: a message that arouses fear.

Chapter 8

Symbols and Style

If language is a system of symbols and the essence of being human, then style lets each of us stamp our own personality on our persuasive messages. This chapter is divided into two parts: symbols and style. The section on symbols considers the characteristics of symbols, denotative and connotative meanings, ultimate terms as persuasive tools, and the relationship between symbols and reality. The second part, on style, examines different types of style and the important stylistic goals for achieving clarity, interest, rhythm, and humor.

Symbols

The McDonald's Arch. The words "puppy," "computer," and "rainbows." The first and second finger straightened up, with the rest of the hand in a fist (i.e. the victory sign). What do these things have in common? They are all symbols. A **symbol** is something that stands for, or represents, another thing. Some of these symbols are words. Others are nonverbal and visual symbols that have been converted into language so that we can talk about them. When we talk about language, we can say that all language is symbolic because it represents ideas and objects. The ability to use symbols is an important feature distinguishing us as human beings. Kenneth Burke, a literary critic, is famous for writing that a human being is a "the symbol-making, symbol-using, symbol-misusing animal" (Burke 1989: 263). Next, we describe the characteristics of symbols.

Characteristics of symbols

Three important characteristics of symbols are that they are arbitrary, adaptable, and conventional. First, symbols are arbitrary. With very few exceptions (for instance the word "buzzing," which imitates the actual sound), there is no objective reason why one word has been selected to represent an idea or object rather than another. Baseball came to refer to the national sport, but it could have just as easily been dubbed batball, glovebat, or diamondball. How did flicking on a lighter at the end of a concert come to be a symbol for a request for an encore? There is no direct relationship between the lighter and the request for more music. Why is applause a symbol of approval, and not hopping on one foot, or patting one's head? The relationship between the symbol and the meaning that has come to be attached to it is arbitrary.

Second, symbols adapt to their circumstances. The meanings of words, for example, have changed over time. "Awful" originally meant deserving of awe. "Pretty" meant crafty, clever, skillfully constructed, fine, and then beautiful. "Tell" was defined as "to count." Words with recent transformations in meanings include "bad" and "gay": Bad can be good (as in "cool") and gay is not just "happy" any longer. Symbols are reflections of the culture and are created, or become more common, when there is a reason to describe particular ideas or objects. September 11, 2001, had a great impact on language: symbols like "ground zero," "Let's roll," "9/11," and "Jihad" became commonplace (Spiegelman 2002).

Third, to say that symbols are conventional amounts to saying that we need to come to some agreement about the meaning of symbols like words. Without this agreement, communication cannot take place. We agree that "baseball" will refer to a game played by two teams of nine players each, who use a hard rawhide-covered ball and a wooden bat in which players score runs. The fact that we have an agreement means that we do not have to explain these details each time we mention the game, because we have agreed that the symbol "baseball" will refer to this particular meaning.

Denotative and connotative meaning

The dictionary meaning of a word is known as **denotative meaning**. But words also have **connotative meanings**, the subjective meanings of words as symbols. These meanings include our reactions to symbols – our attitudes toward these words, which are very much a part who we are. In fact, this is the reason why it is often said that meanings are in people – not in the words themselves. In fact, there are more than 14,000 different meanings for the 500 most frequently used words in the English language (Rothwell 1982). In the example used earlier, we gave the denotative definition of "baseball." There would be little disagreement about this conventional definition, but the connotative meanings for "baseball" are likely to be different depending on your own experiences and background. If you played it, you may have more positive attitudes because of your fond memories of playing the game. Or you might be a disgruntled fan, who has been disgusted about baseball strikes and now has negative attitudes to it. Your attitudes may be influenced by movies you have seen about baseball, such as *Field of Dreams* and *Bull Durham*. In any event, these meanings are much richer and involve more of your own experiences than the denotative meaning. As a persuader, a speaker wants to evoke connotative meanings that will be consistent with her purpose. For example, if the purpose of a message is to secure funding for a new baseball stadium, the speaker will want to remind the audience of their days of enjoyment, either in playing or in watching baseball; she will encourage them to support the proposal by eliciting these positive connotative meanings.

Ultimate terms: god and devil terms

Some symbols are very powerful persuasive tools because they are fixed within the culture and are generally accepted as givens. These symbols are **ultimate terms** and represent an ideal image of the culture and take the form of god and devil terms (Weaver 1953). A **god term** is routinely accepted as positive and carries special persuasive power when used by a speaker because an audience does not question the validity of this symbol. When Weaver wrote in the 1950s, "progress" and "American" were examples of god terms. Today, examples of god terms would be "technology" and "honesty." After 9/11, "American" and "patriotism" have regained or revitalized their status as god terms. A **devil term** refers to a symbol which is hated and rejected without another thought. Back in the 50s, examples of devil terms included "Communists" and "Nazis," whereas today devil terms include "terrorists" and "child abusers."

The use of ultimate terms reveals a persuader's vision of the ideal world (Foss, Foss, and Trapp 2002). Because ultimate terms are also unquestioned by most audience members, they can be very persuasive. When the audience believes that god terms can reasonably be associated with the position a speaker advocates and devil terms can be associated with the alternatives, the persuasive impact of culturally accepted attitudes works in favor of the speaker who can use these terms effectively.

Symbols and reality

Although Burke saw humans as symbol users, he understood that it was through the use of symbols (words and other symbols) that they were able to persuade others to cooperate with them. Burke shows that much of our reality is constructed through symbols. These symbols name things and often do not do so objectively but by evoking an attitude toward the named object. Burke asked, "can we bring ourselves to realize … just how overwhelmingly much of that which we mean by 'reality' has been built up for us through nothing but our symbol systems?" (1966: 5). We come to know the world through the symbols people use to describe it. If you have never been to Tibet, your knowledge of it comes exclusively through the message and symbols others have used to describe the country. Thus, language as a symbolic system is instrumental in shaping what we can know. It is difficult to "know" when we do not have symbols to describe what we know. As a speaker, you use symbols to shape the reality perceived by your audience.

Style

Britney Spears and Hillary Clinton have very different styles of speaking. Imagine the confusion that would occur if they were to switch styles and Hillary started to talk like Britney or vice versa. Neither person would be likely to be very persuasive using the other's style; it would probably be seen as a joke. **Style** is the art of selecting and arranging words and sentences in order to accomplish a speaker's goals. In a speaking situation, it is a manner of producing discourse that others associate with the way a person speaks. Some people have such unique speaking styles that they come to have **signature styles** that are easily recognized by others when they talk. Arnold Schwarzenegger ("I'll be back") and Dick Vitale ("Shoot the rock, baby!") have signature styles that are highly individualized. Their styles of speaking are unique and familiar.

Although it is easy to see that Britney and Hillary have different styles, it is more difficult to say what makes them different. All right, Hillary would probably never say "oops" in public. But beyond that, what makes these styles distinct? We will consider types of style, then describe the elements of style that a persuader can select, so as to increase the persuasiveness of the message through stylistic devices designed to produce clarity, interest, rhythm, and humor.

Oral and written style

The first important distinction is the one between oral and written styles. You have probably noticed that you do not speak exactly the same way you write. In fact, people who do speak the way they write are really difficult to understand. If you have ever had the misfortune of having a paper read at you, you have quickly realized the difference between oral and written styles. There are four important differences between oral and written styles.

Simplicity

An oral style is characterized by shorter sentences and fewer clauses than a written style. The organization of a message is usually less complex in an oral than in a written style.

Repetition

An oral style repeats key ideas more frequently than the written style because the listener must hear the ideas and organizational structure. In contrast, the reader can reread an idea presented in written form to determine the structure if necessary.

Informality

An oral style is characterized by more colloquial, incomplete, even ungrammatical expressions than a written style.

Spontaneity

Responsiveness to the audience, situation, and self are more common in an oral than in a written style (Macaulay 1990; Zarefsky 1999). There is more of an opportunity to interact and adapt in an oral presentation than in a written document.

One of the following excerpts is from an online newspaper and illustrates a written style; the other presents the same information in an oral style. Compare the two examples. Which one illustrates the oral style? Which one illustrates the written style? How do they differ? What characteristics of an oral style can you see illustrated when you compare the two examples?

> EXCERPT 1: A new study shows people who live within a mile of a college campus are more than twice as likely as those living farther away to face public disturbances – vandalism, noise or litter, for example – caused by college students' drinking, and the researchers suggest that limiting the number of bars and liquor stores in these areas would help ease the problem. College students were not viewed as primarily responsible for most negative incidents. But respondents who lived within a mile of a college were more likely to report at least one negative incident caused by college students than were those who lived farther away.

> EXCERPT 2: People living close to campus are more likely to complain about vandalism and noise caused by students drinking than people living a mile or more from campus. But in this study, college students were not seen as the main problem. Not the main problem. Instead, cutting down on the number of bars and liquor stores close to campus would go a long way toward solving the real problem for these neighbors.

The oral style example (excerpt 2) illustrates simplicity. The sentences are shorter and have fewer clauses than the written style example. The average length of sentences in the written example is 35 words, whereas the average length of the sentences in the oral example is 17 words. There is more repetition in the oral style (e.g. "Not the main problem," "close to campus") and some informality with the sentence fragment "Not the main problem."

Types of oral style

But oral styles can also be quite different from each other. When Will Smith was preparing to play Mohammad Ali, he took voice lessons to learn to imitate the signature oral style of the champion boxer. Although there are many ways to individualize a style, the three major oral styles are plain, middle, and grand (Cicero: 1921).

The plain style

The **plain style** is used when clarity is the most important purpose for the speaker and the speaker takes prides in speaking in a straightforward manner. The plain style is often used to teach or educate. This kind of style is illustrated in the following example of a speaker who gave a speech on organic foods.

Simple sentences with few clauses.   The plain style speaker says, "Organic fruits and vegetables cost just a few cents more in your grocery budget" instead of "Organic fruits and vegetables are 2–4 percent more expensive than fruits and vegetables which are grown with insecticide, although this depends entirely on the size of the health food market in the area and that figure can range from no additional expense to about 6 percent."

Simple organizational structure.   The speaker has two main points in the speech: (1) organic fruits and vegetables are better for you, and (2) organic fruits and vegetables cost only a few cents more. She doesn't try to overwhelm the audience with too much information.

Few stylistic embellishments.   The speaker may use humor but introduces very few other stylistic features (e.g. alliteration, repetition, metaphor).

Standard word choices.   The plain style speaker uses "organic" or "natural" foods rather than "macrobiotic," because the first two are standard word choices and less technical terms. For example, this speaker says:

> We are what we eat. And when we eat natural foods, we are healthier. This apple has never been touched by chemicals [holds up an organic apple]. But this apple has been sprayed with a toxic chemical [holds up a regular apple]. You can wash it but the chances of getting it all off are very small. And so it goes into your system. I figure the average person eats an apple a week. By now, that means you've consumed about a 1,000 apples. Each one of them has left a bit of chemical that does not belong in your body.

The persuasive speaker chooses words that will communicate her message clearly to her audience.

Unfortunately, this style has been appropriated by some people who want simply to create the appearance of being straightforward. As receivers of persuasive messages, we are reluctant to believe a speaker who suddenly appears to adopt a plain style or who seems insincere in enacting this style. This would violate the ethical guideline we suggested in chapter 3, that speakers should be honest about their intentions.

The middle style

According to Cicero, the purpose of the **middle style** is to please or to entertain. This style is sometimes referred to as sweet, because audiences have a delightful and pleasant experience when the speaker uses it. The features of the middle style include:

Pleasing words.   Some words are pleasing to listen to because of their sounds. Others are pleasing to listen to because of their content. A speaker who begins with the following illustrates the latter: "It is such an honor to be asked to speak before you tonight. I know that I am in terrific company." This speaker compliments his audience and pleases them by doing so.

Smooth composition.   A smooth composition is one that goes together grammatically and flows when spoken. It does not sound choppy or stilted. Part of this is delivery and part of it is language. Compare the following two statements: "I was raised in Toledo, Ohio, then I went to school in Columbus, finally I worked on a newspaper in Newport" and: "I grew up in Toledo, went to school in Columbus, and got my first job writing for a newspaper in Newport." The second statement has more natural rhythm and flows better when spoken.

Extravagant use of stylistic devices.   The middle style makes use of stylistic devices and exaggerates them for effect. Narratives and humor are especially prominent.

Moderate complexity of ideas and structure.   Compared to the plain style, there are more ideas and more complexity in the structure, but less than in the grand style.

The grand style

In contrast to the plan and middle style, the **grand style** is majestic and impressive. Cicero believed the purpose of the grand style was to persuade and arouse a strong emotional response from the audience. Speakers are fiery and eloquent. This style typically has the following characteristics:

Unusual word choices.   The speaker says, "I suggest that we convoke a meeting of those best-placed to invoke transformation" instead of "I suggest we call a meeting of people who can help create change."

Complexity of ideas and organizational structure.   A speaker using the grand style is likely to introduce more main ideas in the body of the speech and to establish more complex relationships between those ideas for the audience to follow than a speaker who uses the middle style.

Frequent use of stylistic devices.   These devices may be metaphors, similes, narratives, or other such features. The speaker using the grand style often resorts to these devices for clarity, interest, and rhythm. Jesse Jackson often speaks in grand style and his speeches are marked by the frequent use of stylistic devices. Consider an excerpt from his address after the meeting with President Arafat: "Our quest is to promote reconciliation and reconstruction over continued destruction; to choose coexistence over co-annihilation; to give a generation of Israelis and Palestinians a chance to live as neighbors with a shared hope" (Jackson 2002). In this one sentence, Jackson illustrates multiple stylistic devices. There is parallel structure in the image of one thing over another (reconciliation over reconstruction and destruction; coexistence over co-annihilation). He illustrates alliteration in the repetition of sounds with reconciliation and reconstruction, coexistence and co-annihilation, choose and chance.

Complex sentence structures.   The speaker uses sentences with several compound clauses rather than short, simple sentences. Jackson's excerpt above also illustrates the use of multiple clauses that create a complex sentence in grand style. The characteristics of the grand style share some similarities with the written style. Cicero thought each style had a different purpose, but we do not agree with him here. Cicero believed that the grand style was most appropriate for the persuasive situation. We believe that any of the styles can be used in persuasive situations. A persuasive speaker may need to explain, entertain (secure the audience's interest), and persuade in order to be effective. Hence a persuasive speaker may use more than one style in a given speech.

Stylistic Goals

Style is purposeful and a persuasive speaker selects stylistic elements to accomplish particular persuasive objectives. There are four stylistic goals, namely achieving clarity, increasing intensity, establishing rhythm, and creating humor. A persuasive speaker improves understanding and recall of the message by selecting stylistic devices that will achieve clarity. Stylistic devices for increasing interest insure that listeners attend to the message with interest. Persuasive messages with rhythm establish an appropriate mood. Humor is indirectly persuasive through attention, distraction, and liking for the speaker (see box 8.1).

Clarity

Clarity is the quality of speaking in an unambiguous way, so that an audience can understand the speaker. The speaker's ideas are transparent to those who listen the message. The meaning is not difficult to ascertain. Six stylistic devices to achieve clarity are: concrete words, active voice, axioms, concise word usage, ordinary words, and limited complexity.

Concrete words

Concrete words are the opposite of abstract words. A concrete word refers to a specific object which can be perceived, but an abstract word refers to an object that

Box 8.1   Stylistic goals and strategies
Clarity
Concrete words
Active voice
Axioms
Concise word usage
Ordinary words
Limited complexity
Intensity
Vivid description
Visualization
Narrative
Hyperbole
Personification
Similes and metaphors
Rhythm
Repetition
Parallel wording
Antithesis
Alliteration
Rhyme
Humor
The pun
The anecdote
Satire
Irony
The humorous metaphor
The joke

cannot be accessed through the senses. "Big Mac"™ is a concrete word because its referent can be touched and smelled, while "corporate America" is an abstract word because it cannot be directly contacted through the five senses. When a speaker uses abstract words, there is more opportunity for misunderstanding.

Active voice

When the subject of the sentence performs an action, we say that the speaker is using the **active voice**. When the object of an action becomes a (grammatical) subject in the sentence, we say that the speaker is using the **passive voice**. The active voice is clearer: it is not as wordy or ambiguous about who the actor is in the sentence. An example should establish this point. A persuasive speaker who prepared a speech on binge drinking made the following remark: "Students perceive their peers' drinking levels to be higher than they actually are." This statement is phrased in the active voice. In the passive voice, the same remark would be phrased as follows: "The drinking levels of students are perceived by their peers to be higher than they actually are."

In the passive voice, the object (drinking levels) becomes the subject of the sentence. You will notice that the sentence is longer in the passive voice and more difficult to follow.

Axioms

An **axiom** is a wise saying which is widely accepted. It is brief and effective because it rapidly and unmistakably captures the meaning a speaker wants to convey to an audience. Some examples of maxims would be: "Practice makes perfect," or "One who hesitates is lost."

Concise word usage

Concise word usage consists in speaking briefly and to the point. It is contrasted with wordy, lengthy, and long-winded speech. If a speaker wants an audience to follow what is being said, concise word usage is more likely to accomplish this objective. A persuasive speech on the need to change accounting practices used at WorldCom could serve as an example. You could say:

> The Securities and Exchange Commission charged the major global communications provider WorldCom, Inc. with accounting fraud of more than $3.8 billion including allegations that the corporation overstated its income by $3.055 billion in 2001 and $797 million during the first quarter of 2002 and falsely represented itself as a profitable enterprise during 2001 and the first quarter of 2002 by reporting earnings that it did not actually have and by deferring rather than expensing approximately $3.8 billion of its costs.

Can this statement be reworded to be more concise? Another possibility would be:

> WorldCom has been charged with accounting fraud of $3.8 billion. The corporation has been charged with using accounting practices that allowed the corporation to overstate its income and appear to be more profitable than it actually was.

The second statement makes the same point but does so in a much shorter and more understandable way for audience members, who are not financial experts.

Ordinary words

Ordinary words are common or typical for the audience. They are the words an audience can easily grasp. Hence, they can add clarity to the message. Obviously, the training, interests, and education of the audience will influence your choice of what will count as "usual" words, as we discussed in chapter 5. This is not the time to use your ten-dollar words (synonyms from a thesaurus) to impress. You want your audience to understand you so you should choose "simple words" over "uncommon unintelligibility."

Limited complexity

Spoken sentences should not be complex if clarity is the primary goal. **Limited complexity** occurs when sentences are short and have few clauses, so that audiences can easily understand their meaning. Have you had the experience of listening to a speaker such that, by the time he gets to the end of the sentence, you can hardly remember where he started? The speaker lost the audience because too much information was crammed into one spoken sentence. In an interesting persuasive speech on cloning, a student speaker began by describing the three types of cloning by saying: "Most people believe that cloning refers only to copying genes and pieces of chromosomes, but this would be the first type of cloning; while the second type splits an embryo after the egg is fertilized and includes DNA from both the mother and the father, and the third type uses genetic material from only one parent." This sentence has several clauses and, while the information should be retained, it needs to be made into several short sentences in order to be spoken – such as the following: "There are three kinds of cloning. The first and most commonly known kind of cloning copies genes and pieces of chromosomes. The second kind of cloning uses DNA from both parents and splits an egg after it is fertilized into two embryos. The third kind of cloning only uses DNA from one parent" (Human Genome Project 2001). In the second example, the three types of cloning are set out more clearly and each sentence is shorter, so the audience can absorb the material in shorter bursts of information rather than in one large piece of information.

Intensity

Intensity is the vivid and dramatic mood that can be depicted through words. It is the use of stylistic devices to create compelling visual images for an audience. Words generate color and interest. They move audiences to understanding, laughter, and passion. Vivid words can generate attention, an emotional response, and increase recall (Reyes, Thompson, and Bower 1980). Intensity can be established through the six stylistic devices of vivid description, visualization, narrative, hyperbole, personification, and similes and metaphors.

Vivid description

Vivid description uses concrete words and adjectives to provide a striking explanation. A student speaker wanted to provide a stunning depiction of the increase in gambling in the United States and chose to do so through vivid description:

> Legal gamblers lay down more than $50 billion every year in the US. More money is spent for gambling than the money spent in total for sports, movies, music, video games, and theme parks. In 1978, Nevada was the only state with casinos. Today, there are casinos in 26 states. There are lotteries in 37 states. Bingo is played in 46 states. Until 1978, only Nevada had casinos. Now, they're in 26 states. It used to be that you could only play the ponies on race tracks but now there are off-track locations everywhere. In fact, there are only three states that have no legalized

gambling. About 3 million people are considered compulsive gamblers. ("Gambling everywhere?" 1999)

Concrete details of money, years, and states provide vivid description.

Visualization

Visualization asks the audience to imagine themselves in the situation the speaker is describing by actively engaging the imagination in the description. The speaker may describe what the audience sees, smells, tastes, hears, and touches. The speaker may ask the audience to imagine acting and behaving in a particular way, so as to picture their involvement in the environment. A persuasive speaker wanted her audience to get flu shots at the Student Health Center, and used visualization to describe the flu symptoms each of them were likely to experience if they did not take her advice:

> I want you to think about how much it hurts. You have a headache that is pounding at your temples. Your keep coughing – one of those dry coughs that make your ribs hurt and you have a runny nose and a sore throat. All of your muscles ache and you've never felt so tired in your life. You just want to stay in bed. When you take your temperature, the thermometer reads 104°. You feel like death warmed over. You just want to sleep. And you have a test tomorrow! You don't have time to be sick!

This stylistic device would be required in the motivated sequence organizational plan (chapter 6), but could also be used in other organizational plans (e.g. to show how the action would be effective in the AIDA organization, or to show the severity of a problem in a problem–solution organization).

Narrative

A **narrative** is a story which involves the audience members by drawing them into the plot line. In a persuasive speech on noise pollution, a speaker described John's story:

> John loved rock and roll. In fact, he loved rock and roll so much that he spent most weekends at concerts and the closer he could get to the front, the better. But John's ears didn't love rock and roll and continued exposure to over 140 decibels of noise for several hours at a time began to take its toll on John's hearing. At the very young age of 28, John must wear hearing aids to assist him in hearing normal conversations.

The speaker tells a story to involve the audience in the experience of another in order to make them to understand the effects of a problem.

Hyperbole

Hyperbole is an overstatement of significance. A persuasive student speaker who opposed national identification cards uses hyperbole to state his position against this proposal: "Requiring that every American citizen carry a national identification card at all times that is embedded with biometric data that uniquely identifies that individual is tantamount to branding each person with a serial number." Comparing identification cards with branding illustrates hyperbole, because it is an exaggeration to make such a point.

Personification

Personification involves assigning human attributes to an object which is not human, in order to intensify the description of that object. For example, a persuasive speech on Project Echelon, a computer system designed to monitor e-mail communications by the National Security Agency, a student suggested that "Echelon has ears and is listening and if you use certain code words like gun, militia, or anthrax in your e-mail, you are likely to come to the attention of the National Security Agency." In this description, a computer program takes on the human characteristics of ears and possesses the sense of listening.

Similes and metaphors

Both similes and metaphors compare two seemingly dissimilar things for emotional or dramatic effect. **Similes** use "like" or "as" in the comparison, whereas **metaphors** link the two things without these connectors. In a persuasive speech on providing resources for children with dyslexia, a student speaker explained that letters jump and become so confusing that "It's like the words are walking." In this simile, reading is compared to walking – two outwardly dissimilar experiences. A metaphor might suggest that reducing your stress is a jolt of electricity. The metaphor equates two experiences and makes a comparison without using "like" or "as." "He was a lion in battle" compares a man's behavior with that of a lion, trying to create the impression of bravery. Chapter 7 described how metaphors also function as a form of supporting material by using a comparison.

Rhythm

Rhythm is the flow or movement in the speech, and it is established by the patterns of the words and sentences. This pace can set a subdued or excited mood; it can establish a forward motion and audiences can predict what will occur next in the pattern. Rhythm can be established through the five stylistic features of repetition, parallel wording, antithesis, alliteration, and rhyme.

Repetition

Repetition consists in saying the same words, phrases, or sentences again within the same speech. The repetition of an important idea is a way to emphasize its significance to the audience. Repeating a common refrain that the speaker initiates and the audience finishes will allow an audience to predict a repeated pattern and become involved in the speech. In a persuasive speech on road rage, a student used the repetition of the word "increasing" in each one of his phrases, to persuade her audience that new solutions could be achieved to this serious problem: "The public is in favor of increasing enforcement, increasing penalties, increasing involvement by occupants in the car, and increasing the public's awareness of the dangers of road rage according to a national survey of 6,000 drivers."

Parallel wording

Parallel wording involves the deliberate choice of similar or closely corresponding words in phrases and sentences. Parallel wording was chosen by a speaker who gave suggestions for preventing identity theft:

> There are several things you can do to minimize the chances of becoming a victim of identity theft. 1. Protect yourself by keeping good financial records. 2. Protect your personal information by keeping it in a safe place. Always destroy unused credit card offers, old bank statements, etc. 3. Protect your identity by keeping your personal information confidential. Give out your social security number only when absolutely necessary.

The parallel structure repeated similar phrases (e.g. "Protect") in each of the suggestions offered, to reiterate the value of taking action in order to protect oneself from identity theft.

Antithesis

Antithesis is the juxtaposition of two contrasting ideas. An interesting rhythmic balance is established between the two competing phrases, clauses, or sentences. After the decision of the 9th Circuit Court, a student gave a speech on the pledge of allegiance and used the following example of antithesis: "Let us pledge our allegiance to flag and country but our allegiance cannot be pledged to just one God." This example sets up an antithesis between what allegiance should and should not be pledged to by contrasting the two ideas in one single sentence.

Alliteration

Alliteration is the repetition of the same sound at the beginning of words. This stylistic device creates momentum in a sentence through the smooth flow of sounds. In a persuasive speech on the need to improve television programming, a student speaker referred to a pianist in a concert recording by saying: "her fingers fairly flew across the keyboard." The repetition of the "f" sounds in "fingers," "fairly," and "flew" lays down a tempo for the spoken sentence.

Rhyme

The use of **rhyme** involves the same or similar sounds at the end of clauses or phrases. A student speaker who wanted to convince his audience to adopt a pet used rhyme to conclude the speech by suggesting to the audience: "Open your heart and do your part. Adopt a dog or cat." The rhyme of "heart" and "part" creates a strong pattern which establishes a rhythm.

Humor

Humor expresses an idea which is funny or amusing. Used by a persuasive speaker, humor can be entertaining for an audience, but it can also be persuasive by capturing attention (Bryant and Zillman 1989) and distracting the audience from carefully evaluating the message and from engaging in counter-arguing with the message (Cantor and Venus 1980; Sternthal and Craig 1973). Humor encourages peripheral processing of the message rather than central processing using the elaboration likelihood model (chapter 2). Humor tends not to focus on the quality of arguments regarding a speaker's position; this is why it is more likely to encourage peripheral processing of a message. But humor can increase liking a speaker (Weinberger and Gulas 1992), unless the humor is perceived as inappropriate (Derks, Kalland, and Etgen 1995). There are six stylistic devices that create humor: the pun, the anecdote, satire, irony, the humorous metaphor, and the joke.

The pun

A **pun** is a play on words. It consists in the humorous use of words that sound alike but have different meanings. This is considered by some to be the lowest form of humor. If you were giving a speech on the problems of urban sprawl, you might work in the following pun: "Once you've seen one shopping center you've seen a mall."

The anecdote

An **anecdote** is a short, entertaining story about some events. Anecdotes are usually personal and autobiographical in nature. A student began a speech on cell phones and driving with this anecdote:

> When I was driving to class yesterday, I noticed a number of bumper stickers. One said, "Hard work has a future payoff. Laziness pays off now." Another one I came across read, "I'm not a complete idiot, some parts are missing." But my favorite one was the bumper sticker that said, "Hang up and drive" – because the driver of that car was busy talking on a cell phone and nearly ran me off the road.

These bumper stickers are funny and provide context for the speech.

Satire

Satire pokes fun at the flaws and imperfections of others through mockery and sarcasm. For example, a student giving a persuasive speech on the absence of nutritional value in fast foods and on the unknown quality of these foods used Al Astor's satirical commentary on McDonald's top new meal ideas in the light of mad cow and foot and mouth disease. These fake food items included McHaggis, McKnuckles,

Nappy Meal, McScrapple, Gizzard McNuggets, Offal McMuffin, McTripe, Fillet O'Gristle, Quarter Pouder with Head Cheese, and the All-New McBrain Sandwiche (Astor 2001).

Irony

Irony is a humorous way of expressing the opposite of the face-value meaning. It creates an implicit discrepancy between what is said and what is actually meant. Speakers convey that they are speaking ironically through intonation and exaggeration. For example, a speaker could suggest that the ideal college student diet is made up of pizzas, chicken nuggets, and French fries; but we knew from the way the speaker said this that, while most students consume large quantities of these foods, there is no way this can be construed as an "ideal" diet.

The humorous metaphor

A **humorous metaphor** is an implicit comparison between two things which are juxtaposed, and that comparison becomes humorous when it has amusing properties or a witty turn of phrase. For example, George Will used this clever metaphor: "Greed is envy with its sleeves rolled up." Another example, from a student speech on the responsibility of journalists, suggests that "News is often considered the first rough draft of history." These metaphors are somewhat amusing, because the comparisons are unanticipated and involve interesting comparisons that encourage an audience to think more about a topic.

The joke

A **joke** is a story with a punch line. Jokes that are relevant to the topic of the speech are generally more effective, because the audience is receiving the message while laughing at the joke. A speech persuading the audience that eating healthily and exercising is important might incorporate the following joke:

> A woman walked up to a little old man rocking in on his front porch. She said, "I couldn't help noticing how happy you look. What's your secret for a long happy life?" He replied, "I smoke three packs of cigarettes a day, I drink a case of whiskey a week, eat fatty foods, and never exercise!" The woman was amazed and asked him how old he was. He thought for a moment, and replied, "Twenty-six." (*Mamalade Jokes*, n.d)

Jokes are a way to establish rapport with an audience, but you need to consider that jokes that will be offensive to its members will backfire. Some speakers are not particularly comfortable telling jokes and they should choose other forms of humor or other stylistic devices to accomplish their purpose. I have trouble remembering the punch lines of jokes. There is nothing worse than telling a joke and having it fall flat.

Using Symbols and Style in Persuasion

This chapter began by defining symbols and describing their three characteristics. Denotative and connotative meanings of symbols were considered. Weaver's ultimate terms, so-called god and devil terms, were described and their usefulness as persuasive tools was detailed. Finally, Burke's concept that reality is constructed through symbols was discussed. For a persuasive speaker, this means that symbols (particularly language) are very powerful because they can evoke strong reactions and shape reality for an audience.

What does all this mean for a persuasive speaker? First, it means that words that you have chosen may have quite different connotative meanings from those that you have associated with particular symbols. The more you know about your audience, the more you will be likely to determine how much shared experience you have and whether your interpretations are likely to be similar. When you are speaking to an audience formed of people with very different backgrounds and experiences, you need to select your words carefully, so as to avoid offending and creating misunderstandings.

Some topics are more likely to lend themselves to using ultimate terms, but not every message needs to include these kinds of terms. You must avoid overusing these emotionally charged words; you need to use them carefully. These are words audiences react to very strongly, and you should be able to predict your audience's reaction accurately when you use this kind of powerful language, particularly devil terms.

The differences between oral and written style have been delineated. As you design persuasive messages, you need to keep in mind whether the message will be heard or read. Think about the differences we have described in this chapter and adapt your presentation to the situation.

There are three types of oral styles (plain, middle, and grand). So what would determine the style of speaking? Three factors should influence your choice of style: audience, personal preference, and purpose. As we have indicated in chapter 5, analyzing and adapting to your audience is essential in persuasion, and style is another facet of your speech where this adaptation can take place. Do you have any information that suggests that a particular style of speaking would be more effective in persuading your audience to your position? What style of speaking do you feel most comfortable using? Do you have a signature style? What is your purpose? Do you need to explain in order to persuade (plain style)? A speaker who needs to interest his audience in the topic will probably choose the middle style, because this style will help to entertain the audience. Or do you need to motivate your audience with the grand style?

Stylistic goals for achieving clarity, increasing intensity, establishing rhythm, and creating humor have been explained and illustrated. These goals are related to the three types of oral styles. Clarity is the central goal in the plain style; humor is the goal of the middle style; and intensity and rhythm are goals in the grand style. There are many different stylistic devices for accomplishing these goals and for creating a style. Once again, these devices should be selected with the audience in mind. Some speakers believe that they should put a stylistic device at the beginning and the end of their speech; but these should be worked into the presentation throughout all of the parts to achieve the speaker's goals. Style is not just an enhancement, but something important in achieving the ultimate outcome for a persuasive speaker.

Glossary

Active voice: the grammatical situation where the subject of the sentence performs the action in the sentence.

Alliteration: the repetition of the same sound at the beginning of words.

Anecdote: a short entertaining story about some event.

Antithesis: the juxtaposition of two contrasting ideas.

Axiom: wise saying that is widely accepted.

Clarity: speaking in a clear, unambiguous manner.

Connotative meaning: subjective meaning of a word.

Concise word usage: situation characterized by the speaker's being brief and to the point.

Concrete words: linguistic symbols which stand for something specific.

Denotative meaning: dictionary meaning of a word.

Devil term: word generally accepted as negative.

God term: word generally accepted as positive.

Grand style: a style that is majestic and impressive.

Humor: an idea which is funny or amusing.

Humorous metaphor: an implicit comparison in which two things are juxtaposed, and which becomes humorous when that comparison has amusing properties or a contains witty turn of phrase.

Hyperbole: an overstatement of significance.

Intensity: vivid and dramatic word usage.

Irony: a humorous way of implying the opposite of what one is actually saying.

Joke: a story with a punch line.

Limited complexity: speech where sentences are short and have few clauses.

Metaphor: a comparison between two things which is carried out without connectors (contrast with the simile).

Middle style: a style used to please or entertain.

Narrative: story.

Ordinary words: common and typical words from the audience's point of view.

Parallel wording: deliberate choice of similar or closely corresponding wording in phrases and sentences.

Passive voice: the grammatical situation where the object of an action becomes a (grammatical) subject in the sentence.

Personification: the assignation of human attributes to non-human objects.

Plain style: a style that is straightforward and clear.

Pun: play on words.

Repetition: saying the same words, phrases, or sentences in the same speech.

Rhythm: the flow of patterns of words and sentences.

Rhyme: same or similar sounds at the end of clauses or phrases.

Satire: the use mockery and sarcasm to poke fun at flaws and imperfections.

Simile: a comparison between two things, which uses "like" and "as."

Style: selection and arrangement of words, intended to accomplish a speaker's goal.

Symbol: something that stands for, or represents, something else.

Visualization: asking the audience to engage the imagination actively.

Vivid description: the use of concrete words and adjectives to provide striking explanations.

Chapter 9

Hostile, Apathetic, Motivated, and Multiple or Mixed Audiences

We gave a talk recently at another university and a faculty member asked us to explain why he could present the same material for two classes on the same topic and have two entirely different reactions from students. In one class, the students were interested and actively participated in class discussions. In the other class, the students seemed bored to death. But the material and the professor were the same. This professor even used the same jokes in both classes. The first class laughed at his jokes and the second class just looked at him like he was an idiot. So what was different? Of course, the first question we asked at what times the two classes were held. But they were held right after each other, so there was little difference in the time, and neither was very close to lunch (because, in my experience, there is a clear drop-off in attention rate before and after lunch). The most obvious answer, then, was that these two student audiences were quite different and that he needed to adapt his materials to each set. He assumed that all student audiences were the same, but of course they are not.

This chapter furthers the analysis of audiences undertaken in chapter five by describing four types of audiences that a speaker can encounter: hostile, apathetic, motivated, and multiple. For each type of audience, we are going to describe and illustrate the factors that can contribute and explain why audiences are likely to be of a particular type, the cues that a speaker uses to determine the type of audience being addressed, and the strategies used to persuade these kinds of audiences.

Hostile Audiences

A **hostile audience** is antagonistic toward the speaker and/or the message. These listeners are unreceptive and argumentative. A local anti-war group decided to protest the American military's use of napalm at the annual Salute to Veterans Air Show on Memorial Day. This event drew thousands, and, as the name implies, had always drawn a large number of veterans and supporters. The anti-war group could have predicted a hostile audience for their message. According to news coverage of the event, many of the spectators disagreed with the protesters' views of the military and felt that the protesters' message was inconsistent with the purpose of the air show. The air show spokesperson simply said of the protesters, "I don't see them." Editorials appeared in the newspaper after the event, arguing that the presence of the anti-war group was disrespectful and they should not even have been allowed to be on the grounds (Tang 2001). In turn, many of those attending the air show were a hostile audience for the protesters. They strongly disagreed with their message, they were argumentative and unreceptive to persuasive appeals, and the hostility even generated calls for reducing free speech.

In this section, which is on hostile audiences, we will examine the factors that can contribute to hostility; the cues an audience provides that display hostility, and the strategies that persuaders have to adopt in facing hostile audiences.

Factors contributing to hostility

Why are some audiences antagonistic toward the speaker when others are not? There are three primary factors that contribute to hostility from a particular audience: attitudes toward the speaker, attitudes toward the topic, and situational factors.

Attitudes toward the speaker

The first factor deals with an audience's negative attitudes toward the speaker. An audience may be hostile because they dislike the speaker or perceive him/her to have low credibility. Sometimes an audience is hostile to a speaker – even when they agree with the ideas expressed by that person – because of the attitudes they have toward the speaker. A speaker's prior reputation or extrinsic credibility may influence the audience's attitudes (chapter 3).

Listeners may associate negative characteristics with the speaker. For example, they may judge the speaker as unintelligent, dishonest, biased, or insincere. A student in a persuasive speaking class gave a speech on organ donation that made extensive use of his personal experience in contributing a kidney to his mother. He urged others in the class to consider donating an organ to others. After receiving his grade, this student revealed to several students in class that he had not actually given a kidney to his mother but thought that this kind of story would help him do better on the speech. Next, this same student gave a speech on why students should support a tax increase on tobacco products. Many of the students in his audience perceived him to be insincere and untrustworthy, even though this speech was on a completely different topic. They now became a hostile audience for this speaker. They did not trust him.

Previous statements or actions by the speaker may be used by the audience to judge the credibility of the speaker. Dan Quayle, while he was Vice-President and addressing the United Negro College Fund, whose slogan is "A mind is a terrible thing to waste," said "What a waste it is to lose one's mind – or not to have a mind. How true that is" (Petras and Petras 1993: 118). Although Quayle's prior statements often led audiences to prejudge him as unintelligent, controversial prior remarks made by speakers like Pat Robertson on Islam have led some audiences to characterize him as intolerant. On his television program, the 700 Club, Robertson characterized Islam as a religion that was not peaceful, saying: "They want to coexist until they can control, dominate, and then, if need be, destroy" (Zahn 2002). As the longest serving Attorney General of the United States and an alum of Cornell University, Janet Reno was a viable graduation speaker; but some graduating seniors used her past actions as Attorney General during the Ruby Ridge and Waco confrontations to make negative judgments on her integrity, honor, and courage. Based on her past actions, they objected to the decision to invite Janet Reno as a graduation speaker for the graduating class (Pessah 2001). In each of these examples, the previous actions of a speaker were used by audiences to make judgments about a speaker.

Speakers may also be negatively evaluated because of group affiliations. For example, speakers who belong to groups that an audience does not support or feels to be different from the ones its own members belong to may be evaluated negatively even before they begin to speak. A speaker who has ties to a white supremacist group brings that affiliation into the speaking situation.

Attitudes toward the topic

The second factor that determines hostility is the audience's attitude toward the issue addressed in the speech. If its members disagree with the message advocated by the speaker, they are likely to be unreceptive. High levels of ego involvement generate more interest in the topic and less willingness to consider other positions (chapter 2).

In a recent campaign for state representative, one of the issues was abortion. A candidate made the controversial statement that Planned Parenthood was racially motivated. If the audience has high levels of ego involvement and holds a pro-life position, we can predict there will be high levels of hostility toward this candidate.

In another example, a speaker in a persuasive speaking class attempted to persuade her classmates that they should sign a petition expressing no confidence in the student government. While some students felt disgruntled with the actions of the student government, many in the audience did not agree with the speaker and felt that this action was too extreme. They were unreceptive to the position taken in the presentation.

Situational factors

When and where the message is delivered can also influence the audience's reaction to the message. For example, a message that is delivered in the sweltering heat of July may not be received as positively as a message received on a cool spring day. A persuasive message may arouse a more hostile reaction if the situation is a large group and takes on characteristics of a mob.

Hostility cues

Your audience analysis (chapter 5) may reveal that an audience is likely to be hostile. If so, you can take these hostile attitudes into account as you prepare your message. However, an audience may give feedback to a speaker, revealing a hostile attitude while the presentation is being given. And, while many of these cues can be interpreted in multiple ways, a combination of cues that seem to point in the same direction can lead a speaker to infer that an audience is leaning in a particular direction. This discussion will focus on some overt cues that may reveal a hostile audience. It should be emphasized that any of these cues alone may be interpreted differently and that knowing more about audience members allows a speaker to interpret the cues more accurately. Behaviors that may signal hostility include crossing arms, frowning, glaring, facial reddening, shaking head from side to side, and asking barbed questions.

Crossing arms

The nonverbal literature suggests that a posture which involves positioning the arms across the body may be an indication of disagreement. It can be perceived as a nonverbal signal for closing the recipient off from an interaction with the speaker (Mehrabian 1969).

Frowning

Frowning involves a downturn of the mouth and brow. It generally indicates disapproval, annoyance, displeasure, or contempt. It may be used to silence or subdue the speaker.

Glaring

Glaring is giving the speaker a steady and fierce gaze. Eye contact is maintained until the speaker is uncomfortable. It can indicate anger, antagonism, resentment.

Facial reddening

This occurs when the face of an audience member is inflamed. The cheeks are flushed and can generally indicate anger (Tracy 2002).

Shaking head from side to side

When an audience member shakes the head from side to side, this is a nonverbal way to express disagreement with the speaker. The movement says "no" to whatever the speaker is saying at the time.

Asking barbed questions

Hostile audiences may ask very critical questions if given an opportunity, because they want to reveal the weaknesses of the speaker or of the arguments. The tone of voice may be one indication that the question is hostile. Questions can be loaded ("When did you stop cheating on exams?"), set up false dilemmas (e.g. "Are you in favor of letting all of the criminals out on the streets now or never sending them to jail in the first place?"), ask for inappropriate information ("What is your sexual orientation?"), or there may be attempts by the audience member to give a speech. These kinds of questions are often a cue to how hostile the audience (or, more particularly, an audience member) may be to the speaker.

Strategies for hostile audiences

If a speaker anticipates a hostile audience, strategies can be adopted to counteract the negative attitudes toward him/her and the topic. We will begin by examining how a speaker can attempt to modify an audience's negative attitude. As you will recall, this attitude may arise because of a speaker's prior actions, group affiliations, and so on. Audiences vary in their level of hostility, and different strategies may be effective depending on intensity. The ten strategies for dealing with hostile audiences are: introduce humor to defuse hostility; call for a fair hearing; emphasize common ground; refute negative attitudes toward you as a speaker; acknowledge past mistakes; postpone the disagreement; express understanding and respect for the audience's position; reassure the audience; refute the audience's negative attitudes to the topic; and neutralize hostile questions (see box 9.1).

Introduce humor to defuse hostility

A speaker may use self-directed humor to counteract an audience's negative attitudes. This strategy is more likely to be effective if the feelings are not intense

(Clark 1984). Humor can be a very valuable strategy for changing the mood if a speaker can get the audience to laugh. John had been a very visible opponent of the new multicultural requirement on campus. He was asked to speak before the Faculty Council, which was leaning toward endorsing a requirement that students have at least one course with multicultural content. He began his speech by suggesting that he found himself in the very unusual position of generating a great deal of controversy and discussion. It was probably the only time that he could remember he had so many people actually listening to what he had to say! Even if it was to conclude that he was wrong. He said that some of his comments had caused others to call him a few names he had to look up in the dictionary. Still, he was very pleased that this topic was stimulating a thorough dialogue. In this example, John uses self-directed humor by claiming to be surprised to find himself the focus of the attention, and makes fun of himself for not fully understanding the negative comments directed his way.

Call for a fair hearing

A speaker can explicitly ask the audience to listen to the message before making a negative judgment. The speaker calls on the audience to be open-minded and to listen to the arguments and to the evidence. This strategy may be used when the audience is very opposed to the speaker and unwilling to hear the speaker out. A speaker decides to give a persuasive speech on the importance of granting reparations for descendants of slaves. An audience analysis indicates that many in the audience hold attitudes that are hostile to this position. The speaker wants these members to listen to the arguments before making a judgment and chooses the strategy of calling for a fair hearing:

> What I'm going to talk about today is a controversial topic but I know that you will be willing to listen to what I have to say before you make a decision, that you will listen carefully to the arguments before you jump to a conclusion. There is a lot of information to consider and the topic is a complex one. I thank you for your willingness to hear what I have to say on this most important topic.

The speaker compliments the audience on the fairness they will exhibit in listening to him/her, even though they initially disagree with the speaker's position. Calling for a fair hearing encourages an audience to be open-minded to alternative positions on issues. The speaker is asking the audience to consider the quality of the arguments supporting the position and to process centrally the information, according to the elaboration likelihood model (chapter 2).

Emphasize common ground

This strategy calls attention to the areas shared by the speaker and the audience. It suggests that, despite some disagreements or differences, there are still some important shared values. Implicit in this argument is the idea that the speaker and the audience must trust one another (Clark 1984). In 1990, Barbara Bush was invited to be the commencement speaker at Wellesley College. There was considerable controversy about the choice and many of the graduates felt she was an inappropriate one, because her greatest accomplishment had been to be the spouse of the President of the United States. Barbara Bush was not a role model for the contemporary woman. In her commencement address, Barbara Bush repeatedly made the point that the value shared between herself and the graduates of Wellesley was a firm embrace of diversity for women:

> For over fifty years, it was said that the winner of Wellesley's annual hoop race would be the first to get married. Now, they say the winner will be the first to become a CEO. Both of those stereotypes show too little tolerance for those who want to know where the mermaids stand. So I want to offer you today a new legend: The winner of the hoop race will be the first to realize her dream, not society's dream. Who knows? Somewhere out in this audience may even be someone who will one day follow in my footsteps, and preside over the White House as the President's spouse. I wish him well! The controversy ends here. But our conversation is only beginning. And a worthwhile conversation it has been. (Bush 1990)

She interjected some humor into the situation but made the serious point that women have many important choices they can make in their lives. The negative attitudes that she faced from some audience members were misplaced because they actually shared core values that embraced diversity. By extension, that included a diversity of options for women which should have embraced their own choices as well as the choice that Barbara Bush had made for herself.

Refute negative attitudes toward you as a speaker

In this case, the speaker addresses the reasons why the audience has a negative attitude and directly refutes these claims. For example, a speaker who has ties to the white supremacist group may deny any affiliation with that group from the outset of the speech (assuming there are no such ties, of course). She may explain how her name has come to be associated with this group, and how this is an inaccurate statement of her views. She tells the audience that she wants them to know the truth about what groups she does and does not belong to, and the incriminated group is one that she has never belonged to in her entire life.

Acknowledge past mistakes

If an audience is hostile to a speaker because of that speaker's past actions, it may be possible to admit to past faults and show that a new leaf has been turned. Audiences are often quite forgiving if they believe that an individual has really changed and is repentant for past transgressions. Bill Clinton spoke thus at the annual White House prayer breakfast for clergy, after his testimony and address to the nation regarding the Monica Lewinsky affair:

I agree with those who have said that in my first statement after I testified I was not contrite enough. I don't think there is a fancy way to say that I have sinned. It is important to me that everybody who has been hurt know that the sorrow I feel is genuine: First and most important, my family; also my friends, my staff, my Cabinet, Monica Lewinsky and her family, and the American people. I have asked all for their forgiveness. But I believe that to be forgiven, more than sorrow is required – at least two more things. First, genuine repentance – a determination to change and to repair breaches of my own making. I have repented. Second, what my Bible calls a "broken spirit;" an understanding that I must have God's help to be the person that I want to be; a willingness to give the very forgiveness I seek; a renunciation of the pride and the anger which cloud judgment, lead people to excuse and compare and to blame and complain. (Clinton 1998)

Clinton's statement was made to an audience which had heard it before and which was skeptical of his sincerity. He acknowledged that he had not been contrite enough in the past and sought to remedy that in this address. He acknowledged responsibility and asked for forgiveness. Of course, some would never forgive him, but many were willing to give him another chance.

Hostility may also emerge from negative attitudes about the topic. Strategies that can be used to address an audience's strong opposition to the message are indicated below.

Express understanding and respect for the audience's position

When the audience is hostile to the speaker's position because they disagree, this strategy explicitly addresses the disagreement and recognizes that the audience's opinions are understood and valued. Sometimes the speaker can even explain how he/she held the same opinions as the audience at one point, and how his/her opinions changed and why. In a persuasive speech on seatbelts, a speaker used this strategy to show she understood the audience's position:

I know. Seatbelts are uncomfortable. If you're short like me, they cut you right here at the neck. And no matter what you're wearing, they seem to imprint a permanent wrinkle. I confess, I thought all of these things about seatbelts too. And more. Until my sister was with her boyfriend and they were going to a Halloween party. Neither was wearing seatbelts. There was an accident. And my sister went through the front windshield. It is now hundreds of stitches later and multiple plastic surgeries. For me, seatbelts are no longer about being uncomfortable or wrinkled.

The speaker began by acknowledging that there were reasons not to wear a seatbelt and admitted that she felt the same way that the audience did about buckling up. Then, by way of introducing the topic, she explained what had made her change her mind.

Reassure the audience

When an audience believes that the speaker's position works against their best interests, a speaker will need to reassure the audience in order to reduce the hostility.

Self-interest is an important part of ego-involvement. An audience is likely to be hostile to a speaker who advocates a position that will be a threat itself. A college student gave a persuasive speech advocating the requirement of meningitis shots on college campuses. Not surprisingly, his audience, made of college students, was hostile to the proposal because they believed it was against their self-interests: they would have to get the shots they did not want, and the cost of these shots (around $60) would be added to their fees. To reassure his audience, the speaker explained that the shots were less painful than giving blood. He also suggested that the cost of the shots would be subsidized, so that only about half of the cost would be passed on to the student. He argued that this cost was small compared to the probability of saving one's life. His arguments were directed at reassuring his audience that their self-interest would not be negatively affected by his proposal.

Refute the audience's negative attitudes to the topic

The speaker should use what knowledge of the audience's attitude on the topic he/she has, and try to provide a reason to counter these attitudes. To reduce the resistance, the speaker should attempt to focus on the specific points on which the audience disagrees with him/her on the topic. Justice Clarence Thomas' address before the members of the National Bar Association explicitly refuted the basis for a number of negative attitudes from his audience. For example, he used a particular dissenting opinion as an illustration:

> One opinion that is trotted out for propaganda, for the propaganda parade, is my dissent in Hudson vs. McMillian. The conclusion reached by the long arm of the criticism is that I supported the beating of prisoners in that case. Well, one must either be illiterate or fraught with malice to reach that conclusion. (Thomas 1998)

Thomas argued that the audience could not conclude that he supported beating prisoners. The court was ruling on a narrow issue of whether a prisoner's rights were violated under the cruel and unusual punishment clause of the Eighth Amendment. Thomas explained that his decision was based on an interpretation of this amendment and not on whether beating was a moral act. Thus, the audience's negative attitudes about his position on these issues was based on inaccurate information.

Moderate the persuasive goal

Hostile audiences are more difficult to persuade, and you may need to assess whether your expectations are reasonable for your audience. If your audience believes that affirmative action is unfair and should be eliminated and your goal is to convince them that affirmative action programs should be extended, the difference between your positions will make it extremely unlikely that you will be able to accomplish your goal. The positions are too far apart. You may need to moderate your goal and ask your audience to consider why affirmative action programs need to be maintained in their present form.

You may be asking your audience to take an action in your speech. A persuasive speaker knows that a hostile audience is not, initially, in favor of the topic, so that any action that he/she takes must be a small one. Anything more would be asking for too much, given where things begin with that audience. For example, you might be able to ask an audience which is hostile to recycling to place their soda cans in university recycling bins during a single day. This would not be to ask too much of them, and might show them how easy it is to do it. But asking them to begin a compost pile would be out of the question.

Neutralize hostile questions

Although it is tempting to respond to a hostile question with a hostile response, your audience may conclude that you are not being fair to the person asking the question. You want to be perceived as fair, open-minded, committed to your topic, and interested in discussing your ideas. The best way of doing this is by treating the question as if it were asked in a neutral way. If you anticipate a hostile audience and there will be a question–answer period, you should think about possible questions that will be asked and about ways for you to answer them that will not sound defensive. Thinking through your answers in advance is good preparation for this situation.

Specifically, one way to neutralize hostile questions is to acknowledge the importance of the question. Thank the person for asking it. Respond to the question as a legitimate one, even if it is hostile or flippant. If the question is complex, divide it into parts and answer each part separately. If the questioner asks a question with faulty reasoning, explain why you would draw a different conclusion, but do so in a respectful tone of voice. In a persuasive speech that favored ballistic fingerprinting (a database generated by requiring handgun manufacturers to fire weapons and to record the signatures of handguns), the following exchange took place after the presentation:

> QUESTION FROM AUDIENCE MEMBER: Isn't it true that, despite what you've said, the kind of database you're suggesting hasn't really been effective in solving very many crimes?
>
> SPEAKER: This is a very important question and I'm glad that you asked it. At this point, there are only two states – Maryland and New York – that are using the database and it is quite small. If the system were being used widely and in more states, I believe it would be able to solve more crimes. Another kind of evidence for this is that where it is used widely abroad, it has been quite successful in identifying leads in crimes. I don't think we can conclude that something isn't working that isn't really being used yet.

In this exchange, the speaker thanked the audience member for the question and did not react defensively to it. The speaker provided evidence for the position taken in the answer and explained the faulty reasoning of the questioner.

A hostile audience is a challenge for a persuasive speaker. It is unreasonable to expect to convert this audience to your way of thinking about an issue. A more reasonable goal is to convince a hostile audience to listen to your presentation with an open mind. Even this goal can be extremely difficult, depending upon the level of hostility, but you may be able to reach some audience members. Presenting before a hostile audience can certainly get a speaker's adrenaline flowing and forces a speaker to be extremely well prepared.

In this section we have explained why audiences may be hostile and we have presented the cues a speaker can use during a presentation to determine that the audience is displaying hostility, together with a set of strategies for addressing a hostile audience.

Box 9.1 Strategies for hostile audiences

1 Introduce humor to defuse hostility.
2 Call for a fair hearing.
3 Emphasize common ground.
4 Refute negative attitudes toward speaker.
5 Acknowledge past mistakes.
6 Express understanding and respect for the audience's position.
7 Reassure the audience.
8 Refute the audience's negative attitudes about the topic.
9 Moderate the persuasive goal.
10 Neutralize hostile questions.

Apathetic Audiences

An **apathetic audience** is indifferent to the speaker and/or the message. There is a clear lack of interest and the audience is unmoved by the speaker's presence or by the topic of the presentation. Apathetic audiences are not interested in listening to the speaker and feel that nothing will be said that would matter. These audiences would rather be spending their time doing something else. A guest speaker was invited to a college class recently. This class was composed entirely of seniors who were in their last semester, and the speaker's topic was investing for retirement. He faced an apathetic audience because many of these college seniors had not even secured their first jobs! The speaker wanted them to think about saving for retirement when it was at least 40 years away. They were uninterested in the topic and had many other more important things to think about.

Factors contributing to apathy

Some audiences are uninterested because they are bored. We will consider three influences on apathetic audiences: attitudes toward the speaker, attitudes toward the topic, and situational factors.

Attitudes toward the speaker

Audience members may be uninterested in a speaker if they see this person as different from themselves. When the speaker lacks common ground with the audience, the audience may assume that s/he has nothing to say of interest. Graduation speakers often generate this kind of response from audiences. One of the worst examples we witnessed involved a renowned history professor who described Russian history in great detail by way of welcoming incoming freshmen to the university. The speaker failed to establish common ground with his audience. He was enthralled with his historical examples but his audience was incredibly bored. This speaker presented himself as distinct from his audience, and the audience decided that he had nothing to tell them that could be relevant.

Prior experience with a speaker, too, may cause audience members to assume an apathetic attitude toward that speaker. If a speaker was boring on a previous occasion, there is every reason to believe that there will be a repeat performance. At a local peace rally, one of the founding members felt compelled to give a persuasive speech. He did this at every rally and the audience members came to expect a similar presentation each time. The speaker took too much time to express his opinions and appeared not to be interested in what he was saying while he delivered the presentation. He had developed a reputation among the followers as a bore, even though they agreed with much of what he articulated. Many of the followers admitted that they had stopped listening to his presentations and just waited until another speaker began before tuning in. This speaker had an apathetic audience and did not adapt his message to the situation. His persuasive message was not being heard because his past behavior made the audience apathetic.

Attitudes toward the topic

Audiences can be indifferent toward issues. If they feel that a topic is not relevant to them, they may be apathetic toward a persuasive speech on that subject. Why should they care about an issue that affects other people? Or in other places? These topics are not real to them. The issues do not touch them directly, while many other problems do have direct connections to their lives. A persuasive speech on the severity of famine in Africa will seem an issue that is removed from a college student's everyday existence. Even though this issue is important and the consequences are severe, audiences may feel less connected to it than to other domestic issues, which are closer to home. The elaboration likelihood model (chapter 2) would suggest that this low involvement in the topic would lead to peripheral processing.

Sometimes audiences are uninterested in issues because they have little knowledge about the topic involved. Your audience analysis should be able to determine how much your audience knows about the topic in order to determine whether this might be a source of apathy (chapter 5). We live in an age of information explosion, and it is impossible to be well informed on many topics. So on some topics audience members may have some initial apathy simply because they do not know much about the issue in question. We heard a persuasive speech about why SUVs (sport utility vehicles) should be taken off the road. Initially we were apathetic about this issue. We do not drive a SUV, nor does anyone in our family. We had not heard about the recent media campaigns against SUVs (e.g. regarding gas mileage and safety for those who do not drive SUVs) and our apathy came from a lack of knowledge about the topic.

In contrast, apathy can also be caused by overexposure to an issue. When audience members have heard repeated persuasive messages on the same issue, they can become fatigued by the recurrence (Miller 1976). Audiences will be uninterested in repeated messages.

Situational factors

Situational factors may also influence some audiences to be indifferent toward a speaker or a topic. For example, the anonymity that some college students feel in a large auditorium for an introductory required class can set up a situation where a passive and uninterested response is a typical response. In this case, the features of the classroom situation are contributing to the audience reaction.

Apathy cues

You might think that an apathetic audience would not give off any cues about their state. After all, they are indifferent. But this is not the case at all! They can give off cues that they are not interested in the speaker or in what that speaker has to say. And they do not want to be misunderstood. These cues are more powerful indicators to a speaker when they are used in combination; taken separately, any cue can obviously be interpreted in multiple ways. Apathy cues include sighing, minimal eye contact, closed eyes, blank stares, being distracted with other activities, and being unresponsive to questions.

Sighing

Sighing occurs when an audience member inhales or exhales in an extended breath, which is audible to other audience members and to the speaker. In the context of listening to a speaker, it can indicate fatigue.

Minimal eye contact

In this case, very little eye contact is made between the audience members and the speaker. Audience members actively avoid looking at the speaker. In effect, they are signaling that they are not paying attention to the speaker by not even affording that person the basic courtesy of eye contact.

Closed eyes

Apathetic audiences may signal their indifference by closing their eyes on the speaker. They may retreat into their own world, or to sleep, until something more interesting emerges. This cue indicates fatigue, indifference, and unresponsiveness.

Blank stare

When audience members do look at the speaker, they give him/her a vacant look. It is as if they were not there, the space is unoccupied. They are indifferent to what the speaker has to say. They have shut down.

Being distracted with other activities

Audience members are far more interested in other activities than in the speaker or in what that person is saying. Such activities may be doodling on a piece of paper, looking out of the window, or reading a newspaper. But this signals to the speaker that these other activities are more important and more interesting to this audience member than to the speaker.

Unresponsiveness to questions

If a speaker tries to engage the audience, they are unwilling to participate. If there is an opportunity for questions, the audience has nothing to ask. They just do not care.

Strategies for apathetic audiences

Audiences are apathetic for different reasons, and the strategies used to respond to this indifference need to be adapted to the cause of the apathy. Audiences may be apathetic because of the speaker, because of the topic, or because of the situation. The six strategies for dealing with apathetic audiences are: to show how audience members are affected; to show how real people are affected; to establish common ground; to adopt a new approach; to share a startling statistic; and to invite audience participation (see box 9.2).

Showing how audience members are affected

If the audience believes that a topic is not relevant, there is no reason to listen. As we indicated in chapter 6, your audience needs a reason to listen at the very beginning of the speech. A speaker must convince the audience that this is an issue they need to care about by demonstrating that the issue has an impact on them or someone they care about. For example, a student speaker who chose to talk about depression indicated that:

> Thirty-five to forty million Americans will suffer from depression according to the National Foundation for Depressive Illness. That means that the chances are that two people in this class will encounter depression and that four will have a relative or friend who will battle the disease.

These statistics make it clearer that depression is more likely to affect the audience in an important way.

Showing how real people are affected

Although statistics are very useful in establishing the severity of a problem, giving the problem a specific face is important when an audience is indifferent. This makes the problem more real, and an audience may be more likely to become involved. In a speech on the addictive nature of Internet gambling, a speaker told her audience the story of Laura Harbert:

> Laura Harbert is a single mother living in Portland, Oregon. She has two children. And she got hooked. Not on drugs but on Internet Bingo. She would play after her kids were in bed. She said, "These bingo sites – there are hundreds of them – made me feel like I was going out for the evening." Laura Harbert lost several thousand dollars she didn't have to lose by playing Internet Bingo. And when she no longer had any money left in her checking account, the bingo sites wanted her to debit her phone bill in order to pay off her gambling debts. (Horn 2002: 50)

An audience may be moved by the problems faced by a specific person and become interested in the problem.

Establishing common ground

If the audience perceives that the speaker is not worth listening to because they have no shared understanding with the speaker, an important strategy is to point out that there are similarities between the speaker and the audience. We heard a panel of alumni speak about their experiences before a group of students. It was clear that there were many dissimilarities between the panel and the student audience. The panel was much older, they wore suits, and the speakers were no longer students. They were all success-ful writers or businesspeople, been brought back to campus as examples of successful alumni. The first speaker began by remembering how he felt as a student. He described the difficulties he faced and his frustrations in balancing school, work, and a social life. He explained that his grade point average did not reflect his true abilities. He used his own experiences as a student to remind those in his audience that they had common ground. This strategy was an effective way to connect with the audience, and he received many questions from audience members.

Adopting a new approach

If a speaker has a prior reputation with an audience that leads them to expect a dull presentation, the speaker must change the way a talk is approached. If this has hap-pened to you, you probably know it. You have received enough feedback from your prior performance to know that you need to make some changes. Analyze why your previous presentations were not interesting to your audience. What can you do dif-ferently this time? It will be very important to do something quite different at the very beginning of this new talk, so that you will let the audience know that this will not be a repeat performance. A student was involved in the Rotary Club's interna-tional program and studied in Spain for a semester. When he returned, he was asked to speak before the Rotary Club that sponsored his study abroad. He gave a speech but noticed that his audience was not particularly interested in his description of life in Spain. He was asked back to talk about his experiences again when the Club was considering increasing their contributions to the international program. He knew he needed to do something very different from the first presentation. He decided to begin with a couple of interesting slides of Spain. He included some humorous stories of his experiences and asked particular audience members, whom he knew to have participated in the international program, to say where they went and to identify the most important benefit they gained by the experience. In other words, this student changed his lecture-style of giving facts about Spain from his first presentation to a much more interesting and lively talk. He made it clear from the outset that this was going to be a very different presentation from the one he had given previously.

Sharing a startling piece of statistics

If the audience has little information on the topic, they may simply need some interesting data to attract their attention. A startling piece of statistics, by definition, is unexpected and might attract the audience's interest because it is newsworthy. A speaker favoring a flat tax included information about income distribution in the United States. One of the startling statistics that he used was that the average American chief executive officer (CEO) makes 400 times more than the average American worker! While you might expect that CEOs would make more than others, would you expect them to make 400 times more?

Inviting audience participation

It is more difficult to remain indifferent if one needs to participate in an activity. A speaker can ask an audience to visualize a situation that is being described, or the solution to the problem, as in the motivated sequence organizational plan (chapter 6). A speaker can ask even a large audience for a show of hands to a question that is posed. A speaker can build in opportunities for questions from the audience. It might be a good idea to do this during the presentation rather than waiting until the end of the talk. We brought a speaker into a class of 300 students, and one of the techniques he used was bringing a box of red stress balls. As he introduced himself, he threw these out into the audience. Then he asked those students who caught the balls to respond to questions he asked about the video clips he used during his presentation. It was more difficult to remain apathetic when opportunities for audience participation were built into the presentation.

An apathetic audience is a difficult kind of audience to address, because there is such resistance even to listening to the message. The apathetic audience believes that the speaker has nothing of interest to say and, if that attitude is not changed quickly, there will be trouble. This section has described why audiences may be apathetic toward the speaker or topic and how situational factors can contribute to an apathetic response. It has also identified some cues that audiences give off that are associated with apathy and described several strategies for moving an apathetic audience toward greater interest and involvement.

> **Box 9.2**   Strategies for apathetic audiences
>
> 1 Establish common ground.
> 2 Adopt a new approach.
> 3 Show how audience members are affected.
> 4 Show how specific people are affected.
> 5 Share a startling statistics.
> 6 Invite audience participation.

Motivated Audiences

A **motivated audience** has positive attitudes about the speaker and/or the topic. Motivated audiences support the speaker. They, too, can be moved, inspired, stimulated, and enthused through the persuasive efforts of speakers: with a motivated audience, a speaker directs and maintains their support. Keynote speakers at the Democratic and Republican presidential nominating conventions are speaking primarily to those who are motivated audience members – members of their own parties, who already support the party's candidates. These keynote speeches are motivational because they attempt to stir more enthusiasm. In 2000, the keynote address at the Democratic convention was given by Harold Ford, the representative from Tennessee.

> The choice before us – a choice that weighs heavier on my generation than perhaps any other – is what kind of America will we have, not in four years but forty years. Will the amazing advances of tomorrow be fenced off for the few – or will they be tools for all of us to build better lives? At this critical time, America needs a leader with the intellect to understand the complexities we face. A leader with experience who can grasp the challenges of our world. At this critical time, America needs Al Gore. (Ford 2000)

Note that he attempted to inspire his audience, but this message was designed for those who already believed it. It was delivered to active members of the party, who were enthusiastic about their choice for President.

Factors contributing to motivation

What makes an audience motivated to act? Why would audience members be excited to hear a speaker? Some speakers believe that a presentation for a motivated audience is a piece of cake, but they could not be more wrong. Although a motivated audience is on your side, they also usually have high expectations. They want to be inspired, moved, and encouraged. A motivational speaker can fail even though the audience wants the speaker to succeed. There are always the same three factors that can contribute to motivation: attitudes toward the speaker, attitudes toward the topic, and situational factors.

Attitudes toward the speaker

An audience may be motivated by a speaker because that individual has credibility. The audience may have a past experience with the speaker which has created positive judgments of that speaker's credibility (chapter 3), as well as of his/her expertise and trustworthiness. For some audiences, particular speakers are so loved that they are capable of motivating their listeners just through their presence. Following the September 11 attacks, Mayor Rudy Giuliani was one of those speakers. He was able to express the sorrow and outrage that many Americans felt, and many of his remarks motivated others to cope with the disaster. During this period, while the eyes of the country were focused upon him, very few critical remarks were made about his speeches or actions. Audiences are prepared to be moved and stimulated to greater action by those they believe to be great individuals, speakers, and leaders.

A speaker may also use the speaking situation he is engaged in in order to refer to credibility issues (chapter 3). With motivated audiences, this may simply be a reminder that there are reasons why the audience would identify with the speaker. The president of a national fraternity visited the local chapter. He was not someone that the brothers had met before, but he shared their values and held an office that carried a great deal of credibility. When he gave the address at the chapter meeting, it was relatively easy for him to talk about shared common ground before he asked the group to make a renewed commitment to the national organization. The audience developed even more positive attitudes about the speaker as he spoke. A favorable audience became even more energized after his speech.

Attitudes toward the topic

Audiences are highly motivated toward topics when they are ego-involved in the issue, and this means they will be more likely to process the information centrally (chapter 2). It may be a topic of personal interest. We believe very strongly that the government should provide a good education for children with special needs. This attitude comes from our own experience. We have a nephew who has autism, and our extended family has been involved in a fight with the school system to obtain for him the education he deserves. An audience of members of families with children with special needs would be a motivated audience for a speaker advocating increased funding for special education. The challenge for a persuasive speaker is to keep this audience motivated and to give them specific actions that they could believe to make a difference.

Audiences are also highly motivated toward a topic when it is closely connected with their values and personal identity. This makes the issue so important that audience members feel very strongly about it and are quite dedicated to the cause. They are ripe for a speaker whose goal is to move and motivate the audience to action.

An anti-death penalty group held a meeting recently and the guest speaker was a defense lawyer who had been involved in several death penalty cases. The audience members were predisposed toward the topic. Their expressed values of forgiveness, equality, and justice, as well as their personal identities as open-minded and fair individuals, were bound up in their strong attitude to the death penalty. This attitude primed a motivated audience for this speaker who shared their perspective and could encourage action on the issue.

As we listened to the eulogies after the Columbia crash, we realized that audiences are also motivated by a topic when there are shared values. When they can agree on some core ideals, audiences are inspired even in grief. Shared values were expressed in eulogies for the astronauts, which included themes like the importance of that journey, the heroic actions to explore a frontier, the enduring spirit of human beings, and the love of family. These messages were designed by the speakers to encourage, comfort, and inspire.

Situational factors

Situational factors could influence the degree of motivation of the audience toward the speaker or the topic. At a macro-level, when there are periods of change there seems to be a need for direction and motivation. We look to our leaders to help us make sense of things and to inspire us to take particular actions. Many of the keynote addresses at political conventions take up the theme of future directions of the country, suggesting that this or that candidate is the one best suited to lead the country with a particular vision of the future. At a micro-level, a situational variable which can influence the motivation of an audience is the impact of the group itself. An audience composed of like-minded individuals can reinforce itself and create a cycle of continuous enthusiasm.

Motivation cues

Speakers delight in having a motivated audience; as they looks out across that audience, they will recognize some of the cues that we are going to discuss next. These cues indicate that the audience is energized and inspired. They are ready to listen to the speaker and be further encouraged and motivated by the speaker's message. These cues indicate engagement with the speaker and/or the topic. Cues that may indicate motivation include animated facial expressions, applause, positive emotional responses, engaged eye contact, tracking the speaker's movement, and high levels of participation (see box 9.3).

Animated facial expressions

Audience members are excited and their faces convey this excitement. They are lively, spirited, and dynamic. There is a sense of electricity as the speaker gives the presentation. They react as the speaker reacts. In contrast to the hostile audience, there is a great deal of smiling with upturned mouths and brows as one form of animated facial expression.

Applause

Audience members clap their hands and cheer at appropriate places in the speaker's remarks. This generally indicates approval, agreement, and praise.

Positive emotional responses

Speakers with motivated audiences attempt to move, inspire, and stimulate. Speakers often attempt to generate an emotional response from an audience. When they have been moved or inspired, audience members give feedback by reacting emotionally to a speaker's message. If laughter was the desired response, was it elicited by the speaker? Some emotional responses are registered on the faces of members in the audience and can be detected by a speaker who is assessing feedback.

Engaged eye contact

A motivated audience is connected to the speaker and demonstrates this through extended eye contact. Motivated audiences show they are listening by carefully attending to the speaker through eye contact. Indeed, nonverbal meanings may be assessed by paying this kind of attention to a speaker; motivated audiences are observing all that can be taken in from the presentation.

Tracking the speaker's movement

A motivated audience is more likely to follow a speaker's movement. Speakers move as they present their message. A motivated audience does not want to miss a moment of the message; they attend to it most carefully. They monitor a speaker very closely, and this cue indicates that the audience (especially in combination with other cues in this list) is motivated by the speaker and/or by the topic.

High levels of participation

Motivated audience members are more likely to participate in the speaker's presentation. If the speaker asks for volunteers, often more than enough people come forward. If the speaker asks for questions, there are friendly queries from the audience. The speaker may even begin a well-known phrase and invite the audience to finish it. This kind of participation generally indicates enthusiasm for the speaker or the topic.

Strategies for motivated audiences

There are several strategies that a persuader can use in addressing a motivated audience: reinforce similarities with the audience, convey respect for it, use vivid description and imagery, use extended narratives, and attend to the rhythm of the speech.

Reinforcing similarities with the audience

With a motivated audience, the speaker is likely to have good credibility. To enhance this credibility even further, the speaker should remind the audience of the similarities in their values. Essentially, what this strategy does is to say to the audience: "I am one of you and we are together on this." Simons (2001) suggests that a speaker is congratulating the audience for their "right-thinking."

Conveying respect for the audience

Audiences like to be appreciated and, if a speaker is going to ask for more commitment, it is a good strategy to indicate the level of admiration. This can endear a speaker even more to an audience. John gave a speech to presidents of service organizations and he was asking them to become involved in a new service activity. He began the speech by commending them for their service to their communities. Their leadership roles in their various organizations were important to the lives of many other people. By showing respect for their significant work before he asked for an additional commitment, John was able to recognize and appreciate his audience.

Using vivid description and imagery

Dramatic explanations and stirring imagery can go a long way toward moving audiences and visualizing the future in times of change. Chapter 8 provided many specific stylistic devices for creating intensity, a vivid and dramatic mood through language. In a speech given at the First International Drug Peace Day Rally, individuals who have been arrested in the war on drugs are characterized not as criminals but as prisoners of war:

> There is an anguished cry – a cry of sorrow and despair that screams across this nation – but no one can hear it. These cries of sorrow are coming from behind the walls and wire, then dissipate in cornfields and far-off hillsides where our federal government is hiding the prisons! We are a country at war! I am here today to give voice to those cries and bring you a message from the prisoners of war in America. (Callahan 1997)

This speech occurred within a rally organized to support legalizing drugs. This particular audience would have been receptive to a message that used vivid characterizations of the anguish suffered by prisoners of war at the hands of the government.

Using extended narratives

As previously described in chapter 8, narratives can be incredibly powerful in evoking an emotional response from an audience. These narratives are not used as evidence but are ways to amplify or embellish the point being made by the speaker. When the Disabilities Education Act was signed, Judith Heumann, the Assistant Secretary from the Department of Education, gave a speech. This included an extended personal narrative which was designed to motivate the audience rather than persuade them, because the bill had already been passed.

> When it was time for me to go to school, the school officials did not see me – they only saw my wheelchair. And they barred me from class. I was a fire hazard, they said. Well, it was pretty easy for them to push around a kindergarten kid, but my mother was something else again. She is one of the toughest kinds of women you'll ever meet – a housewife from Brooklyn, New York. Without experience, she and my father became activists and my strong advocates. And I finally did get my education. Thank you, mom. Years later, when I applied for my teacher's license, the Board of Education of the City of New York refused me again. I was still a fire hazard. But this time I could fend for myself. I sued them. And I got my license, and I taught elementary school for three years. Today, thanks to the Individuals with Disabilities Education Act, those days have been replaced by the light of hope and opportunity. And the light has given us a brand new vision. (Heumann 1997)

The extended narrative was used to motivate the audience – to show how much progress had been made with the passage of the bill. But, at the end of the speech, the speaker called on the audience to do more:

> We have come a long way, but we know that we can and must do better. Making progress will require continued partnership, aggressive collaboration, and a love for all children. This Act will give disabled young people more opportunities for quality education and meaningful employment than ever before in our nation's history. (Ibid.)

The speaker attempted to motivate the audience to further commitment while praising the accomplishments that have been attained in the present legislation.

Attending to the rhythm of the speech

As we have explained in chapter 8, there are stylistic devices that establish a rhythmic pattern to a speech (e.g. alliteration, antithesis, and parallel structure). These are ways in which a speaker can invite the audience, as a group, to participate in the speech by anticipating the discourse. The audience as a group can participate and be stirred by the speaker's words. In the following graduation speech, Callie Khouri, the screenwriter, motivates her audience through a variety of stylistic devices:

> Don't be afraid to have a dream. Because one of the most amazing things about this life is that dreams can become reality, and I offer myself as living proof. With perseverance, faith, and luck, and by luck I mean, when opportunity meets preparation, truly incredible things can happen to you. I promise you one thing. It won't be easy, but it's easier than spending your life wishing that you'd done something, and feeling disappointed in yourself for never having tried. That's the true hell. So go on and do the thing that scares the hell out of you, because in this world, not unlike Hollywood, the gamble is almost as safe a bet as the sure thing. (Khouri 1994)

She uses an oral style which is marked for its informality. It has repetition, intense language, and simple sentence structures. There was a brief narrative when she made reference to her own success. The humorous metaphor compared pursuing one's dreams to gambling. The rhythmic patterns of this speech helped to draw the audience in to the motivational message.

The present section has described the factors that influence motivated audiences, the cues that indicate an audience's being motivated, and the strategies that a speaker can use with an already motivated audience.

Box 9.3 Strategies for motivated audiences

1 Reinforce similarities with the audience.
2 Convey respect for the audience.
3 Use vivid description and imagery.
4 Use extended narratives.
5 Attend to the rhythm of the speech.

Multiple or Mixed Audiences

A **multiple audience** is made up of audience members with strikingly different attitudes about the speaker and/or the topic. These distinctions can polarize the audience into two (or more) groups. Controversial speakers often attract multiple audiences that include different segments who are hostile and motivated. We attended a talk by Morris Dees, the co-founder of the Southern Poverty Law Center and the chief trial counsel. Dees is best known for successfully prosecuting the Ku Klux Klan for the assassination of Michael Donald and winning a $7 million from the case. His presentation was given before about 300 people in an auditorium on campus, and the audience was clearly mixed in its attitudes toward the speaker and his message. Dees received a standing ovation, but prior to the presentation some members of the audience had passed out a newsletter that labeled his organization, the Southern Poverty Law Center, a "scam," on the grounds that it raised large donations while taking on few actual cases (Winters 1998). At the end of the presentation, Morris Dees answered questions. But he would only respond to written questions, and he sorted through them, indicating that "Some of these questions show that some in the audience really disagree with me." He quoted Harry Truman: "Arguing with people like that is like getting into a peeing contest with a water hose" (ibid.). The motivated audience members supplied most of the questions he was willing to answer. These allowed him to expand on his theme and to answer his critics on his own grounds, or they were complimentary in nature. This presentation was an opportunity for students in our class to get extra credit points. We suspect there were even some apathetic members in the audience, who would rather have been somewhere else (at least at the beginning of the presentation). In this case, the audience had different attitudes about the speaker and the topic.

Factors contributing to multiple audiences

Very few audiences are truly homogenous. Multiple audiences arise because of different attitudes to the speaker and/or the topic among the audience members. There are also three situational factors that can influence the probability of multiple kinds of audiences in a particular case. The present section considers such factors: attitudes toward the speaker, attitudes toward the topic, and situational factors.

Attitudes toward the speaker

Audiences can have different attitudes toward the speaker because they are focusing on different aspects of the individual. It is well known that, when we meet others, we do not always form the same impressions of them. We pay attention to different information in the impression formation process, and we can evaluate the same information differently. It is no wonder that speakers would be evaluated differently as well. While we find Rush Limbaugh's credibility to be low (after all, he made critical remarks about one of the authors of this book!), one of our brothers thinks Rush knows a lot and makes a lot of sense. We focused on the fact that Rush has been critical, while our brother focused on his expertise.

Audiences may have unique reactions to speakers because they have had different prior experiences with them. When this happens, separate audience members bring different expectations to the situation. We saw this happen recently, when a well-known professor was asked to speak to a small group of undergraduate students. Some of these students had been in a large lecture class with this professor in previous semesters. Some had been in small classes with the same professor. After the presentation, we overheard several students talking. It was clear that those students who had attended the large lecture class were surprised by how the professor had acted. He had been much more subdued than in the large class. Students in the small classes thought that this was the way he always talked! Guess which students reacted more favorably to this talk?

Attitudes toward the topic

Audiences may have mixed attitudes toward a topic because it is controversial and has conflicting values attached to it. A persuasive speaker choosing the topic of the insanity defense faced a multiple audience. This is a controversial topic because there have been some high-profile cases in which the insanity defense was used successfully, after which several states have enacted legislation to restrict the use of this defense. There are competing values inherent in the topic. On the one hand, there are victims in these crimes, and the values of justice and of redressing a wrong are salient. On the other hand, issues of fairness and responsibility arise when mental illness is the reason for a person's behavior.

Audiences may have mixed attitudes toward a topic because it represents a complex problem with complicated solutions. The problem of failing to comply with weapons inspections in Iraq was complex and did not have an easy solution. As debate raged over whether war was imminent or more time should be given for further weapons inspections, Secretary of State Colin Powell addressed the United Nations. His speech attempted to garner support for a second resolution, of endorsing force in Iraq by providing multiple layers of evidence that Saddam Hussein was deliberately avoiding compliance with the current weapons inspections. For example, he showed photographic evidence of trucks being loaded and leaving from the back door of an installation while UN weapons inspectors were delayed at the front door. Powell faced a multiple audience. Some members of his audience agreed that further weapons inspections would not be productive, but several countries were unwilling to short-circuit the process.

It is also possible that a problem has different effects, so that audience members may respond to it in different ways. A speaker gave a persuasive presentation on the problem of alcohol abuse before an audience consisting of members of the faculty, students, and the community. The problems were perceived differently by different audience members. Faculty members were concerned about the impact that drinking was having on their classrooms. Students believed that the problems had been exaggerated. Community members were concerned mostly about the noise levels of parties in neighborhoods close to campus. Audience members saw the effects of the problem (and whether there was a problem) from their perspective, and this created a multiple audience for the speaker.

Situational factors

A situational variable that could have some bearing on the probability of a multiple audience is the latter's size. All other things being equal, a larger audience is more likely to be heterogeneous in its attitudes toward speaker or topic. These audience characteristics (size and heterogeneity; chapter 5) can influence the formation of multiple audiences.

Many audiences at a large and diverse institution (like a university) could be heterogeneous. Audiences at other institutions (e.g. in a small business) probably would be homogeneous.

Cues for multiplicity or mixed character

Multiplicity cues are exactly what they sound like – multiple. A speaker receives significant cues that indicate that some audience members are hostile, others are apathetic, others are motivated. Or there can be any of the possible combinations of these three kinds of audiences. You might have an audience with some members who are apathetic and some who are hostile, or an audience with some who are motivated and others who are hostile. Realistically, this is quite common because audiences are rarely entirely homogenous. In the same audience, some will be looking out the window and acting distracted while others will respond with animated facial expressions. The more interesting question is what to do about this mixed reaction.

Box 9.4   Audience cues

Hostile Audiences	Apathetic Audiences	Motivated Audiences
Crossing arms	Sighing	Animated facial expressions
Frowning	Minimal eye contact	Applause
Glaring	Closed eyes	Positive emotional responses
Facial reddening	Blank stare	Engaged eye contact
Shaking head from side to side	Distracted with other activities	Tracking speaker's movement
Asking barbed questions	Unresponsive to questions	High levels of participation

Strategies for multiple audiences

The section on strategies for multiple audiences is different from those that have described discourse strategies for hostile, apathetic, and motivated audiences. Multiple audiences are a mixture of these other kinds of audience within the same group. As a result, the potential discourse strategies have already been described when er discussed each type of audience. But the strategies for multiple audiences concern how a speaker chooses to manage multiplicity: focus on part of the audience, balance attention among the different components, and provide unequal attention to them (see box 9.5).

Focusing on part of the audience

When multiple kinds of audience are present within a larger audience, the speaker may choose to ignore a part of the audience and adapt the presentation to the others. In what kind of situation would this strategy be selected? If the audience is primarily of one kind, but there are a few divergent individuals, the speaker might choose to address the largest group of audience members. For example, a speaker at a rally for Earth Day knew that most of her audience were motivated, only a few were apathetic. She was primarily interested in getting more commitment to act from those who were already motivated, and she directed her remarks toward these members of the audience. She knew that she was unlikely to reach the apathetic members of her audience in her short speech, so she did not use strategies to generate their interest in her topic. Another situation in which a speaker would attend to a part of the audience occurs when only those audience members could enact what the speaker desired. A political candidate delivers a persuasive message to diverse audiences, but will target the message to those who are voters. It is wonderful if a crowd of under-18-year-olds is motivated by a candidate, but they cannot have a direct effect on the ultimate outcome of the election. A candidate will focus only on that part of the audience who votes, and will target the message to this audience.

Balancing attention among the different components of the audience

If the speaker believes that the multiple audiences are represented about equally, then they will require balanced attention during the presentation. A speaker may even acknowledge that there are differences of opinion among the members of the audience about the issues to be discussed, and he could make an attempt to speak to all their concerns:

> I know that some of you wonder why this should be an issue that you should care about. Your health insurance seems just fine. But some of you probably think that what I am going to propose sounds like socialized medicine and I want to reassure you that this is not the case.

In this early statement, the speaker addressed those in the audience who were apathetic toward the speaker's topic; but the speaker also attended to those in audience who were hostile to a proposal that has been linked to socialized medicine.

Some speakers find it easier to divide the speech into half and let the audience know that their concerns will be addressed at a particular point in the presentation. The difficulty with this approach is that part of your audience may not stay with you long enough for you to get to the place in your presentation that is relevant to their concerns. Another possibility is to organize the speech topically and to work material that is relevant to multiple audiences into each topic, so that these audiences may tended to stay with you throughout the presentation. A balanced presentation seeks to provide equal time and attention to each of the multiple audiences in attendance.

Providing unequal attention to the different components
in a multiple audience

Although the previous strategy attempted a balanced presentation, this one explicitly opts for unequal attention in dealing with multiple audiences. It would be chosen when there are unequal numbers of each type of audience. Some numbers are not small enough to be ignored, but they are not large enough for the speaker to feel that they should get equal time either. So, the speaker gives more attention to one kind of audience than another. For example, unequal attention would be the choice if you knew that about 70 percent of the audience was apathetic but 30 percent was motivated. The primary adaptation of the presentation would be geared toward involving the audience but a smaller part of the presentation would take advantage of the motivated audience within this group. You would not want to ignore this important 30 percent.

Multiple audiences complicate life, but they are very common. This section has described why multiple audiences are likely to exist; referenced the myriad of cues that could bombard a speaker faced with multiple audiences; and described the strategies that a speaker has in managing the situation of facing a multiple audience within the same group.

Audiences are essential to the persuasive process, and understanding more about one's audience is very important. This chapter has described four kinds of audiences: hostile, apathetic, motivated, and multiple. For each of these kinds of audiences, we have described the factors that can contribute to its formation and explain why audiences are of a particular type. We have identified a variety of cues that speakers can use even as the presentation is being given to determine the kind of audience they are addressing. Finally, we have suggested a set of discourse strategies that can be used in presentations for each of these audiences. With multiple audiences, we make a special effort to describe particular strategies for addressing different kinds of audiences at the same time, within the same group. How much do you know about your audience?

Box 9.5   Strategies for multiple or mixed audiences

1 Focus on part of the audience.
2 Balance attention to multiple audiences.
3 Provide unequal attention to multiple audiences.

Using Audience Types in Persuasion

To be effective, persuasive speakers need to know as much as possible about their audiences. Not all audiences are the same, and the speaker who treats them as if they were is not as likely to be persuasive. Speakers will gather information about their audiences through an audience analysis (chapter 5), and this will give them information about whether the audience is likely to be hostile, apathetic, motivated, or multiple. The strategies to be adopted for each of the types of audience can be planned in advance by the speaker. For example, if the persuasive speaker knows that the audience is likely to be hostile, then several of the strategies we have described for dealing with this kind of audience should be incorporated into the speech in advance. Any of the strategies for hostile audiences are appropriate; however, you should select the ones that best fit your situation.

But persuasive speakers also need to be alert during the presentation for cues that may indicate that an audience is of a particular type. The audience may be reacting differently than the speaker predicted and adaptations should be made. Some of the strategies we have suggested are easier to implement on your feet than others. Concerning strategies for hostile audiences, you may be able to introduce humor to defuse hostility, call for a fair hearing, emphasize common ground, express understanding and respect for the audience's position, reassure the audience, moderate the persuasive goal, and neutralize hostile questions if you discover that you have an audience that is hostile just as you are delivering your presentation. If you find yourself unexpectedly facing an apathetic audience, we would suggest attempting to establish common ground and inviting audience participation in order to attempt to establish some interest. With a motivated audience, you can reinforce similarities with your audience and convey your respect for them. In each case, we have suggested strategies that do not require extensive planning, constructing an elaborate argument, or providing support for a claim. These strategies can be adopted spontaneously, as you respond interactively to the demeanor of your audience.

This chapter has described what factors might influence audiences' being of a certain type, and has provided strategies for addressing particular types of audience. These strategies allow the persuasive speaker to adapt the message to a particular audience. A hostile audience should be soothed. An apathetic audience needs to be drawn in. A motivated audience can be stirred to action. Multiple audiences must be dealt with carefully, and the size of each contingent group will influence the speaker's choice to ignore or to give a balanced or an unequal treatment to the different groups in the audience.

Glossary

Apathetic audience: a group that is indifferent toward the speaker and/or the topic.
Hostile audience: a group that is antagonistic toward the speaker.
Motivated audience: a group that has positive attitudes toward the speaker and/or topic.
Multiple audience: a group consisting of members with varied (different) attitudes toward the speaker and/or topic.

Part III

Theories of Persuasion

Chapter 10

Consistency Theories of Attitude Change

Social psychologists are interested in what we think – and in the relationships among our thoughts. We know that cognitions are important from the elaboration likelihood model (chapter 2). Psychologists have developed several consistency theories of attitude change, which suggest that, when we have thoughts that are inconsistent, we often change some of our thoughts to restore consistency (the assumption is that inconsistency in our thoughts is unpleasant). Because these thoughts include our attitudes, inconsistency can result in attitude change. Notice that these theories all stress the importance of the audience, because the audience experiences the inconsistency. We will discuss three important consistency theories. The earliest version was Fritz Heider's balance theory. Then Charles Osgood and Percy Tannenbaum developed the congruity theory. Finally, Leon Festinger proposed his cognitive dissonance theory.

Heider's Balance Theory

Heider's theory (1946, 1958) focused on the relationships among three elements, and he used a triangle to depict these relationships. He suggested that we consider a P ("person"), his/her attitude toward another (O, "other person"), and their attitude toward a third thing, an attitude object (for this he used X, since "O" was already used). Using a "+" sign to represent a positive relationship, if P likes (has a positive attitude toward) O, P likes X, and O likes X, we obtain the situation shown in box 10.1.

Box 10.1   Balanced *POX* triad

P (you)

    +   +

(Jordan) O + X (Nike)

For example, if you like Michael Jordan ($P+O$), Michael Jordan likes Nike shoes ($O+X$), and you like Nike shoes ($P+X$), that is a **balanced** relationship, which means that these thoughts are harmonious. However, if for some reason you did not like Nike shoes, we get the situation shown in box 10.2.

Box 10.2   Imbalanced *POX* triad

P (you)

    +   –

(Jordan) O + X (Nike)

Heider's theory declared that this situation is not balanced, and that it would be somewhat unpleasant for you to have these thoughts. Things are just not quite right, less than optimal, when you like Jordan, he likes Nike shoes, but you do not like Nike shoes. It is possible that you could shrug off this inconsistency (balance theory does not predict that attitude change will always result from imbalance); but you might change your attitude.

In this situation, there are three ways to restore the balance: Change any of the three relationships to a different sign. The most obvious way is for you to decide that you do like Nike shoes after all, changing a negative attitude toward Nike into a positive attitude. This would give us the situation depicted earlier in box 10.1. However, as we will see in a moment, there are eight possible triads and half of them are balanced, so you could reduce the unpleasant feeling associated with box 10.2 in other ways too. You could decide that, if Michael Jordan likes Nike shoes, then perhaps he is not such a likeable person (changing your positive attitude toward Jordan into a negative attitude). This triad, shown in box 10.3, is also balanced.

Box 10.3   A second balanced *POX* triad

$$P \text{ (you)}$$
$$- \qquad -$$
$$\text{(Jordan) } O \quad + \quad X \text{ (Nike)}$$

Furthermore, you could decide that Michael Jordan does not really like Nike shoes, changing the *O*+*X* relationship into *O*–*X*. Perhaps you might tell yourself that Jordan only endorses Nike shoes because he is paid so much money. Or you might tell yourself that you were confused: Jordan endorses a different brand of shoes, not Nike. This would create yet another balanced triad, shown in box 10.4.

Box 10.4   A third balanced *POX* triad

$$P \text{ (you)}$$
$$+ \qquad -$$
$$\text{(Jordan) } O \quad - \quad X \text{ (Nike)}$$

We are not saying that these three ways of restoring the balance are equally likely. It may be that your positive attitude toward Jordan is much stronger than your negative attitude toward Nike shoes. If so, you are much more likely to change your attitude toward the *X* (Nike) than toward the *O* (Jordan). However, there are three possible ways of restoring balance in this situation.

As we have suggested earlier, there are eight possible triads, four of them balanced and four imbalanced. Looking carefully at box 10.5, you can see that there is an easy way to determine whether a *POX* triad is balanced or imbalanced: Imbalanced *POX* triads have an odd number of minus signs, whereas balanced *POX* triads have an even number of minus signs.

Box 10.5   Balanced and imbalanced *POX* triads

Balanced triads

P	P	P	P
$+ \quad +$	$- \quad -$	$+ \quad -$	$- \quad +$
$O \quad + \quad X$	$O \quad + \quad X$	$O \quad - \quad X$	$O \quad - \quad X$

Imbalanced triads

P	P	P	P
$+ \quad -$	$+ \quad +$	$- \quad +$	$- \quad -$
$O \quad + \quad X$	$O \quad - \quad X$	$O \quad + \quad X$	$O \quad - \quad X$

Some research has tested the predictions of balance theory. Research has found that balanced situations of the kind described in our example – you like Michael Jordan, Michael Jordan likes Nike shoes, and you too like Nike shoes – are rated as being more pleasant than unbalanced ones (Jordan 1953; Miller and Norman 1976). However, balance theory provided only a partial explanation for the results; it did not explain every pattern that occurred. First, triads with a positive relationship between the two people (P+O) were rated as more pleasant than situations with a negative relationship (P−O). This result was called the **attraction effect**. In other words, some unbalanced triads were rated as fairly pleasant when the two people had a positive relationship. Second, situations in which both people rated the object similarly (P+X and O+X; P−X and O−X) were rated as more pleasant than situations in which the two people disagreed about the evaluation of the attitude object (P+X and O−X; P−X and O+X). This was labeled the **agreement effect**. Again, some unbalanced triads were rated as fairly pleasant if P and O both agreed in their liking (or disliking) for X. So, balance theory predictions were supported in that balanced situations were considered more pleasant, but balance theory did not explain either attraction or agreement.

Balance theory has other key limitations. First, it cannot handle more than three ideas at once (person, other, attitude object). However, many attitudes are complex, composed of several belief/value pairs. Remember the Mini-Cooper automobile from chapter 1? You may have many beliefs and values that contribute to your overall attitude: sportiness, gas mileage, cargo capacity, price, how the car feels, and more. Balance theory simply cannot deal with complex attitudes like these. Furthermore, it seems reasonable that not all attitudes (or beliefs) are equally important or powerful. To return to Michael Jordan and Nike, if you have a very strong attitude toward Jordan and you just do not care about athletic shoes (perhaps you only wear boots, or only sandals), you probably will not experience much imbalance when you realize that you like Mike (a lot!), Mike likes Nike shoes, but you do not like Nike. Third, balance theory ignores the content of messages. We know from chapter 6 that well-organized messages are more persuasive than other messages. Chapter 7 made it clear that messages with good evidence are more effective than other messages. Balance theory, however, says nothing about content. Balance theory was a good beginning in understanding consistency between messages and audiences, but it was no more than that: a start.

Osgood and Tannenbaum's Congruity Theory

Charles Osgood and Percy Tannenbaum developed a variant of consistency theory which they named "congruity theory" (1955). This theory was more limited in scope: congruity theory concerns situations in which a source makes an assertion about a concept, and the audience has attitudes toward the source and the concept. Of course, that is precisely what we want to know in studying persuasive messages. A source making an assertion about a concept is the same as PX in balance theory, the audience's attitude toward the source is the same idea as Heider's PO relationship, and the audience's attitude toward the concept is the OX relationship in Heider's triad. However, unlike balance theory, congruity makes specific predictions about which attitudes will change – and how much. It does this by quantifying two of the three relationships in Heider's triad: the degree of the audience's liking for the source (PO) and the audience's attitude toward the concept (PX). The other relationship, OX, remains the same because congruity theory stipulates that the assertion of the source about the concept can take one of two forms. An **associative** assertion is one in which the source expresses liking for, or agreement with, the concept ("I think Casablanca is a great movie!"). A **dissociative** assertion is one in which the source expresses dislike for, or disagreement with, the concept ("I think that politician is dishonest"). Finally, like balance theory, congruity theory holds that incongruity (like imbalance) is unpleasant and motivates audiences to change their attitudes.

The formulae created by Osgood and Tannenbaum have several implications. First, congruity theory predicts that the audience's attitude toward the source will change along with their attitude toward the concept. Second, when the source makes an associative assertion, the attitudes toward concept and source are expected to move toward each other (the most positive attitude becomes more negative; the most negative attitude becomes more positive) so they meet in the middle. It also predicts that the more extreme of the two attitudes (the one with a larger number, regardless of whether the number is positive or negative) will move more than the more moderate one. A dissociative assertion means that the two attitudes should move further apart.

Consider a case in which a source (Jon, a rock star) makes an associative assertion about hockey: "Hockey is a great game. I like it a lot." First, we need to measure these attitudes, and congruity theory uses a scale from +3 to −3. Shelly would rate Jon (the source, S) at 2, hockey (the concept, C) at −1. We also need to calculate the amount of incongruity, or distance (D) between the source and concept, which in this case would be 3 units: Remember from math that subtracting a negative number, like −1, is equivalent to adding the corresponding positive number, so 2 − (−1) = 3. This relationship is displayed in box 10.6, which shows Shelly's initial attitudes as well as her attitudes after she learns of Jon's associative assertion about hockey.

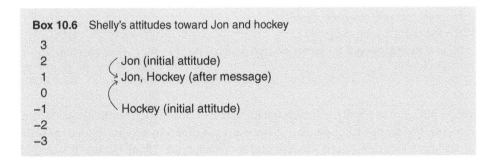

Box 10.6   Shelly's attitudes toward Jon and hockey

3
2   Jon (initial attitude)
1   Jon, Hockey (after message)
0
−1   Hockey (initial attitude)
−2
−3

To calculate Shelly's new attitude toward hockey, we use the formula in box 10.7. Shelly's attitude toward hockey (C) is −1, her attitude toward Jon (S) is 2, and the distance between them (pressure, P) is 3. So we have (2 ÷ [2+1]) (3), or (2÷3)(3), or 2. So congruity theory predicts that Shelly's attitude toward hockey would move 2 units, from −1 to +1.

Box 10.7 Formula to predict change in attitude to concept

$$\frac{|C|}{|C| + |S|} \text{ times P = new attitude toward concept}$$

C = initial attitude toward concept
S = initial attitude toward source
P = Pressure toward congruity
|C| is absolute value of C (ignore the minus sign if there is one), |S| is absolute
value of S

Now consider Shelly's attitude toward Jon, the source. The formula for predicting this attitude change is given in box 10.8. You can see that this formula is similar, but not identical to, the formula used to predict change toward the concept. Here we have (1 ÷ [2+1]) (3), or (1 ÷ 3)(3), or 1 (remember to omit the minus sign for Shelly's attitude toward hockey in this formula). Hence congruity theory predicts that Shelly's attitude toward Jon would move from +2 to +1. This means that Shelly's attitude toward Jon is now the same as her attitude toward hockey, so there is no longer an inconsistency (or, to put it in the theory's terms, no incongruity). The formula also means that extreme attitudes are predicted to undergo greater change than more moderate attitudes.

Box 10.8 Formula to predict change in attitude to source

$$\frac{|S|}{|S| + |C|} \text{ times P = new attitude toward source}$$

S = initial attitude toward source
C = initial attitude toward concept
P = Pressure toward congruity
|S| is absolute value of S (ignore the minus sign if there is one), |C| is absolute
value of C

We do not want to dwell further on the formulae of this theory, but to illustrate how it works. We do need to note that P (pressure) is different when a source makes a dissociative assertion (e.g. if Jon had said something like "I hate hockey. It is stupid and boring").

Congruity theory was tested using a variety of hypothetical situations. Subjects were given a long list of people (potential message sources, such as President Eisenhower or Soviet leader Khrushchev) and concepts (such as communism, democracy), and they were asked to report their attitude toward each one. Later, subjects were given messages which said that Eisenhower or Khrushchev had made a statement about a concept, like democracy or communism. Researchers wanted to explore every option, so some of the statements linked liked sources (Eisenhower) with liked concepts (democracy) and disliked sources (Khrushchev) with disliked concepts: "Eisenhower says democracy is what made this nation great," or "Khrushchev said communism is the best system of government." Other statements associated liked sources with disliked concepts ("Eisenhower said the benefits of communism are not appreciated") and disliked sources with liked concepts ("Khrushchev declared that democracy was more efficient than communism"). After reading these messages, the subjects' attitudes toward the sources and the concepts were measured again. The question was whether reading the message had changed their attitudes toward the concepts in messages which associated positive and negative people and concepts. The data for their initial attitudes toward source and concept were put into the formula, and then their actual attitudes (after reading the message) were compared with the attitudes predicted by congruity theory.

Calculations revealed that the theory's predictions about change in attitudes toward the concept and the source were generally supported: attitudes did tend to change in the direction predicted by the theory. Also, their results showed that attitudes toward sources changed as well as attitudes toward concepts. However, the precise amounts of attitude change predicted were often incorrect (Osgood, Suci, and Tannenbaum 1957). These experimental results led the theorists to propose two corrections to the formula. These corrections were called *post hoc* hypotheses, since they did not arise from the theory, but from research conducted after the theory was stated. In a sense, they are "band-aids" trying to fix errors in the theory's predictions.

The first *post hoc* hypothesis was called the **assertion constant**. It stated that, when a source makes an assertion about a concept, that assertion tells more about the concept than about the source (because, presumably, people are more complex than things). Accordingly, it predicted that attitude toward the source will change less than the original formula predicts. So, when Eisenhower makes a statement about democracy, our attitude toward Eisenhower will change, but not as much as predicted by the formula. Because this hypothesis was developed after looking at the results of their research, it was of course supported by those data.

The second *post hoc* hypothesis was called the **correction for incredulity**. The researchers noticed that, when a source was made to say something implausible – such as Eisenhower praising communism or Khrushchev denouncing communism – the attitude change predicted by congruity theory did not occur. Their explanation was that, when a source supposedly makes an unlikely assertion, the audience will be incredulous, or disbelieving, and not be persuaded by that message. So the theory was amended again, to say that the predictions would hold true except when a source says something that the audience does not believe that the source would really have said.

Evaluation of congruity theory

Congruity theory makes specific predictions about the direction and amount of attitude change that will occur as a result of persuasive communication. These predictions are not perfect but fairly accurate. They are even more accurate when the two corrections are made to the original formula. Balance theory makes no specific predictions about attitude change, so this is a definite improvement.

Congruity theory also has some unexpected advantages. First, it predicts that incongruity will create pressure, not only for change in the audience's attitude toward the concept, but also for change in the audience's attitude toward the source. No theory had predicted change toward the source, but experimental evidence showed that in fact attitudes toward both the concept and the source changed. Second, the theory predicts that more polarized attitudes will change less than moderate attitudes. That prediction was also confirmed by research.

Another advantage is that the correction for incredulity explains why some messages are ineffective. If a message attributes an implausible claim to a source (e.g. that Eisenhower likes communism or dislikes democracy; that Khrushchev likes democracy or dislikes communism), that message will be ineffective, despite the fact that it would appear to create a great deal of incongruity.

One limitation of congruity theory is that, like all balance theories, it ignores message content. There is ample evidence that message factors, like strong arguments or evidence, are significant influences on persuasion. However, congruity theory classifies all messages as either associative or disociative, with no provision for stronger or weaker messages. Second, the corrections it proposes (assertion constant, correction for incredulity) are not predicted by the theory. This means that the theory must be incomplete or flawed in some way.

Festinger's Cognitive Dissonance Theory

Another form of consistency theory is Cognitive Dissonance Theory, developed by Leon Festinger (1957; see also Arsonson 1969; Brehm and Cohen 1962; Wicklund and Brehm 1976). Festinger argues that there are three possible relationships among cognitions (thoughts, ideas): consonance, dissonance, and irrelevance. Two ideas that are consistent, like "I like Michael Jordan" and "Michael Jordan is the greatest basketball player ever," are **consonant**. Two thoughts that are inconsistent, like "I smoke cigarettes," and "Cigarettes can kill smokers," are **dissonant**. Two cognitions that are unconnected, like "Michael Jordan is the greatest basketball player ever" and "Cigarettes can kill smokers," are said to be **irrelevant**. Dissonance theory tells us that dissonance is an unpleasant motivating state (a disagreeable feeling) which encourages attitude change to achieve consonance, thereby reducing our unpleasant feeling. So far, dissonance theory is similar to balance theory.

One of the advantages of dissonance theory is that it can consider more than two cognitions at a time. Another advantage is that it acknowledges that some cognitions are more important than others, and that the importance of cognitions influences the amount of dissonance. Specifically, dissonance theory predicts that the amount of dissonance is influenced by two factors: (1) the proportion of dissonant and consonant cognitions and (2) the importance of the cognitions.

First, consider the proportion of dissonant and consonant thoughts. For example, if you know six good things and four bad things about your friend Bob, you should experience more dissonance than if you know six good things and one bad thing about him. In the example below, think about how much dissonance would exist if you had all four of the dissonant thoughts versus if you only had one of these cognitions. It makes sense that the more inconsistent a person's thoughts are, the more dissonance he or she should experience.

Box 10.9 Cognitions about Bob

Consonant thoughts:
  C1 Bob is funny.
  C2 Bob likes basketball like me.
  C3 Bob likes rock and roll music like me.
  C4 Bob is a loyal friend.
  C5 Bob likes the action/adventure movies like me.
  C6 Bob helped me with algebra in High School.

Dissonant thoughts:
  D1 Bob doesn't like my brother.
  D2 Bob likes those stupid horror movies.
  D3 Bob is really messy.
  D4 Bob goes too far sometimes in making fun of people.

Furthermore, the importance of these good and bad thoughts makes a difference. If your brother is really important to you, the first dissonant thought, that Bob does not like my brother (D1), could create a lot of dissonance. On the other hand, if you are not very close to your brother, this cognition should not bother you as much. Thus, dissonance theory considers all of the relevant thoughts at once, taking into account both the proportion and the importance of consistent (consonant) and inconsistent (dissonant) thoughts. Balance theory and congruity theory can consider only one idea, and neither theory accounts for the importance of ideas.

Dissonance theory suggests that there are three ways to restore consonance. First, one may change a cognition in order to reduce dissonance. If you had new information which suggested that Bob really liked your brother, then the idea that Bob does not like your brother (D1) could change (into C7, Bob likes my brother). This should reduce your dissonant thoughts about Bob. Second, a person who experiences dissonance can add a new cognition. For example, you could decide that Bob just does not know your brother very well, and that, if Bob just got to know him, Bob's feeling toward your brother would almost certainly change. The third way to reduce dissonance is to change the importance of cognitions. You could decide that, because Bob hardly ever sees your brother, you could reduce the importance of Bob's feeling toward your brother, which would reduce your dissonance. One important limitation of dissonance theory is that, unlike congruity theory, it does not predict how dissonance will be reduced in any situation.

An obvious implication of cognitive dissonance theory is that, if you want to change someone's attitude, you could try to create dissonance concerning that person's attitude and hope that desired attitude change would result. However, there are other implications of cognitive dissonance as well. Much of the research on dissonance has focused on decision-making, counter-attitudinal advocacy, forced compliance, and selective exposure to information.

Dissonance after decision-making

Life is filled with many choices for you: Should you go to college? If so, which school should you attend? What major should you choose? Should you join a fraternity or sorority, and, if so, which one? Should you study for tomorrow's test after dinner or go to a movie tonight? Whom should you ask to the dance on Friday? Should you attend the football game on Saturday? Do you want to buy a paperback? If so, should it be a new book by Stephen King (or by someone else)? Rarely do we face a situation in which one option is, without a doubt, the only reasonable choice. Most choices we face in life have both pros and cons. Once we make a choice, however, we accept the disadvantages of that option and give up the potential advantages of other, unchosen, options. Realization of these consequences leads to dissonance that arises after we make a decision: you chose option A, which has drawbacks; you rejected option B, which had its own benefits. Thus, post-decisional dissonance is a form of regret, a worry that perhaps we did not make the best choice.

Cognitive dissonance theory predicts that the amount of dissonance experienced will be related to (1) the net desirability of the chosen and unchosen options and (2) the importance of the decision (Festinger 1964). Specifically, the closer the choices are in their attractiveness (if the unchosen option is almost as good as the chosen option), the greater the dissonance. If two universities look equally attractive (good reputation, affordability, and so on), choosing to attend one instead of the other should create dissonance. On the other hand, if the university we picked is clearly better than the one we rejected, we should experience little dissonance. If the choice is between staying home and watching a boring television show and going out to hear a concert featuring a great band, there will be little dissonance from the decision to attend the concert.

Second, the more important the decision, the more dissonance we should experience. Important decisions usually have more serious consequences than trivial decisions. This means we should experience more dissonance after an important decision, like which university to attend, than after a minor decision, like deciding whether to stay home or go to a concert tonight.

There are several ways to reduce the dissonance that comes from making a decision: you can revoke the decision, increase the attractiveness of the chosen alternative, decrease the attractiveness of the unchosen option, or reduce the importance of the decision. One common way to reduce the dissonance is to adopt both the second and third strategies: to make the chosen alternative look better and the unchosen option look worse (White and Gerard 1981): "I am so glad I decided to attend this university; it is even better than I thought it would be," and "I'm really glad I didn't go to school there, it's not a very good university." This is called the **spreading effect**, because, after the dissonance and the attitude change occur, the two alternatives appear to be further apart (less similar) than before. If the chosen alternate looks much better than the unchosen alternative, there should be little dissonance.

In the automobile industry, some customers who order new cars that are not in stock change their minds between the time they order the car and the time it is delivered to them. This is an example of how post-decisional dissonance (regret) can change attitudes. Donnelly and Ivancevich (1970) found that, when buyers who waited for delivery were given information about their automobile which was consistent (consonant) with their decision (in other words, were given reasons why the decision to buy that car was a good choice), fewer customers backed out of their purchase decision.

Thus, making a decision can cause dissonance, especially if the chosen and unchosen alternates have similar net benefits and if the decision is important. Dissonance can be reduced by revoking the decision, by dwelling on the benefits of the chosen alternative, by stressing the drawbacks of the unchosen option (frequently people do both of the last two things), or by reducing the importance of the decision. It is possible to influence a decision by providing consonant (or dissonant) information.

Selective exposure to information

Festinger declares that dissonance is unpleasant, and that it encourages us to change our cognitions in order to reduce it. Another implication of this theory is **selective exposure**, the idea that people attempt to avoid situations that are likely to create dissonance. Thus, dissonance theory predicts that people will try to avoid exposure to information that they suspect may arouse dissonance – and they may seek out information that is consonant, or consistent, with their attitudes. Research found that people tend to choose consonant over dissonant information (D'Alessio and Allen 2002). That is, we are selective about the information to which we expose ourselves. We have a tendency to seek out consonant information and avoid dissonant information. If so, your audience may be less willing to listen to a message that disagrees with them (audience analysis, discussed in chapter 5, can help you to estimate the audience's probable reaction to your message).

However, dissonance is only one factor among many that influence our exposure to information. For example, curiosity may lead some people to seek out information that disagrees with their current beliefs and attitudes. Second, if we believe that certain information is likely to be useful to us, relevant or important information, we may decide to acquire it rather than avoid it (Freedman 1965). Third, there may be a fairness norm that operates in some situations (e.g. in a trial), encouraging us to seek out relevant information regardless of whether it is consistent with our current beliefs. Thus, a desire to avoid dissonance may sometimes encourage us to be selective about the information we seek, but other factors mean that we do not always try to avoid dissonant information.

Forced compliance

Another area of dissonance concerns what happens when we are forced (or encouraged) to engage in behavior that is inconsistent with our attitudes or beliefs. A very early classic study was conducted by Festinger and Carlsmith (1959). They asked a subject to perform a very boring and repetitive task, pretending that the researchers were studying that task. Actually, they wanted to know whether attitudes would change when subjects experienced dissonance. After completing the boring task (turning spools on pegs; removing spools from pegs and then putting them back), subjects were asked to help the experimenter to convince another subject to participate in the study. Some of these subjects were given $1 to convince the next subject (who was really a confederate helping the experimenter) to agree to work at the task; others were given $20 to talk the other "subject" into participating. Basically, they were asked to lie and say that the task was interesting or fun when they really believed it was boring. Afterwards, they were supposed to report how interesting they thought the task was.

When the subjects tried to convince the "next subject" that the task was exciting and fun, dissonance was likely to occur: "I believe the task I just did was boring; I told someone else that the task was exciting and fun." Because they were paid different amounts of money for their behavior, they were predicted to, and did, resolve their dissonance in different ways. The subjects who were paid $20 could easily rationalize their action by adding a new cognition: "I didn't say the task was exciting because I really believed it was fun; I said it was exciting because I was paid $20."

On the other hand, the subjects who were paid only $1 could not rationalize their behavior that way: "I didn't lie and say it was fun for $1; I must have done it because the task really was fun." They reduced dissonance by changing their attitude about whether the task was boring. In other words, the greater the justification ($20 payment) for engaging in a behavior that conflicted with their attitudes, the easier that behavior was to rationalize. When the behavior could not be rationalized by the justification (payment of only $1), the subjects were more likely to change their attitudes toward the task. So, the key principle of forced compliance is that the less justification is provided for performing the counter-attitudinal behavior, the more the attitude will change.

If you are doing someone a favor, like driving them to a job interview when you really do not want to, you could experience dissonance and might change your attitudes. If there was a really good reason (justification) for doing the favor – say, he is your friend's brother – it is easy to rationalize your behavior: "I don't like Fred; I'm only doing him a favor because he's Joe's brother." If there is no good reason for doing the favor, you might experience dissonance and change your attitude so as to like Fred more than before you did the favor: "There's no reason why I have to give him a ride; maybe I like Fred better than I thought." So, when you perform an action that is inconsistent with your attitude, the less justification you have for that action, the more likely it is that your attitude will change.

Evaluation of dissonance theory

This theory is full of possibilities: It has implications for a variety of situations. It makes predictions about human thought and behavior after making a decision (that is, about post-decisional dissonance). It also makes predictions about whether people will seek information (or commit themselves to selective exposure). It has implications for persuasion as well as for the specific form of persuasion called forced compliance. So cognitive dissonance is a very wide-ranging theory.

Second, dissonance theory has generated literally hundreds of studies. Although it is not always supported (for example, curiosity might interfere with the selective exposure effect), there is no question that this theory has strong research support.

One important limitation is that dissonance theory makes no predictions about how dissonance will be reduced. It lists several options for reducing cognitive dissonance (add consonant cognitions, change dissonant cognitions, alter the importance of cognitions), but surely persuaders want dissonance to be resolved in the way that furthers their goals. If you try to induce dissonance in my girlfriend or boyfriend so as to make them go to a movie with you, you do not want them to change their attitude toward you (to like you less) in order to reduce that dissonance! The fact that the theory does not make specific predictions means that we should qualify the statement on experimental support for this theory. A theory which makes specific predictions can be subjected to stronger tests than vague theories. If the research on dissonance theory had been able to test specific predictions, the empirical support for this theory would be stronger than it is.

It seems likely that some people can tolerate dissonance more than others. Some individuals may be more mentally "tidy," while others may be willing to put up with some inconsistency in their thoughts. Dissonance theory does not take into account such possible individual differences (this limitation applies to all consistency theories).

Summary of Consistency Theories

It is important to understand that, in order to change another person's attitude, you have to disagree with her, at least to a certain extent. If you just parrot back to her what she already believes, there is no reason for her to change her attitude. The idea that you are disagreeing with the audience can be explicit or implicit, but it is always there. Whenever you try to persuade someone, you are essentially suggesting that that person should change their attitude because their current one is wrong. Even if you want to reinforce an existing attitude (rather than convert someone from a positive to a negative attitude or vice versa), you are saying that the other person's positive attitude just is not positive enough. Persuaders must disagree with audiences to obtain change.

A good deal of evidence supports the basic assumption of consistency theory, namely that discrepancy between a message and an audience's attitudes is important for attitude change (Bochner and Insko 1966). Persuasive messages that disagree slightly with the audience usually produce little or no attitude change. Messages that disagree more – or are more discrepant – are likely to yield more persuasion. As we will see in the next chapter on social judgment theory, we must be careful not to go too far when we disagree with our audience. Messages that are extremely discrepant risk failure when the audience rejects them as unreasonable or implausible. Still, discrepancy, when used judiciously, is important in achieving attitude change. The elaboration likelihood model would identify another limitation of consistency theories. Balance and dissonance theory do not make predictions about how consistency will be restored. The ELM indicates that reaction to a message (which creates inconsistency) would depend on the nature of the cognitive responses. If the thoughts are favorable to the message, attitude change is likely to occur, but if the thoughts are unfavorable to the message, persuasion is unlikely. However, neither theory addresses the problem of the kinds of thoughts (favorable, unfavorable) that people have when experiencing inconsistency. But what about congruity theory? Recall that congruity theory's predictions tend to hold up except when a statement is attributed to a source that is implausible or unreasonable. The ELM would explain that, for example, when a liked source makes a plausible assertion, the cognitive responses are likely to be favorable and persuasion is probable. On the other hand, when a source makes an assertion that sounds implausible to the audience (and the correction for incredulity comes into play), the cognitive responses would probably be unfavorable and persuasion unlikely. So, inconsistency can provoke cognitive responses, and different kinds of cognitive responses could account for different outcomes (persuasive/not persuasive).

Using Consistency Theory in Persuasion

The theories discussed in this chapter all agree that attitude change can occur when people confront inconsistent cognitions. Inconsistency – whether thought of as imbalance, incongruity, or dissonance – is considered to be an unpleasant motivating state. When we become aware of inconsistencies, we feel some pressure to resolve the disagreement and restore consistency. Persuaders can make use of this by creating inconsistent cognitions in their audiences. A simple way to do it is to disagree with your audience. Of course, if you disagree too much, your message could be rejected in the same way subjects in the congruity theory research rejected assertions (the correction for incredulity).

Congruity theory is attractive because it is designed around persuasive communication: it describes a source making an assertion (giving a message) about a concept. However, dissonance theory is also attractive, because it can deal with multiple dissonant and consonant cognitions all together.

Consistency theories do not discuss this implication, but we see a connection between (1) inducing inconsistency (imbalance, incongruity, dissonance) and resolving it with attitude change and (2) the problem-solution organizational pattern (and the two related variants, AIDA and the motivated sequence). Inconsistency is unpleasant and motivates the audience who experiences it to resolve that inconsistency. A problem is unpleasant and motivates its victims to take action. Inconsistency is resolved through attitude change (which restores balance, congruity, or consonance). The problem is resolved through the implementation of a solution. This may mean that problem-solution formats could be very useful in arousing inconsistency and in channeling its resolution into the attitude change sought by persuaders.

The idea, from dissonance theory, of regret after a decision can be important for persuaders to understand. Often a persuasive message asks an audience to make a commitment to take action later. The study by Donnelly and Ivancevich (1970) showed how dissonance can help automobile sales by using persuasive messages to counteract post-decisional regret. Whenever your persuasive goal cannot be met by action taken by the audience at the time of your message, you are in effect hoping they will make later (and keep!) a commitment to engage in the behavior you want. Politicians, for example, want voters to like them and to vote for them when election day rolls around. Whenever you persuade for behavior that does not involve immediate action, your audience may regret their agreement with your message. Thus dissonance underscores the importance of reinforcing your audience, so that their agreement with you may not "wear off".

Finally, consistency theory does not say so, but we would say that providing strong reasons for your disagreement (ideas that probably would impress this audience, on the basis of audience analysis (chapter 5), supported by strong evidence (chapter 7), would make it less likely that your audience would reject your message out of hand. In other words, even though consistency theories ignore content, it would be easy to incorporate it into their theories. For example, one could theorize that "Messages with strong evidence will create more inconsistency (incongruity, dissonance) than those without such evidence."

Glossary

Agreement effect: the principle that situations where both people rate the attitude object similarly are perceived as being more pleasant than situations where the two people disagree.

Assertion constant: a hypothesis which states that, when a source makes a statement about a concept, the assertion will influence attitudes to that concept more than attitudes to the source.

Associative assertion: an assertion whereby the source expresses liking of a concept.

Attraction effect: the principle that, when two people in a triad have a positive relationship, (perceived) imbalance is reduced.

Balanced: ideas that are consistent.

Consonant: ideas that are consistent.

Correction for incredulity: the principle that, when a source is claimed to have said something that the audience considers implausible, persuasion will not occur.

Dissociative assertion: an assertion whereby the source expresses dislike for a concept.

Dissonant: thoughts that are inconsistent.

Irrelevant: concepts that are not related.

Selective exposure: the idea that people attempt to avoid situations or information which are likely to create dissonance.

Spreading effect: the principle that two alternatives appear to be further apart after a decision is made.

Chapter 11

Social Judgment/Involvement Theory

This theory of attitude change, developed by Muzafer Sherif and Carl Hovland (1961; and later by Carolyn Sherif (1967)), is different from other consistency theories (chapter 10) for two reasons. As its name suggests, it is a model of judgment, which means that it declares that the audience interprets or judges a message. Specifically, a listener judges how much the message agrees or disagrees with his or her own attitude. Second, social judgment/involvement theory (SJ/I) holds that the degree of a listener's **involvement** in the topic of the persuasive message – that is, how important a topic is to that listener – is an important factor in attitude change. As with the other consistency theories, the elaboration likelihood model would focus attention on the thoughts the audience had when they compared the position advocated in the message with their own attitudes.

Protagoras was a Greek sophist, or traveling teacher, in the fifth century BCE. He rebelled against the idea that there were absolute truths. Instead, he declared that "Man is the measure of all things" (see the discussion by Schiappa 1991). Without going into the philosophical details of his statement, we can observe that one person may think a summer day is hot, while another believes it is only pleasantly warm. Two friends can see the same movie and one will like it while the other will hate it. And of course two people can hear the same persuasive message but have quite different reactions to it. Social judgment/involvement theory offers one explanation for the fact that two people can react so differently to the very same message.

When we teach this theory in class, we bring in three buckets of water: hot, cold, and room temperature (tepid). We ask two students to volunteer to participate in a "science experiment." One puts a hand into the hot water and another one puts a hand into the cold water – but they are not told anything about the temperature of the water in any of the three buckets. Then we ask them to take their hands out of the bucket and place them into the third bucket (of lukewarm) water, both at the same time. We ask them to describe the temperature of the water in the third bucket. What do you think happens?

The student whose hand was in the hot water says the water in the third bucket is cool, while the student whose hand was in the cold water describes it as warm. Both these students put their hands into the same bucket of water, yet they described it differently. The reason why they give different answers is that they have different comparison points (or **anchors**, in the language of SJ/I). The water felt warm to the student whose hand had just been in the cold water (this person's anchor point), but it felt cool to the student whose hand had just been in the hot water (the other person's anchor point – a different anchor). Protagoras would have been happy to see his point demonstrated this way. This process is just what social judgment/involvement theory says happens when people hear or read a persuasive message. Each audience member judges the main idea of the message, how much it agrees or disagrees with the persuader, by comparing the message with his or her own anchor points, which in social judgment/involvement theory is the audience members' existing attitude on the message topic.

Of course, if we really wanted to know the temperature of the water in three buckets we would use a thermometer. We have clever devices which measure the temperature accurately and objectively. We could easily find out that the water in one bucket was 40 degrees, in the second was 70 degrees, and in the third was 100 degrees. However, we do not have any such thing as a "message thermometer." We have to make judgments about the position advocated in a message (how much a message agrees or disagrees with us) because there is no accurate or objective way to measure message position. SJ/I holds that the process of judging, or perceiving, the position of a message is important to understanding how persuasion works. Notice that this theory reinforces the importance of the audience generally in persuasion – as well as the importance of audience analysis (chapter 5). Different audiences may interpret, and react to, the same message in different ways.

The Nature of Social Judgment/Involvement Theory

We will first describe the nature of social judgment/involvement theory. Then we will assess its strengths and weaknesses. Finally, we will offer advice on using SJ/I in persuasion.

First, we will discuss the audience's own attitudes and what is called the three latitudes: acceptance, non-commitment, and rejection. Then we will describe two processes of perceptual errors, assimilation, and contrast. Finally, we will explain what SJ/I says about involvement.

Latitudes of acceptance, non-commitment, and rejection

First we have to understand the audience's attitudes. Then we can see how a listener's attitudes relate to perceptions (judgments) about persuasive messages. As indicated above, each audience member's current attitude on the message topic is his or her anchor point. SJ/I assumes that we judge the position of a message by comparing it to our own attitude: Does the message agree with my attitude? If not, is the message more positive or more negative than my own attitude? In other words, is the position advocated in a message **discrepant**, or different from, my own attitude – and, if so, how much discrepancy is there between the message position and my attitude? As mentioned in chapter 10, to change a person's attitude, we have to disagree with him or her. If you like baseball and I want you to dislike it, I have to say negative things about baseball (statements with which you might disagree). Hopefully, I can give you good reasons to support my negative position on baseball and you will consider changing your attitude. If you like baseball a little and I want you to like it a lot, I still have to disagree with you, telling you "Baseball isn't just nice – it is wonderful!" Again, I have to give you good reasons for you to change to a more favorable attitude toward baseball. The key is to disagree enough to change the audience's attitude, without going so far as to alienate them.

Luckily, most people are reasonable and flexible, willing to easily tolerate a little disagreement. The range of acceptable or plausible attitudes is called the **latitude of acceptance**, and the anchor point is at the center of this latitude. Sherif and Sherif (1967) explain that "[t]he latitude of acceptance is simply [the] most acceptable position plus other positions the individual also finds acceptable" (p. 115). On both sides of the latitude of acceptance are two **latitudes of non-commitment**. These are positions which disagree moderately with the person's own attitude (anchor), but are not so discrepant that he or she actually rejects them. Sherif and Sherif define the latitudes of non-commitment as "the positions that [the individual] does not evaluate as either acceptable or objectionable" (ibid.). But if we move too far away from the audience's own attitude, we reach the **latitudes of rejection**, message positions that the person actively rejects as wrong: "the position most objectionable to the individual ... plus the other positions also objectionable" (ibid.). Every message that could be given on a topic must fall somewhere on a continuum of pros or cons about the topic. First, listeners must judge where your message falls, and then they can compare your message with their own attitude to see if, and how much, you disagree with them.

If we map out potential message positions on a topic, like gun control, we can visualize these three latitudes. Figure 11.1 is an attitude/message diagram, which displays the attitude and message positions on a given topic which are possible for Pat. In this case, the topic is gun control and Pat has an attitude of about +0.3 toward

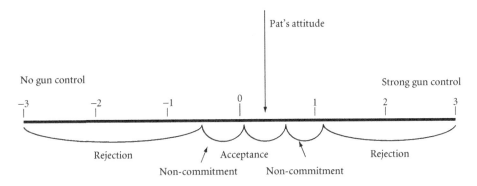

Figure 11.1   Pat's attitude

gun control, a very mildly positive attitude. Pat's own attitude (before listening to the message) is identified. The latitude of acceptance includes her own attitude as well as those positions that are similar enough to hers to be acceptable. The two latitudes of non-commitment, on each side of the latitude of acceptance, represent positions which Pat is not willing to accept but which are not extreme enough for her to reject them. The latitudes of rejection encompass all of the remaining possible message positions which Pat would reject as unreasonable (or too extreme). In this case, Pat rejects both extremes: messages advocating no gun control and messages advocating very strict gun control. Notice that, because Pat has a slightly positive attitude, the right latitude of rejection is somewhat larger than the left latitude of rejection.

In the second example, illustrated in figure 11.2, we have another listener, John, who has an extremely positive attitude (about +2.8) toward gun control. Notice that, because his own attitude is so extreme, he has only one of each of the three potential latitudes, and the latitude of rejection is quite large for him.

In the third example, figure 11.3, we display Jenny's attitudes – someone who has a moderately negative attitude toward gun control (−1.7). We can see that she has two latitudes of non-commitment, one latitude of acceptance, and one latitude of rejection.

We can create four simple rules for these latitudes. (1) There is always one and only one latitude of acceptance, and the listener's own attitude lies at the center,

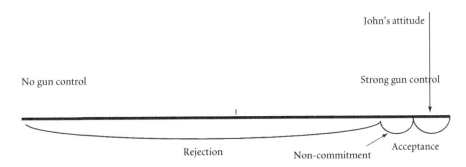

Figure 11.2   John's attitude

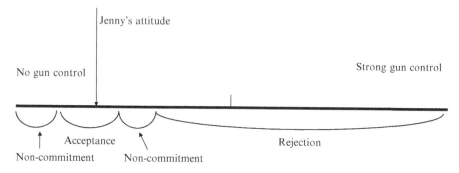

Figure 11.3 Jenny's attitude

anchoring it. (2) There must be at least one latitude of non-commitment (and no more than two) and at least one latitude of rejection (and no more than two of these as well). Extremely positive or negative attitudes may have only one of each latitude. (3) There may be two latitudes of non-commitment (one on each side of the latitude of acceptance) if the person's attitude is less extreme. (4) Finally, if the person's attitude is closer to the middle of the continuum, there can be two latitudes of rejection, but if so, there must be two latitudes of non-commitment as well.

Now we can consider how a listener's own attitude (anchor), and his or her latitudes of acceptance, non-commitment, and rejection influence perception of message positions. In figure 11.4, we have Pat again (with a slightly positive attitude), who listens to a persuasive message advocating a slightly (more) positive message toward gun control. The numbers in the figure represent the positions of three different messages that Pat could hear. Message 1 (few controls on guns) falls into her latitude of acceptance and is likely to be at least somewhat persuasive. But even if Pat agreed completely with this message, little change could occur in Pat's attitude. Message 2, which

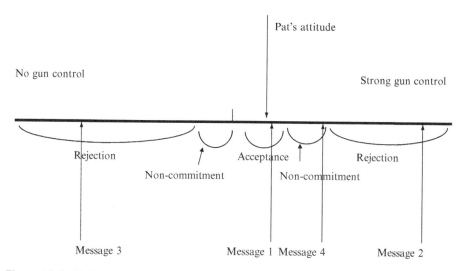

Figure 11.4 Pat's attitude

advocates fairly, but not extremely, strict gun control, falls into the right latitude of rejection. Message 3, which advocates few controls, falls into the right latitude of rejection. Neither message 2 nor message 3 is likely to be very persuasive; both would probably be rejected by this listener, although they would probably be rejected for different reasons (each one is too discrepant from Pat's own attitude, although in opposite directions). Probably the most persuasive message would be one at position 4, which advocates moderate gun control: it does not disagree enough with Pat to fall into the latitude of rejection and be dismissed. It disagrees enough, though, to create a reasonable amount of attitude change, even if only accepted partially.

From these examples – that message 1 should be somewhat persuasive and message 4 more persuasive, but messages 2 and 3 would be unpersuasive – we can examine SJ/I's predictions. When a message falls in the latitude of acceptance, as message 1 does (or in a latitude of non-commitment), SJ/I predicts that the greater the difference between the message and the listener's existing attitude (called **discrepancy**), the greater the persuasion (so message 4 should be more effective than message 1). However, too much discrepancy will move the message into the listener's latitude of rejection (messages 2 and 3), which means that they should not be persuasive. And we can see that this makes sense. We are less likely to be persuaded by people who take very extreme positions in their messages: Extreme positions, in general, do not seem as reasonable as more moderate positions. In fact, SJ/I predicts that messages which fall into the latitude of non-commitment, like message 4, are likely to be most persuasive. Specifically, SJ/I predicts that the more discrepant a messag'e is from a listener's own attitude (the greater the difference between the audience attitude and the position adopted in the message), as long as the message does not fall into the latitude of rejection, the more attitude change is likely to accompany that message. Notice that ELM would explain that an extreme message is likely to be unpersuasive because it is likely to evoke unfavorable thoughts.

Furthermore, when a listener's attitude changes after seeing or listening to a message, his or her latitudes will shift. The latitude of acceptance is always centered around the individual's attitude. So, if the attitude changes, the latitude of acceptance will shift along with it. The latitudes of non-commitment and rejection will also shift along with the latitude of acceptance. See figure 11.5, where the latitudes shift after Pat's attitude changes in favor of stricter gun control. Pat's attitude, and her latitudes, are displayed before and after a persuasive message.

Perceptual errors: assimilation and contrast

However, there is more to the process of perceiving, or judging, a message position than to determine which latitude that message falls into. Social judgment/involvement theory also identifies two different processes of perceptual distortion, called assimilation and contrast. These two effects occur when a message is very close to the listener's own attitude (assimilation) or is very different from the listener's own attitude (contrast). In a way, the choice of name is unfortunate, because "assimilation" sounds as if it might be a good thing. If you "assimilate" a message, one might think that means that you accept or integrate it into your own beliefs. But, as SJ/I uses the term, "assimilation" is an error in judgment which actually works to reduce a message's persuasiveness.

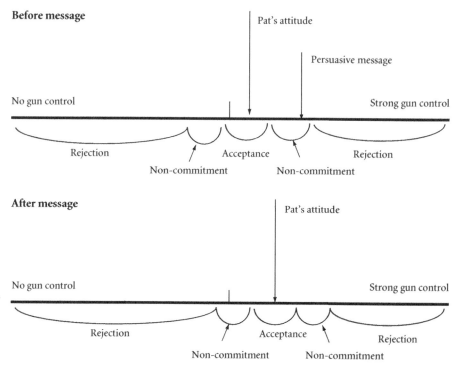

Figure 11.5 Pat's attitude

In figure 11.6, we have one message that is plotted with arrows in two places on the continuum of message positions (the two arrows are placed right next to each other because they are meant to be just a little different). One arrow represents the actual message, the other, the message as perceived by Bob. SJ/I predicts that, when a message actually (as stated by the persuader) falls in the latitude of acceptance, near the listener's own attitude, it will tend to be **assimilated**, or perceived by the listener as being even nearer to his or her own attitude than it really is. This perceptual error minimizes differences between the message and the listener's own attitude. Thus, in figure 11.6, the perceived message is nearer to Bob's own attitude than the actual message is. This means that assimilation is an error, a process of misperception. After Bob has judged the position of the message, that message can create an attitude change. However, relatively little discrepancy between the perceived message and Bob's own attitude will mean that very little attitude change should result. Thus Bob can think to himself something like this: "Hey, this person's message [as I perceive it] is almost exactly the same as my own attitude, so I do not really have much reason to change my attitude." If a listener believes that a message basically echoes his or her own attitude, there is no reason to change that attitude (in fact, the message in question could reinforce the listener's existing attitude rather than changing it). The theory predicts that the closer the actual message is to the listener's own attitude, the more assimilation (and the less attitude change) will occur.

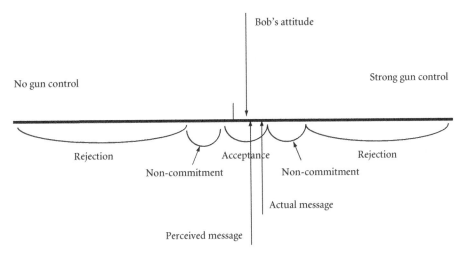

Figure 11.6 Bob's attitude

In figure 11.7, the other process of perceptual distortion, contrast, is depicted. SJ/I predicts that, when a the actual position of a message falls into the latitude of rejection, it will be **contrasted**, or perceived as even further away from the listener's own attitude than it really is. This perceptual error exaggerates the difference between the message and the listener's own attitude. Because messages falling into the latitude of rejection are unlikely to be persuasive, this means that contrast does not help the persuader either. The theory also predicts that, the further an actual message is from the listener's own attitude, the more contrast will occur. In this example, the message falls into Sally's latitude of rejection. However, because the message is far away from her own attitude, SJ/I predicts that Sally will contrast the message,

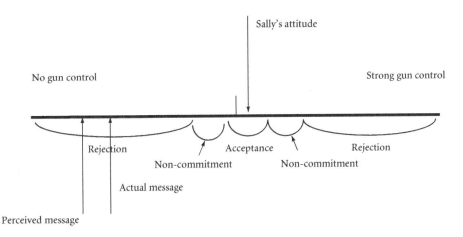

Figure 11.7 Sally's attitude

perceiving it to be even further away from her own attitude than its real position is. Because she thinks the message really disagrees with her (is quite extreme), Sally is not likely to be persuaded by it.

So assimilation and contrast are both perceptual processes in which the listener decides on the position advocated in a persuasive message. Both are errors of perception: in assimilation, a message is perceived to be closer to the listener's own attitude than it really is; in contrast, a message is perceived to be further away from the listener's own attitude than it really is. Not all messages are contrasted: only those that are near to the listener's own attitude (which are assimilated) and those that are rather far away from the listener's own attitude (which are contrasted). Furthermore, neither process is helpful to the persuader. Messages that are assimilated are thought to be quite similar to the listener's attitude, so there is little reason for listeners to change their attitudes. Messages that are contrasted fall well into the latitude of rejection and for that reason are not likely to be very persuasive.

The role of involvement

People vary in the extent to which they are involved in a topic. Some are highly involved. The topic is very important to them (or relevant, or salient) and it may affect them personally. Others may not care about a given topic (or may not care very much), and then they are said to be less involved in that topic. For example, in 1999 two high school students killed thirteen people in Columbine High School in Littleton Colorado (and then committed suicide themselves). Although there are exceptions, gun control probably became more relevant to people who lived in the area, probably causing them to be involved in the topic of gun control. Those who attended Columbine High School, or whose children attended it, and who knew the victims of this tragedy, were probably highly involved in this topic. In other states, those with children in high school were probably less involved in the topic of gun control than those who live in Littleton, but they were probably more involved than their neighbors who did not have children of school age. The point is that people vary in the extent to which they are involved in a topic.

SJ/I acknowledges that listeners vary in their involvement, and it makes specific predictions about involvement and persuasion. Specifically, those listeners who are less involved in a topic will have wider latitudes of acceptance and narrower latitudes of non-commitment than those who are highly involved. Figure 11.8 depicts Tom's attitudes, a person who is relatively uninvolved in gun control. Karen, in contrast, is highly involved in gun control. Karen has a much smaller latitude of non-commitment and, correspondingly, larger latitudes of rejection than Tom, because she is involved in the topic (Sherif and Hovland 1961).

This prediction means that persuaders, who should not want their messages to fall into the listeners' latitudes of rejection, have to take less extreme positions in order to be persuasive with those who are highly involved in a topic. This is a reasonable prediction: those who do not care much about a topic (who are uninvolved in that topic) are probably more willing to tolerate a difference of opinion, or a discrepant message, than those who care greatly about that topic. The prediction

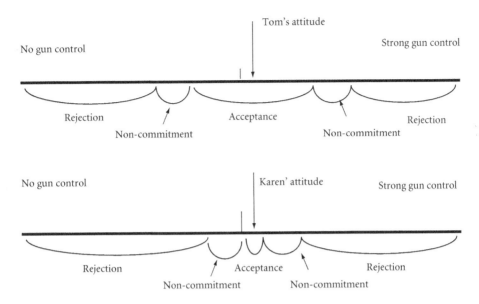

Figure 11.8   Tom's attitude

also means that those who try to persuade people who are highly involved in a topic may have to settle for smaller levels of persuasion than those who persuade the uninvolved. Audience analysis should reveal the type of audience one is facing.

SJ/I explicitly recognizes that listeners interpret (perceive) messages – the position advocated in a persuasive message may not be clear, objective, and unambiguous. Sometimes people make mistakes when they perceive a message (such as assimilation or contrast). These statements are common sense, but social judgment/involvement theory explains how such processes work.

Listeners judge a message's position according to their own attitudes, which serve as anchor points. The closer a message is to a listener's own attitude, the more likely it will be assimilated or perceived as even clolser than it really is. The further a message is from the listener's attitude (the more discrepancy there is between message and listener's attitude), the more likely it is for the message to be contrasted, or perceived as even more discrepant than it really is. Once a listener has judged a message position, we can determine how much persuasion is likely to occur. The more discrepancy there is between a perceived message position and the listener's attitude, the more attitude change is likely to occur, provided that the perceived message does not fall in the latitude of rejection. Messages which appear to fall in the latitude of rejection are not persuasive.

This means that social judgment/involvement theory predicts a **curvilinear** relationship between discrepancy and attitude change: as discrepancy increases, attitude change first increases and then decreases, like an upside-down "U." With too little discrepancy, there is little reason to change one's attitude. This is exacerbated by the process of assimilation: if a message is close to the persuader's own attitude, it will be assimilated or perceived as even less discrepant than it really is.

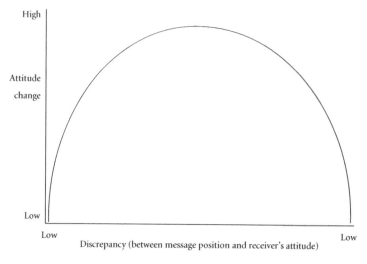

Figure 11.9 Curvilinear relationship between discrepancy and attitude change

Because discrepancy is viewed as necessary for attitude change to occur, messages that have been assimilated offer very little reason for the listener to change his or her attitudes. Figure 11.9 shows that, as discrepancy increases, attitude change first increases and then decreases. Change increases at first, because greater discrepancy provides more reason to change. However, when discrepancy becomes too large, the message falls into the listener's latitude of rejection, which reduces effectiveness.

Box 11.1   Summary of social judgment/involvement predictions

1   Listeners who are highly involved will have narrower latitudes of acceptance and wider latitudes of rejection.
2   Messages that fall near the listener's own attitude (anchor) will be assimilated, or misperceived as closer to the attitude than they really are.
3   Messages that fall far from the listener's own attitude (anchor) will be contrasted, or misperceived as further from the attitude than they really are.
4   As discrepancy between perceived message position and listener's attitude increases, attitude change increases – until the perceived message falls in the latitude of rejection.

Evaluation of Social Judgment/Involvement Theory

The discussions of Social Judgment/Involvement theory offer research in support of this theory (Sherif and Hovland 1961; Sherif and Sherif 1967; Sherif, Sherif, and Nebergall 1965). Other studies have found support for the curvilinear relationship between discrepancy and persuasion, although there are some exceptions (Eagly and

Chaiken 1993). There has also been some support for the prediction that highly involved people are less susceptible to persuasion than those who are less involved (Johnson and Eagly 1989; note that they distinguish between different kinds of involvement, an idea discussed below, and SJ/I predictions are not supported for each kind of involvement).

This theory has several strengths compared with other consistency theories. First, it realizes, and helps to explain, the role of perception in persuasion. It seems obvious that two different people may perceive a single message differently. SJ/I can help explain when and how this happens. In consequence, the theory can explain how the perception of messages influences persuasion. Second, there is a lot of empirical evidence, as noted above, for a curvilinear relationship between discrepancy and persuasion. The processes of assimilation and contrast, and the latitude of rejection, all help explain why this occurs. Third, there is considerable evidence that involvement in the topic of a persuasive message plays an important role in persuasion, and the theory makes use of this concept.

But SJ/I also has some limitations or weaknesses. First, Sherif and Hovland (1961), in their initial formulation, limit the effects of assimilation and contrast to messages that are more ambiguous or open to different interpretations. Some messages take positions that are fairly clear, and the audience has less leeway in interpreting those messages, in comparison with more ambiguous messages. The authors explain that "we would not expect that a communication taking a clearly black or white stand on an issue would be subject to such displacement" as assimilation or contrast (p. 149). For example, a message that advocates "no abortions under any circumstances" would be difficult to misinterpret. On the other hand, a speech arguing that "abortion should be limited to situations when it is justified" leaves unstated which (and how many) situations would be considered justified, as well as what kinds of justification the speaker thinks would be acceptable for abortion. The latter message should be more susceptible to assimilation and contrast than the former.

Second, except for message position, SJ/I ignores message content. There is much evidence that several message variables, like evidence or argument quality, affect persuasion. Social judgment theory, like other consistency theories, does not take into account any of these important message variables. It is possible, for example, that a message which falls in the latitude of rejection might not be rejected if it has strong evidence for its position (chapter 7). Messages that are extremely discrepant, at the far end of the latitude of rejection from the listener's own attitude, may almost always be rejected. However, some of messages that fall in other parts of the latitude of rejection might be persuasive if the message is strong. Third, social judgment/involvement theory ignores the effects of source credibility, another factor that can influence attitude change (chapter 3).

There are also some questions which can be raised about the theory itself. It is not clear when a listener makes a judgment about the position of a persuasive message. Is the message judged before attitude change takes place, as this theory assumes? It is possible that the process is actually reversed, and the position of a message is judged after we decide whether to be persuaded by it. Messages which are persuasive (which change a listener's attitude) may then be perceived as falling into the latitude of acceptance. The listener could think something like this: "That message was persuasive. It must have been near my own attitude." On the other hand, messages that fail to persuade people may, after they have failed, be judged to fall into the latitude of rejection: "That message wasn't persuasive at all. It was really different from my own attitude."

Some have raised the possibility that the latitudes are not really specific to particular topics, but reflect a person's general persuasibility (Eagly and Telaak 1972). People who are relatively easy to persuade have wide latitudes of acceptance, while those who are difficult to persuade have wide latitudes of rejection. There are also questions about whether there are different kinds of involvement (O'Keefe 2002). Is involvement an indication of a topic's importance? Is it an indication of how often a topic is encountered by a listener? The common cold, thankfully, affects far more people that malaria, but malaria is a more serious disease. Which one should be considered more involving?

Finally, there are questions about some of the research on social judgment/involvement theory. It is difficult (but not impossible) to change an audience member's involvement level. Studies by Sherif and Hovland (1961) compared groups of involved people with other groups, who were uninvolved. Because they did not randomly assign subjects to involved and uninvolved groups, it is possible that those people who were in the involved group differed in other ways from those in the uninvolved group (that is, in addition to the differences in involvement). If true, differences in attitudes between these groups could have been caused by the different levels of involvement – as the researchers assumed – or by other differences between the groups. As O'Keefe (1990) explained, "the high-involvement participants had more extreme attitudes than the low-involvement participants," which could mean that differences between the groups were caused by the extreme attitudes rather than by involvement levels (p. 40). Thus more research needs to be conducted to understand this theory.

Using Social Judgment/Involvement in Persuasion

One implication of SJ/I is that persuaders should realize that audiences interpret messages. What you mean to say in your message is probably clearer to you than it will be to them. There is also a possibility that your audience will misperceive your message (through assimilation or contrast). Both processes of misperception work to reduce the effectiveness of a message. Second, SJ/I underscores the importance of audience analysis. Highly involved audiences can be more difficult to persuade. This may be because involved listeners have narrower latitudes of acceptance, as SJ/I suggests, or because they are more difficult to persuade (less open-minded), as Eagly and Telaak suggest. Third, the curvilinear relationship between discrepancy and attitude change is very important. As discrepancy between perceived message and attitude increases, attitude change goes up for a while, but then (when the message falls in the latitude of rejection, according to SJ/I), more discrepancy reduces persuasion. As we observed in chapter 10, you must disagree with your audience if you want to change their attitudes. However, too much disagreement is less likely to be effective.

Notice that consistency theories fail to explain that too much discrepancy can be ineffective. The elaboration likelihood model would explain this curvilinear relationship by suggesting that higher levels of discrepancy increase unfavorable thoughts.

Finally, we want to return to the idea of hostile audiences from chapter 9. One source of hostility is disagreement with the position you advocate in your message. SJ/I would explain this phenomenon through the notion of a message which falls into the audience's latitude of rejection. In other words, when you develop a persuasive message that falls into your audience's latitude of rejection, you risk making your audience hostile. Clearly, you would want to moderate (tone down) the position you take in a message intended for such an audience. If you make a more moderate claim, their level of hostility should be reduced.

Glossary

Assimilation: the position advocated in a message is incorrectly perceived as being nearer to that of the audience than it is.

Anchors: comparison points or points of reference.

Contrast: the position advocated in a message is incorrectly perceived to be further from that of the audience than it is.

Curvilinear: evoution pattern in which, as one variable (discrepancy between message and audience's attitude) gets larger, another variable (amount of attitude change) first gets larger, then smaller.

Discrepancy: the difference between the position advocated in a message and the listener's attitude.

Discrepant: the position advocated in a message is different from the listener's attitude.

Involvement: relevance or importance of a topic to a listener.

Latitude of acceptance: the range of message positions that are acceptable or plausible for an audience member.

Latitude of non-commitment: the range of message positions that an audience member neither accepts nor rejects.

Latitude of rejection: the range of message positions that a listener actively rejects.

Chapter 12

Theory of Reasoned Action

Many people think that influencing the audience's behavior is the "bottom line" in persuasion. Can you get a job offer? Can you make a sale? Can you win an acquittal for my client? The theory of reasoned action, developed by Martin Fishbein and Icek Ajzen (1975; Ajzen and Fishbein 1980), confronts the relationship between persuasive messages and behavior. Reasoned action can be seen as an improvement over consistency theories (chapter 10). First, as indicated, reasoned action is concerned with the relationship between messages, attitudes, and behavior. However, this theory also recognizes that there are situations and factors which limit the influence of attitude on behavior. For example, if our attitude leads us to want to go out but we have no money, our lack of money will prevent our attitude from actually influencing our behavior. Therefore reasoned action predicts the **behavioral intention,** which concerns what a person would like to do or plans to do. This is a compromise between only trying to predict attitude change and continuing to predict behavior. Because it separates behavioral intention from behavior, reasoned action also discusses the factors that limit the influence of attitudes (or behavioral intention) on behavior.

Second, reasoned action adds a new element, norms (the expectations of other people), to help predict behavioral intent. That is, whenever our attitudes lead us to do one thing but the relevant norms suggest we should do something else, both factors influence our behavioral intent. For example, John's attitudes may encourage him to want to read a Harry Potter book, but his friends may think this series is childish. Does John do what his attitudes suggest (read the book) or what the norms of his friends suggest (not read the book)? Another reason this theory is particularly useful to persuaders is that it outlines many options available to persuaders for changing the audience's attitudes. The elaboration likelihood model would discuss the cognitions identified in reasoned action as favorable or unfavorable reactions to messages.

Factors Influencing Behavioral Intention

Specifically, reasoned action predicts that behavioral intent is shaped by two factors: our attitude toward behavior (AB) and our subjective norms (SN). Each of these two factors is broken down into smaller parts. The **attitude toward behavior**, which is the extent a given behavior is seen as positive or negative, has two components: belief strength and evaluation. **Belief strength** (BS) is basically the same concept as "beliefs" from chapter 1, where beliefs are "facts" or statements that can be verified as true or false. **Evaluation** (E) is essentially the same idea discussed under "values" in chapter 1 – judgments of worth. So these basic concepts in the theory of reasoned action should be familiar.

The second component of reasoned action which influences behavioral intent is the **subjective norms**, which reflect the extent to which a person is aware of the expectations of others and the extent to which that person wants to comply with those expectations. Subjective norms also have two components: **normative beliefs** – what I believe others would want or expect me to do (NB) – and **motivation to comply** – how important it is to me to do what I think others expect (MC). In short, AB and SN jointly determine BI (behavioral intent). These two components of subjective norms are also quantified. These concepts, and their relationship to behavioral intention and behavior, are depicted in figure 12.1.

Reasoned action quantifies each of the elements in the process. Belief strength, evaluation, subjective norms, and motivation to comply can be measured with attitude scales, as shown in box 12.1. In this example, we are trying to predict the likelihood that Fred will participate in a recycling program. His behavioral intent is predicted from his attitude toward this behavior and from his subjective norms on this topic. Fred's AB is made up of his belief strength ($BS = +2$ in this example) multiplied by his evaluation ($E = +1$). Fred's subjective norm is comprised of his normative belief ($NB = -2$) times his motivation to comply ($MC = +2$). Inserting these values into the formula yields a behavioral intent of -2. This means that reasoned action predicts that it is unlikely that Fred will start recycling.

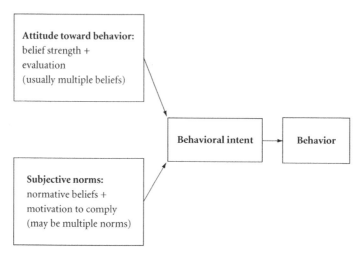

Figure 12.1 Theory of reasoned action

In most cases, attitudes are more complex that this one, with more than one relevant belief and/or more than one norm. The complete formula includes $\Sigma\ (BS \times E) + \Sigma\ (NB \times MC)$, which means that you need to sum together all of the $(BS \times E)$ pairs and all of the $(NB \times MC)$ pairs. The full formula also acknowledges that AB and SN are not always equally important, so each component of the formula is weighted (w_1, w_2) to reflect their relative importance: $\Sigma\ (BS \times E)w_1 + \Sigma\ (NB \times MC)w_2$.

Box 12.1 Predicting Fred's behavioral intent for recycling

Attitude to behavior
Belief strength (BS)   Recycling reduces the demand for scarce resources
                                   false –3___ ___ ___ ___ ___ _X_ ___ +3 true
Evaluation (E)   Protecting scarce resources is
                    unimportant –3___ ___ ___ ___ _X_ ___ ___ +3 important
Subjective norm
Normative belief (NB)   My friends think recycling is worthwhile
                                   false –3___ _X_ ___ ___ ___ ___ ___ +3 true
Motivation to comply (MC)   My friends' opinions on recycling matters to me
                                   a little –3___ ___ ___ ___ ___ _X_ ___+3 a lot
Basic formula: behavioral intent = $(BS \times E) + (NB \times MC)$
                    $(2 \times 1) + (-2 \times 2)$
                        $2 + -4$
                          -2

Understanding how these elements work together also tells us how to change a person's behavioral intent. For example, if we want to encourage Fred to recycle, we could try to change his NB from −2 to a positive number. If we could persuade Fred that his friends thought recycling was somewhat worthwhile (+1), that would change his behavioral intent from −2 to 4, which would mean he is likely to recycle. Or, if we could convince him that he should do what he thinks is right instead of following his friends, that could change his MC from +2 to −1. His BI would then become 4 (because −2 × −1 = +2).

This theory reveals that we have many options when trying to persuade someone. First, we can attempt to alter their attitude toward a behavior. There are six different ways to change the AB in the direction you seek (see box 12.2). For example, suppose you wanted to persuade your roommate, Chris, to go and see a new movie. Based on his belief/evaluation pairs (see below), Chris has a neutral attitude toward this movie. Belief 1/evaluation 1 make him tend to have a positive attitude, but the addition of belief 2/evaluation 2 (which incline him toward avoiding the theater where this movie is showing) makes his attitude toward going to see the movie in this theater neutral. You could try to tip the balance in favor of going to see the movie by increasing the strength of belief 1 (option 1): "It isn't just a few people; everyone says this is funny" or "This movie isn't just cute, its hilarious." Or, you could use option 2 and attempt to alter the evaluation: "I know you really, really enjoy a good laugh at the movies."

Box 12.2 Changing the attitude toward behavior

1 Strengthen the belief strength of an attitude which supports your persuasive goal.
2 Strengthen the evaluation of an attitude which supports your persuasive goal.
3 Weaken the belief strength of an attitude that opposes your persuasive goal.
4 Weaken the evaluation of an attitude that opposes your persuasive goal.
5 Create a new attitude with a belief strength and evaluation which supports your persuasive goal.
6 Remind our audience of a forgotten attitude with a belief strength and evaluation which supports your persuasive goal.

Either of these options has the potential to make Chris's attitude more favorable toward seeing the movie, and, hopefully, change it enough to overcome his distaste for that theater (box 12.3). It is also possible to make Chris's overall attitude more favorable by working against these unfavorable cognitions. For example, in response to belief 2, you could try to alter the belief strength (option 3): "They remodeled the Checker Theater; it is much nicer." Or you could try to alter the evaluation of that negative attitude (option 4): "The important thing is the movie, not the theater." So you can encourage a more favorable attitude toward behavior by counteracting unfavorable belief/value (B/V) pairs.

Box 12.3 Chris's attitude toward behavior (going to see the new movie)

Belief (1): I heard someone say that this movie is pretty funny.
Evaluation (1): I like comedies.

Belief (2): The Checker Theatre, where the movie is playing, is pretty decrepit.
Evaluation (2): I like to go to theaters that are nice.

Furthermore, you can try to make Chris's attitude more favorable by adding new belief/evaluation pairs, which is option 5. For example, you could explain: "I heard the soundtrack to this movie is great!" or "I know you really like this actor (which is an evaluation, by the way) – did you know he is in the movie?" Finally, option 6 indicates that you can make an existing attitude more favorable by reminding him of a forgotten attitude: "Remember how you said those plush, reclining seats in the Checker are great?"

It also possible to combine several of these options to create a message that tried to alter several of Chris's beliefs or evaluations. But keep in mind the discussion in chapter 1: If you change both parts of a belief/value pair, no attitude change will result (the audience will hold the same attitude, although for the opposite reasons).

So reasoned action begins by analyzing attitudes into their components (beliefs, evaluation) and revealing the options persuaders have to persuade an overall attitude by changing one or more of the parts that make up that attitude.

Box 12.4 Changing subjective norms

7 Strengthen a normative belief which supports your persuasive goal.
8 Increase the motivation to comply with a norm which supports your persuasive goal.
9 Weaken a normative belief which opposes your persuasive goal.
10 Weaken the motivation to comply with a norm which opposes your persuasive goal.
11 Create a new subjective norm which supports your persuasive goal.
12 Remind the audience of a forgotten subjective norm which supports your persuasive goal.

Furthermore, reasoned action also adds the concept of subjective norms. To the extent that our audience's behavior is determined by the members' norms, we can influence it by changing those norms. This creates six additional options for persuaders to consider (see box 12.4). For example, option 7 suggests that you could try to strengthen an existing normative belief: "Everyone knows that you shouldn't sit home on a Friday night." Another possibility (option 8) is to increase the motivation to comply with that norm: "Our friends all think it is really important to go out on Friday." If Chris thinks it is not on to go to a movie with a roommate instead of a date, you could try to weaken this normative belief (option 9) or the motivation to comply with that norm (option 10). Furthermore, option 10 indicates that you could try to create a new norm: "Everybody knows you gotta go see movies made by this director." You can attempt to create a new norm, which supports a favorable attitude toward behavior: "You know, it is important to support theaters like the Checker; it is so much better than 40 screens at the mall" (option 11). It is also possible to remind the audience of a subjective norm which supports a favorable attitude (option 12).

> **Box 12.5**   Chris's subjective norms (going to see the new movie)
>
> Normative belief 1: It is wrong to stay home on Friday night.
> Motivation to comply 1: My friends think staying home is moderately uncool.
>
> Normative belief 2: Movies should be seen with dates not roommates.
> Motivation to comply 2: My friends think going to a movie with a roommate is
> moderately uncool.

Finally, the fact that there are two influences on behavioral intention, attitudes and norms, gives one final possibility for persuasion (see box 12.6).

> **Box 12.6**   Final method of changing behavioral intent
>
> 13   If one component (attitudes or norms) supports your persuasive goal more
> than the other, make that component more important than the other.

Suppose Chris had two favorable belief/value pairs, one unfavorable belief/value pair, and one favorable and one unfavorable subjective norm. Chances are his attitude will be more favorable than his subjective norms (because he has two favorable B/V pairs). Then you could try to make the AB more important than the SN ("Don't be like everyone else. Do what feels right to you"). This kind of appeal might reduce the importance of subjective norms for Chris and result in a more favorable attitude toward the behavior.

So this theory gives persuaders thirteen different options for changing a person's attitude (six ways to change an attitude toward a behavior, six ways to change the subjective norms, and one way of changing the relative importance of attitude and norms: see box 12.7).

Limitations to the Prediction of Behavior

Reasoned action adds a new variable between attitudes (and norms) and behavior: that of behavioral intent. An important question, therefore, is: How does behavioral intent relate to behavior? Reasoned action states that three factors influence whether (or how much) behavioral intent shapes our behavior. First, we must have control over our behavior (volitional control). If Steve has no cash (and if his credit cards are maxed out), then he cannot take his girlfriend to the movies. Similarly, Jill's attitude (and the norms of her friends) may lead her to want very much to attend Harvard Law School, but she cannot make them admit her. We cannot always get what we want (what our attitudes lead us to desire and what norms suggest we should want), because we do not have complete control over the world around us.

A second reason why behavioral intent may not yield the expected behavior is that attitudes and behavior must be measured at the same level. When my intention

Box 12.7 Summary of reasoned action suggestions for persuasion

Changing attitude toward behavior (AB):

1 Strengthen the belief strength (BS) of an attitude which supports your persuasive goal.
2 Strengthen the evaluation (E) of an attitude which supports your persuasive goal.
3 Weaken the belief strength (BS) of an attitude which opposes your persuasive goal.
4 Weaken the evaluation (E) of an attitude which opposes your persuasive goal.
5 Create a new attitude with a belief strength and evaluation which supports your persuasive goal.
6 Remind our audience of a forgotten attitude with a belief strength and evaluation which supports your persuasive goal.

Changing subjective norms (SN):

7 Strengthen a normative belief (NB) which supports your persuasive goal.
8 Increase the motivation to comply (MC) with a norm supporting your persuasive goal.
9 Weaken a normative belief (NB) which opposes your persuasive goal.
10 Weaken the motivation to comply (MC) with a norm opposing your persuasive goal.
11 Create a new subjective norm which supports your persuasive goal.
12 Remind the audience of a forgotten subjective norm which supports your persuasive goal.

is to buy a new car, I might not buy a Ford Mustang. So the fact that I did not purchase a Mustang does not indicate that my behavioral intent did not affect my behavior (I could have bought an Eclipse). If I want to go to college, I might not attend the University of Southern California. Again, knowing that I did not go to USC is not a reason to think that my behavioral intent had no influence on my behavior; I may attend another university.

The idea that behavioral intent (or attitude) and behavior must be measured at the same level may seem somewhat silly, but some researchers thought to have discovered that attitudes did not influence behavior. They measured attitudes and behavior differently. For example, one study asked people about their attitude toward snakes ("Do you like snakes?"). Most people said "No," indicating an unfavorable attitude. However, that study asked people if they wanted to touch a snake, and most said "Yes." The researchers concluded that behavior does not reflect attitudes, because all of these people had negative attitudes toward snakes but they agreed to touch them (which is a positive behavior). Clearly, willingness to touch a snake could reflect simple curiosity. A better behavioral measure would have been to ask these people if they wanted a snake for a pet. It seems likely that everyone who displayed a negative attitude ("I don't like snakes") would also have a negative behavior ("No, I will not take a snake for a pet"). Or you could change the attitude measurement, from "How much do you like snakes?" to "How much would you like to pet a snake today?" So attitudes or behavioral intent must be measured at the same level.

Third, we know that attitudes do change over time. Behavioral intent and behavior must be measured at the same time for us to expect that they will relate. Reasoned action states that attitudes, together with subjective norms, determine behavioral intent. This means that, if a person's attitude (or subjective norm) changes, his or her behavioral intent will probably change as well. So if we learn people's behavioral intent and then wait to measure their behavior several weeks or months later, that behavior may correspond to their current behavioral intent, and not to the behavioral intent we observed in the past. Jill may want to attend Harvard Law today, but a year from now she might prefer the University of Michigan Business School.

Chapter 1 discussed three other factors that determine how much attitudes influence our behavior. Although reasoned action does not talk about these three additional factors specifically, they are relevant and worth mentioning again. Attitudes formed through direct (rather than vicarious) experience with the attitude object exert a greater influence on behavior. Our attitudes are more likely to influence our behavior when involvement is high (when the attitude concerns something that we care deeply about). Finally, the normative component will be more influential than the attitudinal component for people who are high in self-monitoring (people who care about the reactions of others; who very much want to make a favorable impression on others).

Evaluation of the Theory of Reasoned Action

There has been a great deal of research on the theory of reasoned action (see e.g. Ajzen and Fishbein 1980; Sheppard, Hartwick, and Warshaw 1988). This research is generally supportive of reasoned actions' predictions: Behavioral intent can be fairly accurately predicted from attitudes toward behavior and subjective norms. Several scholars have confirmed the predictions of the theory of reasoned action via meta-analysis, which is a statistical method of combining the results from many individual studies conducted by different scholars (see the discussion by Hale, Householder, and Greene 2002). Kim and Hunter (1993b), for example, investigated the relationship between attitudes and norms, behavioral intentions, and behavior. They found that attitudes have a stronger relationship with behavioral intentions than with behavior and that behavioral intention has a stronger relationship than attitudes with behavior, which is what you would expect if behavioral intentions are a "bridge" between attitude and behavior. Their study also indicated that there is a stronger relationship when the attitude is more relevant to the behavior, and that volitional control also influences the relationship, as the reasoned action predicts.

Various studies have revealed that these predictions of reasoned action hold in a variety of situations such as consumer behavior (Fishbein and Ajzen 1980), environment (Hamid and Cheng 1995), health (Hausenblas, Carron, and Mack 1997), and voting (Fishbein, Ajzen, and Hinkle 1980). However, this research shows that, of the two components, attitude is a better (more accurate) predictor of behavioral intent than subjective norms. O'Keefe (2002) points out that the relationship between the attitudinal component and the factors that contribute to it (evaluation, belief strength) is stronger than the relationship between the subjective norm component and its two parts (normative beliefs, motivation to comply).

Thus it is useful to add the idea of subjective norms, because sometimes they can influence our behavior, but in general attitudes are a more important influence on behavior. Reasoned action complicates our understanding of persuasion (which is a drawback), because it inserts another variable into the process: messages > attitudes > behavioral intent > behavior (and note that the elaboration likelihood model would insert another variable, cognitive responses, between messages and attitudes). However, human behavior is quite complex, and that may well mean that a theory which is too simple will not work well for understanding human behavior. Reasoned action is well supported by research and explains some of the reasons why an attitude (or behavioral intent) will not result in the expect behavior. Persuaders can find it useful because it outlines thirteen different options for persuading audiences (six ways to change the attitudinal component, six ways to change the normative component, and one way to alter the relative importance of attitudes and norms). Reasoned action is also useful because it helps persuaders to see what kinds of obstacles can prevent attitudes from causing behavior (e.g. lack of volitional control). Persuasion cannot always be expected to succeed, and it is useful to understand when and why it might not work.

An important limitation of reasoned action is that, like consistency theories and social judgment/involvement, it does not address other aspects of content (beside beliefs, values, and norms). But we know from chapter 6 that the way a message is organized can influence its persuasiveness, andchapter 7 has demonstrated that evidence can also affect attitude change from persuasive messages. Nor does reasoned action discuss how source credibility influences persuasion (chapter 3).

Using Reasoned Action in Persuasion

Reasoned action is useful to persuaders for several reasons. First, it can help you decide which ideas to use or what arguments to make in your speech. You audience analysis (chapter 5) can help you determine your audience's likely AB (belief strength, evaluation) and SN (normative beliefs, motivation to comply). You need to see which of these are consistent and inconsistent with your persuasive goal. You can reinforce or strengthen the components of AB and SN which are consistent with your purpose, and you can weaken or change the components of AB and SN which are inconsistent with your goal. Your research on the topic may uncover other reasons that support your purpose (ABs, SNs), which your audience analysis reveals your audience does not know or has forgotten. Persuading your audience to add these new ideas can change their attitudes in your favor.

Second, reasoned action identifies many (thirteen!) options for creating attitude change. Make a favorable belief stronger. Decrease the intensity of an unfavorable evaluation. Create a new favorable belief/value pair. And so on. A persuader should never complain, "I have no idea what to do to change my audience's attitudes," with all of the options identified by reasoned action.

For example, assume that you want to get your friends to join you in volunteering at a local shelter for the homeless. Because you know your friends, you know something about their attitudes on the subject (see box 12.8). Currently, there are three parts to their attitude to behavior: volunteering takes too much time, the homeless are unpleasant, and they are lazy. All three of these factors incline them against volunteering. They also have one normative belief (volunteers are geeks) which, again, discourages volunteering. (Of course, your friends do not have exactly identical attitudes, but assume this summary to be a good reflection of their attitudes generally.)

Box 12.8   Cognitions about volunteering at a homeless shelter

Belief strength (1):	Volunteering is time consuming.
Evaluation (1):	My time is very valuable.
Belief strength (2):	Homeless people are unpleasant (e.g. rude, smelly).
Evaluation (2):	I do not like spending time around people who are unpleasant.
Belief strength (3):	Homeless people are lazy.
Evaluation (3):	Lazy people do not deserve handouts.
Normative belief (1):	My friends think people who volunteer are geeks.
Motivation to comply (1):	I care what my friends think.

With this understanding (an audience analysis) of their attitudes, you can devise a persuasive message to change their behavioral intentions. You can attempt to change their three beliefs with arguments like these:

B1 (time-consuming): I volunteer and it only takes an hour a week. That isn't very much.

B2 (unpleasant): Like any other group, some homeless people are unpleasant, but others are friendly, helpful, and have a sense of humor.

B3 (lazy): It is a myth that all homeless people are lazy. With the economy in trouble, unemployment is increasing. I've met these people; a few are lazy but many are hard-workers who are just having bad luck.

N1 (geeks): I volunteer and hope you don't think I'm a geek!

These are not the only things one can say to change these beliefs and norms (see box 12.7), but they illustrate the process.

You can also add new beliefs or norms that support your goal of encouraging your friends to volunteer at the homeless shelter:

B4: Volunteering can make you feel good about yourself [BS]. I feel like I've helped other people, like I've made a difference. This is very satisfying [E].

M: Volunteering is a service activity you can put on your resume for job applications [= NB]. Employers really like to see community service on a resume [MC].

Of course, you could probably think of other reasons for volunteering that could be used, if you wanted to make other new beliefs and norms for your audience. This shows how understanding your audience's beliefs and norms can help you to change their attitudes in line with your goal.

Third, it is important to understand the relationship between attitude toward behavior and the behavior itself. We must realize that, even when our audience changes its attitudes in the direction we advocate, that does not necessarily mean that they will do what we hope. Not only does this mean that we will have more realistic expectations about what persuasion can accomplish; we may be able to identify obstacles to behavior that we can overcome. For example, if we want our audience to donate blood, we need to persuade them to have favorable attitudes toward blood donation. However, they need to know where (and when) they can give blood. They may also need transportation to the blood drive. So we need to not only to persuade them to have favorable attitudes toward our goal, but we will be more effective if we can create circumstances that will make it possible for them to engage in the desired behavior.

Theory of Planned Behavior

One of the authors of the theory of reasoned action, Icek Ajzen, has developed another theory, which adds another element to TRA. The theory of planned behavior (TPB) starts with the TRA model and adds to it another key element: perceived behavioral control. Perceived behavioral control represents the extent to which people think they can perform a behavior. For example, I may be persuaded to desire a particular car; however, I may not think I have enough money to buy it. In this case, my perception that I do not have enough money will prevent me from performing the behavior my attitudes and norms incline me to perform. Or, my daughter may persuade me that skiing on the advanced trail would be great fun; however, my beliefs about my inability to ski could stop me from attempting the run. Ajzen divides perceived behavioral control into two elements, as with attitudes and norms. First, there are control beliefs (e.g. how much money I have, my skiing ability). Second, he identifies the power of the potential control factor. In these examples, how important is my bank balance (perhaps I can get a loan; if so, my present finances may not be very important in the decision to buy that car)? How important is my ability to ski (very important if I want to avoid broken limbs!)? This theory incorporates the concept of volitional control into the theory, rather than adding it to the interpretation of the theory (as TRA does). Ajzen has a helpful webpage devoted to the TPB (2006). The idea of perceived behavioral control is similar to Witte's concept of self-efficacy in fear appeals (chapter 7).

Glossary

Attitude toward behavior: degree to which the behavior is viewed as favorable or unfavorable.

Behavioral intention: what a person would like to do, or plans to do.

Belief strength: belief, potentially verifiable cognition ("facts").

Evaluation: value, judgment of something's worth.

Motivation to comply: the extent to which a person things it is important to comply with the others' norms or expectations.

Normative beliefs: what a person believes the others want or expect that person to do.

Perceived behavioral control: the extent to which a person believes that he or she can perform desired behavior.

Subjective norms: the extent to which a person is aware of the expectations of others and is prepared to comply.

Part IV

Critical Consumers of Persuasive Messages

Chapter 13

Persuasion in Advertising

Chapter Contents

Advertising is a pervasive form of persuasion. In 2001, advertisers spent $231 billion in newspapers, magazines, broadcast TV, Cable TV, radio, yellow pages, direct mail, business publications, internet, and miscellaneous advertising outlets ("Coen's spending," 2002). Statistics also suggest that about half of the advertising dollars spent worldwide are spent on American consumers (Douglas and Craig 2002). Advertising must be considered a significant form of persuasion on the basis of expenditures and economic impact.

What companies do you think spend the most on advertising? You may be surprised at the list, but you need to remember that some of the advertisers are not targeting you as a primary audience for their messages. You may not have been exposed to as many of their messages as their target audience. The top five advertisers are General Motors, Procter and Gamble, Ford Motor, Pepsi, Pfizer, and Daimler Chrysler ("100 Leading," 2002). What were your guesses?

Social commentators suggest that the average person in the US is exposed to over 3,000 advertising messages per day (Shenk 1997). If you buy a book at the bookstore, there is a good chance that an advertisement for magazines or credit cards will be included in the bag along with your purchase. When you go to class, the bulletin boards are filled with advertisements for magazine subscriptions, apartments, and printing services. Your mail probably includes offers for credit cards, loans, and pizza coupons. When you get a credit card bill, the company often includes some special offer or new product. If you receive coupons in the mail or on your door, advertisers are trying to reach into your pocket. You may even find advertisements in with your paycheck! Do you get them in e-mail messages? If you surf the web, you cannot escape being exposed to multiple advertising messages. The movies you rent have products advertised within the films, trailers for other films and ads for music cds. If you attend a sporting event, there are ads on the score boards and on the sides of the arena. The students attending the sporting event wear hats, shoes, t-shirts, and jackets with logos for Nike®, DKNY®, Georgetown, and the Kansas City Chiefs.

In an interesting twist, two high school seniors offered to become walking advertisements by covering their bodies, cars, and dorms with corporate logos in exchange for college tuition (www.chrisandluke.com). They were willing to be spokespersons to other college students and FirstUSA® was chosen from among twenty companies to foot the bill for the first year of college tuition (Kellogg 2001). In the future, your college roommate may be another source of advertising. Would this offend you? Advertising is also important to understand as a form of persuasion, because it is virtually everywhere. It is commonplace in our culture.

This chapter begins with a description of the nature of advertising. Then we consider consumer behavior and why advertising is persuasive. In the next section, an explanation is given about how advertisers research consumers, so that they can adapt their messages. The persuasive effects and ethical implications of subliminal advertising and deception in advertising are considered. Finally, we take a look at questions to consider in critiquing an advertisement from the receiver's point of view.

The Nature of Advertising

Because we are all bombarded with advertising, we may feel we already understand it, but it is useful to consider carefully how advertising has been defined and what are its different types. When we are exposed to advertising, we are generally attending to the message as consumers rather than as students of persuasion. We will be looking more carefully at advertising and using some of the concepts from earlier chapters to analyze and evaluate these persuasive messages.

Advertising is persuasive communication designed to sell goods, services, and ideas to consumers. It uses a variety of media to deliver the persuasive message. There are many types of advertising.

The first way of distinguishing types of advertising is to consider what is being advertised. **Product advertising** promotes the sale of either tangible goods or services. A tangible good has form and substance. It is something that can be felt or touched. A service provides an intangible function; service advertising often emphasizes quality, uses testimonials about the benefits derived from the service, or focuses on the quality of the employees (Russell and Lane 1996). An ad for Reebok® Classics shoes advertises a tangible good (figure 13.1).

The ad for The Ritz-Carlton Golf Club and Spa℠ describes the quality of this resort as a "masterpiece," "luxury residences," "legendary service," "lavish," and "exclusive" (figure 13.2).

The advertisement is selling the service provided at this facility. **Non-product advertising** promotes an organization's corporate identity or mission rather than a specific product. In the ad by Weyerhaeuser™, the corporation is depicted as environmentally aware; the ad shows a dragonfly in front water, bushes, and trees.

Figure 13.1   Ad for Reebok. © 2002 Reebok International Ltd. All Rights Reserved. Reprinted with permission

A masterpiece is in the works.

THE RITZ-CARLTON GOLF CLUB & SPA™
JUPITER

ESTATE HOMESITES. LUXURY RESIDENCES. SEASONAL HOMES. SIGNATURE GOLF & SPA.

The Ritz-Carlton Golf Club & Spa—a premier real estate opportunity with legendary service and amenities in
the tradition of The Ritz-Carlton. Grand Addison Mizner style architecture. An exclusive Jack Nicklaus Signature
Golf Course. A lavish 15,000-square-foot spa. Only 20 custom Estates, designed with The Ritz-Carlton touch;
34 exclusive Residences, artfully designed on your behalf. 285 pristine acres. Only 54 keys, ever.

To arrange a preview, call 561-626-8676 or toll free 866-352-7489, or visit 106 Ritz-Carlton Club Drive, Jupiter, Florida.

This is not an offer to residents of New York, California, New Jersey or in any state where prohibited by law.

Figure 13.2   Ad for Ritz-Carlton. © The Ritz-Carlton Golf Club & Spa, Jupiter. Reprinted with permission

The copy says, "At Weyerhaeuser, we believe that taking care of business and taking care of wildlife don't have to be mutually exclusive." The goal of this advertisement is to create positive attitudes about the corporation rather than sell its paper towels.

A second way of classifying advertising is by considering its source. What kind of company, corporation, or foundation is behind the advertising? **Commercial advertising** promotes products, services, or ideas with the goal of securing a profit (for instance the advertisements for Reebok® and the Ritz-Carlton℠). **Non-commercial advertising** is sponsored by a charitable or non-profit institution, civic, religious, or political group, and the intention does not involve making a profit. The non-commercial advertisement sponsored by the Make a Wish® Foundation persuades others to help children with life-threatening illnesses to achieve their wishes while there is still time.

Advertising can also be differentiated by a third characteristic: its target audience. **Consumer advertising** is directed toward individuals who may buy a product for themselves or for someone else's personal use (e.g. the ad for Reebok® shoes). **Business advertising** persuades individuals to buy a product for use in a company. Business advertising can be subdivided into three main categories: trade, professional, agricultural. **Trade advertising** is aimed at middlemen who buy products for resale to customers. For example, an advertisement appearing in *Restaurant News* for Coke® is targeted at increasing sales to restaurant owners, who then resell the product to their customers. **Professional advertising** is directed toward individuals who are licensed under a code of ethics or a set of professional standards. The Joel Berman Glass Studios™ advertisement for corrugated glass panels appeared in *Architectural Record* and is targeted at architects rather than general consumers; general consumers are unlikely to be in the market for corrugated glass. **Agricultural advertising** persuades individuals in farming or agribusiness to purchase related products and services. An example is the internet advertising for EzyRun, a baler twine which is targeted toward agricultural users. The ad provided several statistics on product features.

A fourth classification divides advertising into type by medium. **Print advertising** includes newspapers and magazines. **Broadcast advertising** consists of radio or television. **Out-of-home advertising** includes outdoor and transit ads (e.g. for using commercial transportation). **Direct mail advertising** delivers a variety of persuasive messages through the postal service. **Internet advertising** is the largest growing market in advertising. **Yellow pages advertising** is also a significant market, and delivers local advertisements to consumers through telephone books. Although these are the largest of the advertising media, there are others which include table tents, shopping carts, cinema, and ATM machines to – mention only a few.

A fifth way of looking at advertising is to consider its geographic reach. **International advertising** is aimed at multiple foreign markets, even though companies adapt their messages for each geographic market. **National advertising** is designed for customers in several regions of the country. **Regional advertising** is directed toward customers in a particular area of the country where the products are sold. Advertisers buy local media or regional editions of national media, to reach the consumers. **Local advertising** is intended for customers in one city or locality and advertisers most frequently use local media or direct mail to reach their target audience.

And, six, advertising can even vary by purpose. If the goal is short term, **promotional advertising** seeks to generate immediate action from its recipient. Promotional advertising may include coupons to persuade consumers to make a purchase. This kind of advertising may be particularly important when an advertiser is introducing a new product. St. Ives® skin care is introducing a new lotion and uses action advertising to generate immediate sales. It combines coupons for the new product as well as adding coupons for their existing line of products, hoping to generate sales for several products. If the goal is more long-term, **brand advertising** may be used to establish the image of a product or reinforce familiarity with the product's name and package. We can return to the Reebok® ad as an example of awareness advertising. The ad focuses on the visual image of the product and does not make textual claims about its benefits. Instead, it strengthens familiarity with the brand name, image, and product look.

Although this list of types of advertising is not exhaustive, it gives you an idea of the variety of different kinds of advertising that are used to persuade. Types of advertising can be classified by what is being advertised, source, target audience, medium, geographic market, and purpose.

Consumer Behavior: Why Advertising Works to Persuade Consumers

To understand why advertising is persuasive, we need to examine why people buy. The three primary influences on consumer behavior are individual, social, and situational.

Individual influences on consumer behavior

Individual influences are internal or personal factors that influence consumer behavior. Three individual processes that influence this behavior are perception, learning, and motivation.

Perception

Perception is the individualized process of attending, selecting, and organizing sensory stimuli so as to make them meaningful. Advertisers are interested in the perception process because it is the initial step in determining whether a consumer even pays attention to advertising. Furthermore, two individuals who attend to the same advertisement may perceive it in a different way. This reiterates one of the basic assumptions of social judgment/involvement theory that we described in chapter 11. Such variability is due in part to the perceptual screens that individuals use to reduce stimuli to a manageable level. Unwanted messages are filtered subconsciously through physiological and psychological screens.

Physiological screens limit the messages through the use of the senses. For example, a consumer who is color-blind will screen out much of a print or video advertisement. The most common color blindness is for red or green and affects about 10 percent of the male population. Advertisers must keep in mind that there are physiological screens that should be considered in composing an advertisement. Psychological screens limit attention to messages on the basis of personality, human needs, self-concept, interests, attitudes, beliefs, past experiences, and lifestyle. We never attend to cigar advertisements because of our anti-tobacco attitudes and our view that cigars stink. Our psychological screens have effectively limited our attention toward this advertisement. What kind of advertisements do you screen out?

Advertisers are trying to get past consumers' perceptual screens, so that persuasion can take place. Because consumers are bombarded with stimuli, it is not surprising that these screens are well developed. This process of focusing on some things and ignoring other stimuli is selective exposure, an idea we have previously discussed in chapter 10. The concept of selective exposure is important to advertisers because their goal is to place their ads in media outlets that will reach audiences who are not screening out their messages.

Learning

"**Learning** is the process by which people acquire knowledge and experience that results in a permanent change in behavior" (Reeber 1995: 411–12). As it relates to advertising, learning is the process by which consumers acquire product knowledge and experience that affect their buying behavior. Advertising is a means for providing product information in order to persuade consumers to change their buying behavior. Learning and persuasion are closely related.

Learning generates attitudes toward products. As we indicated in chapter 1, an attitude is a learned and relatively enduring predisposition to act. Advertisers want to create many favorable attitudes toward their product, be it a good, service, or even the company itself. Advertisements for the New Shades of Herbal Essences Color® (a new hair color product) tell readers that the product has "intense color and shine" and "exhilarating shades that hold on and hold true." The model featured in the ad illustrates the New Feisty Pumpkin shade and declares: "New Feisty Pumpkin … any more intense and the Color Cops would bust me!" This advertisement attempts to create brand interest, a curiosity and openness toward the brand, by establishing a positive set of attitudes toward the product. Unlike other hair color products that offer the same old dull shades, this new product positions itself as bold and trendy.

Learning fosters buying habits. A **buying habit** is a patterned purchasing behavior that has been learned and has become so automatic that it is difficult to change. Advertisers want to instill buying habits for their products, also known as brand loyalty. Why do many of our buying behaviors become habitual? It is easy. Buying by habit is easy because you do not have to make a decision. You simply grab a product off the shelf. You do not have to make comparisons on price. You do not have to read anything to make an assessment of quality or talk to anyone about the merits of various alternatives. You get the same product because that is what you have always bought. If you had to evaluate every product each time you made a purchase, you would be unable to function. You cannot handle this much information. In fact, research suggests that, even when we are initially making a buying decision, most of us are likely to cope with only one or two brands in a particular product category (Ries and Trout 1986).

Buying by habit is also more secure. You buy a product because you like it. It performs the way you expect. We like Heinz ketchup because it is thick and not watery, like other brands. We know we can count on it. In other words, you feel safe in purchasing the brands you know. It is a risk to try a new brand. It may not perform up to your expectations. What brands do you buy through habit?

Advertisers obviously want to create brand loyalty. Brand loyal consumers can be counted on to make continuous purchases no matter what the competition is doing, and their maintenance costs the advertiser less than a new customer. Habit in buyer behavior is so important that advertisers recognize they must persuade three types of audiences: brand loyals, switchers, and novices. Brand loyals need to be reinforced for their continual purchase of the brand, or simply need to see advertising that supports their perception of the product. For example, Apple computer users (and Mac users) were extremely brand loyal and much of their advertising reinforced product loyalty through clear identification of the product line. Switchers need to be persuaded to leave their old brands through incentives or comparisons that show the new product's advantages over the competition. In the ad for cleaning products (Brillo®, Scrub Free®, Clean Shower®), switchers are encouraged to "Stop messing around with other cleaners!" and offered a coupon incentive to use the products advertised. Novices must be shown the way to brand loyalty. They have purchased the product but have not committed to it. Advertisers offer incentives to deepen the level of commitment and reinforce the initial purchase decision in their persuasive efforts. When magazines attempt to get first-time subscribers to resubscribe, they often use direct mail advertisements with inducements to secure this commitment. We recently received one of these mailings that offered a free subscription for a friend if we were to resubscribe to the magazine.

Motivation

Motivation is the third individual process; this is the need, wants, or desire that may cause a person to act. Advertisers attempt to relate their products and services to the perceived motivations of consumers. They want buyers to see their products and services as a way of satisfying their needs, wants, and desires. The classic model of human needs is Maslow's hierarchy of needs (1970) (see box 13.1). The hierarchy has five levels; it begins with basic physiological needs and progresses to self-actualization. The hierarchy assumes that basic needs must be satisfied before higher level needs will be addressed. Advertisers appeal to the needs in this hierarchy.

Figure 13.3 Cartoon: "I'm really motivated to sell to you." © 1999 Ted Goff. Reprinted with permission

Box 13.1 Maslow's hierarchy of needs

Need	Product	Appeal
Self-actualization	Air Force Reserve	"This is a challenge that will take you above and beyond anything you ever expected."
Esteem	Crest® White strips™	"In just two weeks you'll get a noticeably whiter smile."
Social	Bacardi® Mixers	"Instant Pool Party."
Safety	Mercedes Benz	"Security. Unlike any other."
Physiological	Post® Shredded Wheat	"It's the good-tasting way to help drive away your hunger."

Source: Maslow (1970)

Maslow's hierarchy is a classic treatment of motivation, but Settle and Alreck (1989) provide a model of horizontal needs that was designed for advertising in particular (see box 13.2). Their typology suggests fifteen distinct needs. In contrast to Maslow, they argued that individuals strive to attain multiple needs simultaneously, without regard to any hierarchy.

Box 13.2 Settle and Alreck's horizontal needs

Need	Product	Appeal
Achievement	Mass Mutual Financial Group	"Climbing the ladder of success takes stamina, know-how, and a little luck. We have investments and insurance opportunities that can help."
Independence	Novell® Net Business Solutions	"Microsoft wants more money from you. And they'll do whatever it takes to get it. If you want to move your business in a direction where you stay in control of your software costs, then head straight to Novell."
Exhibition	Toyota Corolla	"The New Corolla. It just wants to have fun."
Recognition	Samsung LCD Monitor	"To avoid the distraction of fellow admirers, you may need to close your door."
Dominance	Dodge Intrepid	"Everything has its place. Behind you."
Affiliation	Tyson® Chicken	"You'd give her wings to fly if you could. You give her quality chicken that's all natural because you can. It's what your family deserves."

Box 13.2   Settle and Alreck's horizontal needs—cont'd

Need	Product	Appeal
Nurturance	Hershey's® Hugs & Kisses	"Have you hugged and kissed your kids today?"
Succedanea	Costa Rica vacation	"100% soothing. Warm hospitality. Soothing climate."
Sexuality	Victoria's Secret	"Very sexy. Provocative fragrances for him and her."
Stimulation	Kodak Film™	"Share moments. Share life."
Diversion	Bally's®	"Some things never go out of style. Like Bally's Las Vegas. Where you'll find delicious, award-winning restaurants, white-hot casino action and entertainment that smolders like the business end of a Cahaba [cigar]."
Novelty	Color Xerox®	"Break out. Go beyond black and white. There's a new way to look at it."
Understanding	Smithsonian Study Tours	"Love to travel? Love to learn? Take the Smithsonian on your next trip."
Consistency	Adobe® Acrobat® 5.0	"Windows. MacO5. Palm. Yes, we can all get along."
Security	Ford Taurus	"Top-selling vehicle in my class to have earned double five-star: the government's highest front crash test rating, four years in a row."

Source: Settle and Alreck (1989)

Rossiter and Percy (1997) used the literature on motivation to generate a set of negatively and positively originated motives for purchasing a product (see box 13.3). They suggested that **negatively originated motives** for buying are situations in which the buyer is in a negative mental state (i.e. a bad frame of mind) and must seek information to reduce that mental state. For example, an individual faces a problem: coffee stains on her teeth that she wants to remove. To do so, she encounters advertising promising that a product will whiten her teeth and she purchases the product. An advertisement for Starbucks Doubleshot™ coffee emphasizes that it will "get you going" because it is "invigorating" (figure 13.4). The product addresses a bad frame of mind (being tired) and indicates that the product can give the consumer a "doubleshot™" of energy.

Positively originated motives suggest that the individual will benefit in some way, and the advertiser persuades the consumer that buying the product will be advantageous. These motives are transformational, since the buyer believes that a desired alteration will occur. An advertisement for a spa persuades us that we will receive sensory gratification through massages and the opportunity for relaxation and play.

Box 13.3 Rossiter and Percy's purchase and usage motives

Motives	Products	Appeals
Negatively originated motives		
Problem removal	Threaded	"More than 100,000 prostate cancer survivors across two generations are living proof that Threaded treatment can cure prostate cancer."
Problem avoidance	Ban®	"Finally, a maximum strength anti-perspirant that helps prevent shaving irritation."
Incomplete satisfaction	Royal Velvet® Towels	"Introducing the larger, more luxurious classic bath towel. Vast."
Mixed approach-avoidance	Amstel® Light	Always satisfying. Never watered down. Amstel Light. The beer drinker's Light Beer.
Normal depletion	Air Wick® Air Freshener	"Stands up to the toughest odors. Lasts up to 6 weeks."
Positively originated motives		
Sensory gratification	Panasonic® Digital Camera	"Taking your images further than film ever could."
Intellectual stimulation or mastery	The Rosetta Stone Language Library	"Conversing in a foreign language is a major social and business asset and brings new life to the worlds of travel, entertainment, and relationships."
Social approval	Bacardi® Silver Beverage	Malt"Your night just got more interesting."

Source: Rossiter and Percy (1997)

An ad for the new Discover® 2000 card proclaims that 95 percent of adults said it was unlike anything they'd ever seen. 90 percent said it was "an engineering masterpiece." The ad suggests that when you use the card you'll get "a lot of envious stares and questions." This advertisement motivates consumers through social approval: it suggests that you need one of these cards to be among those carrying the latest engineering masterpiece and you will want others to envy you for possessing the card.

Whether motives are hierarchical, horizontal, negatively or positively originated, advertisers are trying to convince consumers that their products satisfy your needs. Motives represent needs. But motivation is individualized, because people are not motivated by the same needs, wants, and desires. Advertisers must adapt their messages to the different motivations of their audiences. An advertiser of coffee may find that some consumers are motivated by taste (sensory gratification) while others are more concerned with the amount of caffeine (problem avoidance). Although it is impractical to create a different message for each consumer, advertisers can create different messages for different groups of consumers.

Figure 13.4   Ad for Starbucks. © Pepsi Cola. Reprinted with permission

Social influences on consumer behavior

Social influences consist of the impact of society or community on buying decisions. In particular, social influences on consumer behavior include the household, social class, and reference groups.

Household

One possible social influence on consumer behavior is the household. A **household** includes people living under one roof, no matter what the blood relationships may be between those individuals. These include students sharing rooms together, single parents, people living alone, step families, gay or lesbian couples, married couples with or without children, and other configurations. Households are social and economic units that make buying decisions. Advertisers have investigated two primary issues related to the influence of households on buying decisions. First, they have been interested in how children in families learn to become consumers. Second, they are also interested in who makes the buying decisions in families.

Advertisers want to know how children learn to buy products. Evidence indicates that children model their consumer behavior of that of the adults in their household. They learn from the behavior of their parents and caretakers when they go shopping with them and observe what products are purchased. Children also learn when given products, or the withdrawal of these items, are used as reinforcements or punishments. Some theorists believe that the way children are learning to consume is changing as parenting styles change. There is evidence that the household exerts less influence on children's consumer behavior as working parents take less active roles in care taking than in past generations (Bagdikian 2000). As families spend less time shopping together, children are modeling less of their consumer behavior on their parents' buying behaviors and more on those of their peers.

Advertisers are also interested in who makes buying decisions in the household, so that they can persuade the right target for their advertising. Societal changes that altered family structure have influenced who makes buying decisions. With the multiplicity of possible family configurations, there are greater possibilities for who might have the role of decision-maker in buying given product. Single families, divorced families, and step families are but three examples of types of families which have altered the traditional decision-making roles. Roles have also changed in families, and the modification in gender expectations have created other changes in decision-making. For example, women now purchase half of the new cars, and advertisers who fail to advertise to this audience will lose a significant part of the market ("Women Call the Shots," n.d.).

Social class

Traditional social class categories in the United States are based on a hierarchy defined by money, power, and respect. The four primary categories have been upper-class Americans (14 percent of the population), middle-class (32 percent), working-class (38 percent), and lower-class Americans (16 percent) (Coleman 1983). Advertisers believed that social class was an important influence on buying behavior, as it affected the amount of disposable income available to spend as well as the way people spend their money.

Advertisers also investigated similarities in attitudes among individuals within the same social class. For example, upper-class Americans were likely to buy prestige brands and self-image appeals were particularly persuasive with this audience. Working-class Americans valued family ties and were likely to respond to persuasive appeals which suggested that a task could be made easier with an appliance (Coleman 1983).

More recently, advertisers have realized that social class is much more complex. First, changes in family circumstances (e.g. divorces, retirements) often alter traditional social class groupings, even though attitudes (and sometimes their related buying behavior) do not change. In addition, the upward mobility of many people with a wide variety of attitudes have really changed the meaning of "middle class."

Some theorists would even argue that social class is an outdated concept for classifying consumers and that it should be replaced with geo-demographics, a composite of income, education level, neighborhood, and other lifestyle variables which describe more accurately the social influence on buying behavior. For example, Microvision's lifestyle categories classify individuals into fifty categories. The following is a sampling of some of those categories:

Upper Crust: Metropolitan families, very high income and education, manager/ professionals

Movers and Shakers: Singles, couples, students, and recent graduates, high education and income, managers/professionals, technical/sales; average credit activity

Stars and Stripes: Young, large school-age families, medium income and education, military, precision/craft

Social Security: Mature/seniors, metro/fringe, singles and couples, medium income and education, mixed jobs

University USA: Students, singles, dorms/group quarters, very low income, medium-high education, technical/sales. (Arens 1999: 141)

Individuals in the same lifestyle group tend to have similar attitudes and buying behavior. Advertisers use this information to design messages and select media to reach their target markets.

Reference groups

A **reference group** is a unit that a person values. As a result, that group can influence the attitudes and behavior of a person. A reference group can be people with whom you have direct contact (e.g. a peer group) or it can be a group that you aspire to be like, even though you do not have any personal contact with the members of that group (e.g. the National Basketball Association (NBA) players).

Reference groups can influence what products you buy as well as the brand you buy of a certain product. Whether you purchase a graphing calculator or a sports car can be influenced by your reference group. The brand of perfume, jeans, and beer you purchase are also likely to be influenced by your reference group.

How do reference groups influence your actions? Because we want to identify with our reference group, it influences our actions through a group affiliation process. When we buy a product that is associated with our reference group we are expressing a connection with that group. Advertisers persuade the consumer that he/she can be like the person portrayed in the ad, and if this person is part of the reference group for the buyer, the ad has primed the affiliation process.

Reference groups also influence your actions through a normative process. The reference group provides approval for buying behavior it endorses and disapproval of buyer behavior it finds objectionable. In many junior high and high schools, the pressure to conform to norms of dress is strong, and reference groups reward those who follow the norms and ostracize those who do not fit in. But this kind of socialization can be much more subtle. When you go to see a movie because your friends have been raving about it or you purchase a CD because everyone you know is listening to it, your reference group is exerting influence on your buying behavior.

Reference groups also influence behavior through an endorsement process. Because you value the opinions of the reference group or of the members of that group, endorsements of a product or brand can influence your buying behavior. To promote sales, the Gatorade® ad uses an endorsement from Derek Jeter encouraging fans to associate themselves with this baseball player and to value his opinion of the product.

Cultural influences on consumer behavior

A third source of influence on buying behavior is culture. A **culture** is defined as:

> the deposit of knowledge, experience, beliefs, values, attitudes, meanings, hierarchies, religion, notions of time, roles, spatial relations, concepts of the universe, and material objects and possessions acquired by a group of people in the course of generations through individual and group striving. (Samovar and Porter 1994: 11)

This definition of culture is packed with meaning and we can consider several components within it. First, a culture is the accumulation of knowledge, experience, beliefs, values, attitudes, meanings, hierarchies, religion, ideas about time, space, the universe, and even material objects and possessions. For example, cultural attitudes to numbers and colors influence advertising and marketing. Like the number "13," which is considered bad luck in some cultures, the number "4" is viewed negatively by some Asian Americans, and marketers targeting this group have learned not to package items in groups of four to such audiences. Red is a lucky color, but green is perceived negatively by some Asian Americans (DeGroat 2002). Second, culture is acquired over the course of several generations. Culture is learned both consciously and unconsciously, through a process of learning that is called enculturation. A culture is capable of change through invention and diffusion. **Invention** is the process of creating new practices that members of the culture come to accept. **Diffusion** is the process of integrating those practices within one's own culture.

There are also subcultures within a culture. A **subculture** is a group of people who have a set of values, meanings, and norms which make them distinct from people in the larger culture. "In the United States, ethnic group members include African Americans, Asian Americans (Japanese Americans, Chinese Americans, Korean Americans, and so on), Mexican Americans, Polish Americans, Irish Americans, Native American Indians, and Jewish Americans just to name a few" (Collier 1994: 38). Subcultures are defined by ethnic identities, racial identities, and religious identities in the United States. In Canada, the two majors subcultures, Anglophones and Francophones, are defined by language (Arens 1999).

African American subculture

Subcultures influence product preferences, brand loyalty, and amount and type of media exposure. For example, African Americans represent 12 percent of the

US population and spend 600 billion dollars per year. Marketing research suggests that this subculture purchases only 2 percent of the trucks and vans but 10 percent of the televisions, radios, and stereos. They also purchase 28 percent more baby products than other consumer groups, and make up 19 percent of the market for toiletries and cosmetics. They watch ten hours of network and cable television a day and are readers of morning newspapers. Black-oriented media has increased (BET, BlackAmericaWeb.com, *Black Living*, *Ebony*), and advertisers have increased advertisements specifically targeted to members of this subculture.

Hispanic subculture

According to the US Census Bureau, there were 37 million Hispanics in 2001; this subculture is a unique market for advertisers. Hispanic markets are concentrated in six large cities: Los Angeles, Miami, San Francisco-San Jose, Chicago, and Houston. The median age of Hispanics is twenty-four, compared to the US median age of thirty-two years. Household size is also larger, averaging 3.5 persons (compared to 2.7 for US households in general). Hispanics spend 454 billion dollars a year on products/services. Marketing research suggests that Hispanics spend more than other subgroups on groceries and are loyal to brands. Name brands are important in their purchase of several product categories. Hispanics have access to Spanish-language media and spend 15.8 hours watching Spanish television and 7.5 hours watching English television per week. They are more influenced by advertisements in Spanish-language media than by advertisements in English (Korzenny and Lanusse 1997). Because Hispanics spend more time online than other groups and are willing to buy consumer electronics, baby supplies, and travel through the internet, advertisers are developing Spanish-language websites (Swartz 2003).

Asian Americans subculture

As another example, Asian Americans represent 2 percent of the US population but are considered to be the fastest growing minority group in the United States. They have higher household incomes and graduation rates than other cultural groups. This makes this market particularly attractive to advertisers, because Asian Americans spend 254 billion dollars a year in products and services. Marketing research indicates that Asian Americans are status conscious, likely to buy premium brands, and purchase high tech products. Asian Americans spend more time online than any other subgroup (Kornblum 2001) and read newspapers more, but they watch television, listen to the radio, and read magazines less than average (Downey 2002).

Situational influences on consumer behavior

Situational influences are those factors in the environment that have some effect on our buying decisions. We will examine how the time of year, as well as the time of day, can influence a purchase. The location where you purchase and use the product also influence your buying decision. Finally, we investigate the influence of persuasive messages on your decision to buy.

Time

Time is an important situational influence on consumer behavior. Some products are seasonal purchases. You are more likely to buy gloves and snow blowers in the winter. Suntan oil and swimsuits are summer purchases. Advertisers who pay attention to consumer behavior allocate more of the advertising budget to those months when sales are higher. Even the time of day can influence consumer behavior. Fast-food restaurants sell more at lunch than at dinner (Vanden Bergh and Katz 1999).

On some occasions, time influences consumers to make quick buying decisions because there is an emergency. The tire must be replaced, the phone is dead, or the refrigerator has stopped working. These are not purchases that can be delayed while you do comparative shopping, so time has altered your usual buying behavior.

Location

The location of purchasing and consuming a product also influence consumer behavior. First, advertisers must insure that consumers know where to purchase their products. They need to get them into the store, and then they need to present the product in a way that will close the deal. Almost three quarters of brand selections are made within the store (Vanden Bergh and Katz 1999). This means that the store display and placement of the product within the store can be critical in persuading the consumer to buy. This is why manufacturers pay premium prices for good locations for their products in supermarkets. The cereal aisle in your local supermarket is not haphazardly arranged. The children's cereals are on the lower shelves, where little ones can get to them and put them in the cart. For the adults, those items at eye level are occupying prime real estate in the supermarket aisle.

The location for the consumption of the product also influences consumer behavior. People behave differently in public from they do in private. This is true of their consumption behaviors as well. We know for example that people consume different beers in a restaurant or bar from the ones they drink at home. They are more likely to purchase and consume a premium and/or import beer in a bar or restaurant, whereas for home consumption they purchase a cheaper brand . We also use products in different ways depending on our consumption location. One of our sisters lives in a very hilly area of California and she must replace the brakes in her car far more frequently than we do, because we live in a relatively flat area of Missouri. Hence the way we consume the product (a car's brakes) is influenced by the place where we do it.

Persuasive messages

Consumer behavior is influenced by persuasive messages about the product. These messages may be word-of-mouth endorsements of a product by a credible individual.

When one of our brothers tells us that the new Harry Potter book is terrific and we buy a copy, his personal endorsement has influenced our buying behavior. Persuasive messages may also involve any form of advertising for a product or service. The present chapter has been about this kind of persuasive message.

"Understanding consumer decision making helps advertisers provide the most persuasive information at the most appropriate time in the decision making process" (Vanden Bergh and Katz 1999: 210). In this section, we have described how consumers behave by considering individual, social, cultural, and situational influences on their buying decisions. We have also illustrated how this information is used by advertisers to adapt their persuasive messages to the appropriate target audience.

How Advertisers Research Consumer Behavior

Just as we have emphasized the importance of audience analysis in other persuasion contexts, here too it has to be said that advertisers must know their audience. For advertising, the audience is the consumer. Advertisers collect and analyze research on consumer behavior. Specifically, advertising research consists of target audience analysis, message research, and media research.

Target audience analysis

As we have explained in chapter 5, it is essential to analyze the audience. For an advertiser, it is important to analyze the target audience because an advertising campaign designed for the wrong audience is a waste of money. **Target audience analysis** determines who buys the product and what are the characteristics of this audience. This kind of analysis reveals the demographic characteristics of the potential buyers such as sex, age, ethnicity, education, and so on. The research also uses psychographic information of the kind we described earlier – such as values, attitudes, and lifestyle – to get a better understanding of the product's buyers. This information is obtained through surveys and focus groups. Some of the information may come from industry surveys conducted by trade associations. Researchers also wants to know how much the target audience knows about the product category, how aware they are of brands in that category, how they make decisions to buy, and what media they use. An analysis often includes a study of competitive products and what the audience knows about them. Advertisers can use syndicated research services such as Competitive Media Reporting (www.cmr.com) or Nielsen Monitor Plus (www.nielsenmedia.com) to gather data on a competitor's expenditures by brand, medium, and geographic areas.

Message research

Message research tests the effectiveness of advertising messages with target audiences. It includes concept and copy testing. **Concept testing** asks potential consumers to evaluate the basic idea for an advertising campaign before its development. The major benefits of the product are described briefly. Concept testing is usually done when there are several ways the product could be positioned and the advertiser is trying to determine which one is likely to be the most effective with the target market. A new running shoe could be positioned primarily for its comfort for the wearer or for its aerodynamic design. Concept testing with the target audience will allow the advertiser to determine which of these benefits is most important to consumers. **Copy testing** is a methodical pre-testing of a completed advertisement on the target audience. This research exposes target audiences to advertisements and then measures several kinds of effects including recall, persuasion, and commercial reaction. **Recall** asks the target audience to tell what they remembered about what was read/ said in the advertisement or what they saw visually in the advertisement. An advertisement's persuasiveness can be assessed by asking consumers to rate the brand or their interest in purchasing the brand. **Commercial reaction** is a global measure of the consumer's favorable or unfavorable response to the advertisement. Message research is better when it uses multiple measures of effects, including recall, persuasion, and commercial reaction. According to Maurice Parisien, an experienced marketer with Marketing Direct, Inc., the most persuasive message "weaves both an emotional and rational message into the advertising, recognizing that people make purchase decisions on both an emotional and rational level" (2003).

Media research

Media research gathers information about the size and demographics of various media. It is used to make those media buys that match product's audience best. The Audit Bureau of Circulations (www.accessabc.com) provides information on the number of subscribers and the number of readers per copy to calculate the total audience for print media. Simmons Market Research Bureau (www.smrb.com) and Mediamark Research (www.mediamark.com) use extensive interviews to obtain information about magazine readership, product use, other media use, demographics, and lifestyle characteristics.

Information about national television audiences is provided by Nielsen Media Research (www.nielsenmedia.com). A random sample of 5,000 households' viewing patterns is measured through **people meters**. These devices measure the channel the television set is tuned to and who is watching the television. The meter records the station, network, or satellite, as well as channel changes. Each individual in the household is assigned a personal viewing button, and periodically the people meter requests that viewers record who is watching the program. Information about local television audiences is also collected by Nielsen, but the methods are different. In this case, between 400 and 500 households in 55 major markets are sampled with set meters. These record only the channel that the television is tuned to, but they are supplemented with viewing diaries of what programs individuals watched during a specified period of time. This kind of media research is used to project ratings and share of the market. **Ratings** are the number of households tuned into a particular program, divided by the total number of households with television sets. So if

400,000 households are tuned into *Friends* for a particular week and there are one million television households, *Friends* has a rating of 40 for that week. **Share** is determined by dividing the number of households tuned into a particular program by the number of households actually using their television sets. For example, if there are 400,000 households tuned into *Friends* and 800,000 households using their television sets during that time period, the share of the market would be 50. Programs with higher ratings and shares of the market can deliver a larger audience for advertising.

Media research on radio collects similar information regarding listenership and audience characteristics. The two most common research services are both offered by Arbitron: Radio's All Dimension Audience Research service, which specializes in assessing network radio and gathers information through telephone interviews, and Arbitron Radio (www.arbitron.com), which uses diaries to investigate local radio listening behavior.

Target audience analysis, message, and media research are critical for advertisers to understand their target audiences, product preferences, attitudes, reactions to advertisements, and media habits. These data can be used to design more persuasive messages, which will reach the appropriate audience and be sensitive to the influences on buying behavior we discussed in the earlier section of this chapter. This is the way that advertisers do audience analyses. You can see how important audience analysis is, both in this context and in the contexts we have described earlier for the persuasive speaker (chapter 5 and chapter 9).

Advertising as Persuasion: Ethical Issues

Advertising has been the subject of disapproval and criticism in some places. For example, critics have accused advertisers of taking advantage of children by targeting them for inappropriate and excessive advertisements (Dobrow 2002; McDonald and Lavelle 2001). The ethics of advertising controversial products (e.g. tobacco, alcohol) has come under scrutiny (Elliott 1993; Nagle 2002). This section will take up two ethical issues in advertising that have received a great deal of attention: subliminal advertising and deception and exaggeration in advertising.

Subliminal advertising

One of the most common ethical questions in advertising and persuasion concerns the use of subliminal advertising. Before we can consider the ethical implications, we need to define this form of advertising and describe the research on its effectiveness.

Subliminal advertising uses what is, essentially, a secret message inside ads, which is processed without conscious awareness. In video or audio clips, pictures or words which last for for a hundredth or a thousandth of a second are inserted or embedded into messages. Printed advertisements embed pictures or words into other images (e.g. "Sex" spelled out in the ice cubes of a Gilby's gin ad: Key 1973).

"Only your subconscious mind can see it. It says, 'You must buy Acme Thermoplex Couplings.' The ad agency let us have it for a song!"

Figure 13.5 Cartoon: "Only your subconscious mind can see it ..." © Ted Goff. Reprinted with permission

The interest in subliminal advertising began with a study by James Vicary. He claimed that he inserted subliminal messages to "Drink Coca-Cola" and "Eat popcorn" on a movie screen at 1/2000th of a second, every five seconds. Popcorn sales increased in the theater by 57.5 percent and Coke® sales increased by 18.1 percent. However, subsequent attempts to replicate his experiment (to duplicate his results in a similar study) were unsuccessful. Critics argued that Vicary's experiment was seriously flawed because there was no control group who did not receive the subliminal message. Although Vicary explained his results as being caused by the subliminal messages, critics argued that, without a control group, his results could be explained by other factors (e.g. seeing Coca-Cola® advertisements prior to coming to the theater). Critics also argued that his results could be explained by the fact that the movie that was being watched was *The Picnic*. It featured food, and subjects in this study may have eaten more popcorn and consumed more Coca-Cola® because of the movie and not because of the subliminal messages. Some critics have even argued that Vicary's results were actually a well-executed publicity scheme rather than an actual experiment (Rogers 1992).

Since this first experiment, there have been many tests of the effects of subliminal messages. Most studies show that there are no effects, or that the effects last only for seconds (Gable, Wilkens, and Harris 1987; Pratkanis and Aronson 1992; Smith and Rogers 1994; Theus 1994; Vokay and Read 1985). By contrast, the few reports which show that subliminal messages work have not been replicated and have serious methodological weaknesses (e.g. no control group). So, although subliminal advertising sounds interesting, the evidence is quite strong that subliminal advertising does not work.

Nevertheless, 75–80 percent of Americans believe that advertisers use subliminal advertising and that it is effective (Rogers and Seiler 1994; Rogers and Smith 1993; Zanot, Pincus, and Lamp 1983). But advertisers deny using subliminal advertising (O'Toole 1981; Rogers and Seiler 1994). If a message is below conscious awareness, it is difficult to prove that it is being used. On the one hand, why would advertisers use subliminal advertising when the evidence is so compelling that it does not work? They would be better off spending their time and money developing messages that are within consumers' conscious awareness. On the other hand, one could argue that it probably costs very little extra to airbrush "sex" into the ice cubes of the print ad, and, if there is a chance that it works, why not go ahead and do it?

This brings us finally to the ethics question. If subliminal advertising is being used by advertisers, is it an ethical practice? You will remember that in chapter four we described several ethical perspectives for evaluating behaviors. The human nature perspective is appropriate for evaluating subliminal advertising, because its effects may threaten a person's human abilities. This approach asks two central questions: Does the practice insure that the audience can make a rational choice? Does the practice preserve the humanness of the audience? If subliminal advertising is effective and influences behavior without our conscious awareness, it does not allow us to make rational choices. Subliminal advertising treats human beings as passive agents and attempts to manipulate their behavior. It does not respect their humanness. So, according to the human nature perspective, subliminal advertising would be assessed as an unethical practice. This evaluation assumes that subliminal advertising works. Other ethical perspectives could also be used to evaluate this practice. Advertisers, of course, would argue that is a moot point, since they claim that subliminal advertising is not used. Furthermore, subliminal advertising does not reduce human beings to passive agents or remove their ability to make rational choices when there is compelling evidence that it does not work. Thus, ultimately, subliminal advertising should not be judged as unethical.

Deception and exaggeration

Ethical questions are raised when advertising is deceptive, although advertising that makes use of exaggeration to sell products is pervasive, persuasive, and accepted. What is the difference between deception and exaggeration? According to the Federal Trade Commission, **deception** occurs when an advertisement makes a representation or omission that misleads consumers. A three-part test is used to identify deception. First, the ad must have made a representation or omission that was likely to mislead consumers. Second, the advertisement must be considered from the perspective of a reasonable consumer. Third, the representation or omission must have influenced the consumer's decision. If it did not affect the consumer's buying behavior, there was no impact and the deception would not be "actionable." An interesting application of this test can be made in the case of soft drink ads which use plastic ice cubes (they are easier to photograph as they do not melt under hot lights). Because these advertisements are not making claims about the ice cubes and thus are not influencing consumers' buying behavior through the use of plastic ice cubes, this representation of "ice cubes" is not considered deceptive under these guidelines (Russell and Lane 1996).

When a company is producing persuasion unethically in the US, by using advertising which is considered deceptive, a claim can be filed with the Federal Trade Commission (FTC). These claims can originate from the consumer, from competitors, or from the FTC staff. The FTC investigates and, if it finds that the advertisement is deceptive, the advertiser is asked to sign an agreement to end the deceptive practice. Advertisers who continue the practice are fined. Advertisers who refuse to sign the agreement are issued a cease and desist order and the case comes before a court.

> Some of the most common of the deceptive practices in advertising identified in court decisions have been false promises, small-print qualifications, and partial disclosures. False promises occur when an advertisement makes a promise that the product cannot fulfill. Dietary supplements are notorious for making outrageous claims. The FTC filed a complaint against the maker of a bee pollen supplement that claimed in advertising to prevent breast tumors, heart disease, constipation, moles, asthma, colds, arthritis, and improve sex drive. (Peeler and Cohn 1995)

Small print qualifications are considered deceptive when they qualify or nullify what appears elsewhere in the advertisement. For instance, a car dealer in Seattle advertised very low monthly payments but in small print described a "purchase option" of several thousand dollars. This actually was a large balloon payment the consumer paid after the initial payment period. The FTC ruled that the advertising emphasized the small monthly payments and hid the large payment in small print. Since adequate information was not provided to the consumer, the small print qualifications were deceptive (Moser and Rogers 2002).

Partial disclosures leave out important information that the consumer needs in order to interpret the claim. Gerber Foods™ made the claim in its advertising that "Four out of five doctors recommended Gerber baby food products." This was based on a survey of 562 pediatricians. The results were that 408 pediatricians recommended baby food, only 78 recommended specific brands, and, out of these, 67 recommended Gerber. Gerber got their figures by telling consumers about the pediatricians who recommended specific brands of baby foods because 67 of 78 recommended Gerber (or about four out of five pediatricians). But the FTC concluded that this claim was misleading, since Gerber failed to include those pediatricians who did not recommend a particular brand. When this information is included, Gerber products are only recommended by 16 percent of those surveyed. Because Gerber did not provide all of the information and consumers used this information to make inferences about nutritional value, the FTC insisted that Gerber be prohibited from making these deceptive claims.

On the other hand, exaggeration in advertising is quite common. It is also known as puffery, because copy writers exaggerate the praise for the product by puffing up the claims. It is commonly accomplished through subjective claims. For example, Herbal Essences hair color claims that their product provides "True Intense Color." This is not a statement that can be objectively verified. The language of exaggeration in advertising is broad, ambiguous, and sweeping in its endorsement of the product or service. Consider the copy for the Golf Club and Spa[SM]: "A premier real estate opportunity with legendary service and amenities in the tradition of The Ritz-Carlton." The adjectives create amplified praise through the use of "premier" and "legendary" as descriptors, but these are not objective factual claims.

It is important to remember that advertising has multiple goals. One goal is to sell a particular product or service. Another goal is to provide product information that will make the product appear to be most appealing to the consumer. This helps to explain why some advertisers resort to deception and why exaggeration is commonplace in advertising copy.

Are these practices ethical? Deception is clearly an unethical practice. Even using the legal perspective on ethics, it is unethical to deceive consumers. Certainly, using the human nature perspective, deception does not allow individuals to make rational choices because they do not have access to important information necessary for decision-making.

Exaggeration is more difficult to assess on ethical grounds. Are consumers aware that advertising which uses exaggeration is not providing factual information about products and services? Are they savvy and critical evaluators of advertisements, or are they taken in by the exaggeration? Advertisers would argue that consumers fully expect and enjoy advertisements that use some hyperbole. Advertising would be boring if it had to stick entirely to the dry facts of the matter. Critics argue that advertisers should provide consumers with the information they need in order to make buying decisions and should not create unrealistic images and exaggerate product benefits through language. They argue that this is an indirect form of deception and that some consumers are particularly vulnerable to these kinds of claims (e.g. children). You could argue that exaggeration in advertisements is not unethical for adults but is unethical when targeted at children (using the situational perspective from chapter 4). It is important to consider a set of questions you should use as you evaluate advertising messages in the next section.

Using Advertising in Persuasion

Some of you may be involved in marketing careers and will be able to use this material on persuasion and advertising to design more effective persuasive messages. But more of us will be receivers of persuasive advertisements. And, as receivers of persuasive messages, we need to be active in evaluating the messages aimed at us as audiences, if we are to avoid being influenced inappropriately.

In this chapter we have discussed the ways advertisers use persuasion to adapt messages to consumers. In this last section, we want to focus on how you, as an expert in persuasion and an informed consumer, can assess and critique advertisements. We suggest a set of questions that should be asked to assess an advertisement, and we will use the ad from Starbucks™ (figure 13.4) to illustrate this kind of analysis.

1 *What type of advertising is being used in this advertisement?*

The advertisement is for a commercial product. Although this company also advertises to businesses and trade (e.g. grocery stores), this particular advertisement is aimed at the consumer. It appeared in *In Style* magazine, a consumer publication and print medium. The advertising campaign is national, supporting sales primarily in grocery stores and retail outlets in the United States.

2 *What is the primary purpose of the advertising?*

The purpose of the ad is to reinforce affiliation with the Starbucks™ brand and to highlight this new product in the line of Starbucks™ coffee products. The prominent display of the logo on the can underlines brand affiliation and promises implicitly that this product will have the same quality the consumer has come to expect.

3 *Are there perceptual screens that influence your reaction to this advertisement?*

Yes. Although we can certainly understand the difficulty of getting going without some sort of stimulant, we are not coffee drinkers, so our natural instinct is to use perceptual screens to ignore advertisements about coffee products. We are clearly not the target market for this ad. We paid attention to it for this chapter. What are your perceptual screens?

4 *What learned behaviors do you have that are relevant to this advertisement?*

Many learned behaviors are habitual and those that would be relevant for this advertisement would include behaviors regarding coffee consumption, espresso consumption, and brand loyalty to Starbucks™. For example, if you are someone who drinks coffee and believe that it is essential to get you going, you are more likely to accept the claim of this advertisement at face value. A consumer with strong brand loyalty to Starbucks™ products will also be likely to use these learned behaviors to make a buying decision about this new product.

5 *What needs or motives are appealed to in this advertisement?*

Using Settle and Alreck's horizontal needs, this advertisement appeals to achievement needs. The people in the ad need to get going so they can achieve more. In fact, they are visually portrayed as climbing a ladder and scaling the sphere. There is also an appeal to novelty by reminding consumers that this is a new product. Rossiter and Percy would argue that Starbucks™ is using a negatively originated motive because Doubleshot™ addresses problem removal. If you can't get going, then Starbucks Doubleshot™ will take care of this problem for you.

6 *What benefits are claimed for this product/service? What evidence is provided to support these claims?*

The claim is that this product will invigorate the drinker and get him/her going. Even the name "Doubleshot™" implies that there is more caffeine in this product than in other coffee products, so that the user will get the necessary jolt to move forward. No factual evidence about caffeine content is provided in this advertisement, although the product is clearly identified as espresso.

7 *What image is created for the product/service and the user of this product/ service? How realistic is this image?*

The claim that this product will invigorate the user is expressed visually in the print ad by showing a male person below the can attempting to climb a sphere. They appear to have some difficulty (as one person climbs part of the sphere, it has slipped from its proper location). On the other hand, the person above the can appears to be walking confidently toward the sun as he swings his arms. The image created for the product is one of energy, spirit, and vigor. Coffee drinkers tell me that espresso has more caffeine and is capable of giving the drinker a needed kick. A double espresso would increase the impact.

8 *Who influences the decision in your household to buy this product/service? Is this advertisement aimed at the person in your household who makes the buying decision about this product?*

The buying decision for this product would seem to be influenced by the person who is most likely to actually consume this product. The product is not likely to be shared.

9 *Who is the audience for the product/service? Can you make any inferences from the advertisement about who the advertiser thought the audience was in terms of lifestyle or demographic characteristics?*

The advertisement seems to suggest that the product is aimed at upwardly mobile males. All of the figures portrayed in the ad are men, and the motives emphasize achievement. With some investigation, we discovered that the product was aimed at a demographic group older than the usual 18–24 age group. But the figures seem instead to be those of males college age, dressed in khakis, and they represent a younger age group.

10 *Do you think reference group influences attitudes to his product/service? If so, does the advertisement make use of this in the appeals?*

Yes. A reference group can play an important part in shaping attitudes to this product. If your reference group has strong positive attitudes to Starbucks™ and to coffee drinking, there is a good chance that you will too. If your reference group uses caffeine to get going, you are more likely to accept this as a natural course of events. If your group has strong negative attitudes, this is also likely to influence your opinions. However, the ad itself does not make use of reference group attitudes in its appeals.

11 *How do cultural influences impact your reactions to this advertisement? How should this advertisement be changed for different subcultures?*

You may have noticed that all of the figures depicted in this advertisement are male and all appear to be fair skinned against darker backgrounds. In fact, rather than incorporating diversity, the figures look remarkably alike. It would be useful to investigate cultural attitudes about the use of caffeine as a stimulant, because this is the only benefit mentioned in this ad.

12 *Do situational influences influence the advertisement for this product/service? How?*

This product can be purchased in grocery stores or retail outlets. This could influence buying behavior. Consumers would be more likely to consume this product on the go as they try to get going. This is unlikely to be the kind of coffee that consumers will linger over at the Starbucks™ coffee bar. But nothing in the advertising copy appeals to these situational influences.

13 *Are there ethical concerns in the advertisement?*

We do not see any ethical concerns in this advertisement. Our only complaint is that there is no factual information provided for a consumer to make a rational decision about the product, but our friends who are coffee drinkers assure us that knowing that this is a double shot of espresso is sufficient information for those who are in the target audience.

Advertising is an important form of persuasion. It is designed to sell products, services, and ideas to consumers. Types of advertising can be differentiated by what is being advertised, source, target audience, medium, geographic market, and purpose. The three primary influences on consumer behavior are individual, social, and situational. Advertisers conduct target audience analysis, message research, and media research to gather information to increase their ability to persuade consumers. There are ethical concerns regarding advertising, and the two issues of subliminal advertising and deception/exaggeration in advertising have been discussed in detail. Finally, a set of questions for analyzing advertisements allows receivers to be critical consumers of advertising messages.

Glossary

Advertising: persuasive communication designed to sell goods, services, and ideas to consumers.

Agricultural advertising: persuades individuals in farming or agribusiness to purchase related products and services.

Brand advertising: establishes the image of a product and familiarity with the product's name and package.

Broadcast advertising: ads that appear on radio or television.

Business advertising: messages persuading another company to buy a product.

Buying habit: patterned purchasing behavior that is difficult to change.

Commercial advertising: messages promoting products, ideas, or services to make a profit.

Concept testing: asking potential consumers to evaluate the basic idea for an advertising campaign before its development.

Consumer advertising: messages aimed at people who buy a product for themselves of for someone else to use.

Commercial reaction: global measure of the favorable response from a consumer to an advertisement.

Copy testing: a methodological pre-testing of a completed advertisement on the target audience.

Culture: the combination of knowledge, experience, beliefs, values, attitudes, meanings, hierarchies, religion, ideas about time, space, the universe, and material objects and possessions transmitted over time.

Deception: when an advertisement makes a representation or omission that misleads consumers.

Diffusion: the process of integrating new ideas and practices with culture.

Direct mail advertising: ads sent through the postal service.

Household: group of people living under the same roof regardless of blood relationships.

Individual influences: internal or personal factors that influence consumer behavior.

International advertising: design to sell to consumers in multiple foreign markets.

Internet advertising: advertising on the world wide web.

Invention: the process of creating new practices that members of a culture come to accept.

Learning: process by which consumers acquire product knowledge and experience that affect their buying behavior.

Local advertising: designed to sell to consumers in one city of locality.

Message research: test of the effectiveness of advertising messages with target audiences.

Media research: gathering information about the size and demographics of various media.

Motivation: the needs, wants, or desires that cause a person to act.

National advertising: designed to sell to consumers in several areas of a country.

Negatively originated motives: situations where the buyer is in a negative mental state.

Non-commercial advertising: sponsored by a charitable or non-profit institution without the intention of making a making a profit.

Non-product advertising: promotes organization's corporate identity or mission rather than a specific product.

Out-of-home advertising: includes outdoor and transit ads (e.g. on buses).

People meters: devices that record the channel viewed on the TV and who is watching.

Perception: individualized process of attending, selecting, and organizing sensory stimuli to be meaningful.

Positively originated motives: situations where the product is perceived to be advantageous.

Print advertising: ads appear in newspapers or magazines.

Product advertising: promotes the sale of either tangible goods or services.

Professional advertising: directed towards individuals who are licensed under a code of ethics or set of professional standards.

Promotional advertising: generates immediate action from recipient of the advertisement.

Rating: number of households tuned in to a program divided by the total number of households with television sets.

Recall: asking the target audience what they remember about an advertisement.

Reference group: a set of people a person values.

Regional advertising: persuasive sales messages aimed at those living in a city or locality.

Share: number of households tuned in to a program divided by the number of households using their television sets.

Social class: divides potential customers by income levels.

Subculture: a group of people who have a set of values, meaning, or norms that make them distinct from those in the larger culture.

Target audience analysis: describes who buys a product and characteristics of this audience.

Trade advertising: aimed at those who buy products for resale to consumers.

Traditional social class: hierarchical categories in the United States that are defined by money, power, and respect.

Yellow pages advertising: persuasive sales messages in telephone books.

Chapter 14

Persuasion in Political Campaigns

Political campaigns are an important part of our democracy. They allow citizens to have input into their government by selecting one candidate, and the policies he or she favors, over another candidate. Of course, at times all candidates sound alike: Everyone wants to lower taxes, improve education, safeguard retirement benefits, strengthen the economy. Because so many voters agree on certain goals, candidates naturally support some of the same ideas. Nevertheless, there are differences between the candidates. In 2000, for example, George W. Bush proposed tax cuts for every-one; Al Gore recommended tax cuts targeting the middle class. Bush supported private school vouchers, which Gore opposed. Bush wanted to allow workers to invest social security into the stock market, a plan not endorsed by Gore. A political campaign allows candidates to explain and justify their ideas, and each citizen has the opportunity to vote for the candidate who, in the opinion of that voter, has the best mix of ideas. This means that political campaigns educate voters (and there is evidence that campaigns generally and campaign messages specifically do help people in learning about the candidates and their issue positions; Holbert, Benoit, Hansen, and Wen 2002) and allow voters to choose their elected officials and to chart the general course of government.

This chapter will discuss political campaign discourse. Because few people become political candidates, our emphasis (like in chapter 13 on advertising) is designed to help you see how persuasive messages operate in our society rather than to teach you how to create political messages yourself.

Politicians seem to talk all of the time, and they produce messages on many other topics, of course. Newly elected presidents give inaugural addresses; senators and representatives give speeches in Congress about pending legislation. This chapter will focus on persuasive campaign messages. There are thousands of political cam-paigns for many offices, from dog-catcher to president. Most research, however, has investigated presidential campaigns, and the present chapter will reflect that empha-sis. Finally, the chapter focuses on political campaign messages, which means that it will not discuss other important activities such as fund-raising, polling, or organiz-ing a campaign staff and volunteers (see e.g. Shea 1996).

Political Campaign Communication

Figure 14.1 is a simplified version of the political campaign process (it leaves out political interest groups like the National Rifle Association or the Sierra Club, which

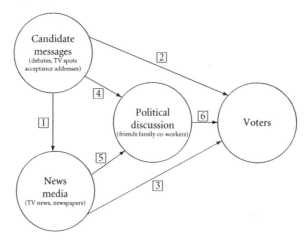

Figure 14.1 Campaign information flow

sometimes create political advertisements that discuss the relative merits of candidates). On the left are the two primary sources of information, candidate messages and the news media. Candidate messages take a variety of forms, such as television spots, debates, stump speeches, Internet sites, radio spots, newspaper advertisements, direct mail brochures, campaign buttons, and bumper stickers. Arguably, the three most important persuasive message forms are television spots (because so many are broadcast repeatedly), debates (because of the huge audience, because of the fact that voters can learn about both leading candidates, and because they last longer than a 30-second television advertisement) and acceptance addresses (because the presidential nominating conventions tend to attract large audiences, although not as large as debates, and these speeches are also longer than TV spots). Therefore this chapter will focus on these three message forms, but it is important to keep in mind that candidates use a variety of persuasive means to reach voters.

The other primary source of information, besides messages from the candidates themselves, is the news media. Again, this part of the diagram represents a wide variety of specific information sources. There are three major television broadcast networks (ABC, CBS, NBC) and several cable news channels (e.g. CNN, FoxNews, MSNBC) and thousands of newspapers. Candidates also attempt to reach voters through other kinds of programming: Bill Clinton appeared on MTV in 1996; in 2000 Bush and Gore appeared on several television shows, including the ones hosted by Leno, Letterman, and Oprah. We want to note that entertainment shows like "Saturday Night Live," "Politically Incorrect," and "The Daily Show" are not news programms, but they make jokes which are usually based on the candidates' actual behavior and statements. This means that some "real" learning can occur from watching these programs too.

In the middle of figure 14.1 we see political discussion. From time to time – more frequently and more heatedly with some people than others – citizens engage in discussion with one another about politics (e.g. taxation, health care, national defense), the candidates' positions on these issues, and the character of candidates. People, to varying degrees, talk with family, friends, and co-workers about politics and candidates. Sometimes we are persuaded by what others tell us about politics in informal conversation.

Finally, voters are represented on the right-hand side of the campaign information process. Campaigns are designed to provide information for voters, who ultimately decide the outcome of the election with their votes on election day. The point of figure 14.1 is to show the various kinds of persuasive sources of information about political candidates and their policy proposals, which are available to voters during a campaign.

The arrows in figure 14.1 show the direction of information flow during political campaigns. Political candidates and the news media originate messages with information about the candidates and their issue stands (which is why both candidate messages and the news are on the left-hand side of the figure). However, some information from the candidates' messages goes to the media (arrow 1), who then, in turn, pass it along to the public. In other words, both candidates and the media originate information, but the media also filter, interpret, and pass along some information from the candidates.

Some persuasive information moves directly from the candidates to individual voters (arrow 2) as they watch political television spots, debates, or candidate speeches or are exposed to other candidate messages. Some persuasive information travels directly from the news media to voters (arrow 3) as they watch the news or read the newspapers. As just mentioned, some of what people see, hear, and read in the news originates with the news and some is filtered by the news, coming indirectly from candidate messages (arrow 1) via arrow 2. Some information from candidate messages (arrow 4) and some information from the news (arrow 5) go to some people (the public) and, then, in political discussion, it moves to (other) voters (arrow 6). This process is very complicated, and, if an accurate diagram were constructed for several voters, it could be much more detailed (telling which television spots, debates, or other messages were seen; telling which news programs or newspapers were read). The figure for each voter would be a little different, because no one sees exactly the same television commercials and television news, reads the same newspapers and newspaper articles, or has exactly the same political discussions as any other voter. So, figure 14.1 shows the overall flow of persuasive information, the potential information sources available to voters.

Keep in mind that this diagram is about messages (information sources), not about voters. Voters vary in how much attention they pay to campaigns and in which messages they hear, read, or watch. Some people are "political junkies," who actively seek out information about the candidates and their policy positions. Some people are turned off by politics and actively avoid exposure to political information. We believe that most voters are probably in the middle between these two extremes, learning about the candidates through information that happens to come their way, usually without going out of their way either to seek or to avoid political information. Figure 14.1 is about the major potential sources of information. Different voters will be exposed to different combinations of messages.

A great deal of research has documented the effects from candidate messages emanating from sources like television spots (Benoit 1999; 2001) and debates (Benoit, McKinney, and Holbert 2001). Which sources of information (media) have the most influence on voters? Given the complexity of the campaign as depicted in figure 14.1, we want to stress the studies that compare more than one information source. Two studies, one on the 1972 presidential campaign (Patterson and McClure 1976) and one on the 1984 presidential campaign (Kern 1989), found that four times as many voters learned more issue information (e.g. a candidate's stand on education or taxes) from television spots than from the news. Brians and Wattenberg (1996) reported that presidential television spots created more issue knowledge than watching television news or reading newspapers during the 1992 campaign. Holbert, Benoit, Hansen, and Wen (2002) examined the effects of multiple information sources in the 1996 presidential election. Political advertising, political discussion, and the first presidential debate, all had significant effects on issue knowledge; watching television news and reading newspapers did not have a significant influence. Finally, Benoit, Hansen, and Holbert (2007) studied the 2000 presidential campaign. They found that television news, televised spots, debates, and newspaper reading, but not political discussion or the Internet, contributed to issue knowledge.

What can we conclude from these studies of six different presidential campaigns? First, the impact of these information sources on issue knowledge appears to vary from campaign to campaign. This seems reasonable, because the quality (of the debates, of television spots, of news coverage, or of other messages or media) probably varies from one election to another. We should not expect – and we do not find – that the same messages or media are equally effective every year. This kind of fluctuation from campaign to campaign is particularly important given the fact that new media, like cable television with its news networks and the Internet, are emerging and becoming more important with the passage of time. Still, there are some consistent patterns in this research. It may seem odd, but, in every one of these campaigns, television commercials were important persuasive influences on issue knowledge. Newspaper, television news and political discussion emerged only once as important factors. While debates were found to be significant influences in only two campaigns, these were the only campaigns in which these studies looked for possible effects from debates. So one conclusion is that television ads and debates are important and fairly consistent persuasive influences on voter knowledge, but the news (and political discussion) appears to be less important.

The fact that news programs do not have a significant impact on issue knowledge may be another surprise. However, news media have a well-documented tendency to focus more on reporting what is termed the "horse race": who has raised the most money, who is ahead in the polls, which states are being contested and which states are being conceded, who will be allowed to debate (e.g. in 2000 Ralph Nader was not included in the presidential debates). These questions are news, but they do not help voters decide who will be a better president (see e.g. Lichter and Noyes 1995; Patterson 1980; Robinson and Sheehan 1983; Farnsworth and Lichter 2003).

With this understanding of the basic sources of information available to voters, and this understanding of the importance of candidate messages like television spots and debates, we can turn to an understanding of the nature of presidential campaign messages.

The Functions of Political Campaign Messages

Political campaign communication has one clear goal: to persuade voters that one candidate is a better choice than his or her opponent(s). There are a few exceptions to this rule (candidates who run not because they believe they can win but in order to champion a cause). However, serious candidates campaign so as to attract enough votes to win the election.

Candidates do not have to persuade voters that they are perfect. When two candidates contest an office, voters only have three options: to vote for candidate A, to vote for candidate B, or not to vote at all (actually, they can write in another candidate's name, but write-in candidates almost never win). This means that candidate A does not have to be perfect; it is enough to appear to be better than, or preferable to, candidate B (and candidate B only has to appear the same). Furthermore, candidate A does not have to persuade everyone that he or she is a better choice than candidate B; the candidate who convinces a majority of those who actually vote in the election will win. Because elections are comparative – a matter of deciding which candidate is a better choice – it follows that candidates have three options to attract votes: acclaim (self-praise), attack (criticizing opponents), and defense (rejecting attacks).

Acclaims: self-praise

An **acclaim** is essentially a boast about a candidate's own positive qualities. Ordinarily, people have some norms of modesty which suggest that we should not acclaim ourselves as much as to risk appearing to be braggarts (Benoit 1997). However, politicians are expected to "blow their own horns," so voters will be persuaded of their strengths or positive qualities. For example, in the 2000 presidential campaign, television spots provided several instances of acclaims. One television advertisement for Governor George W. Bush ran: "Why vote for George W. Bush? Because he believes in family. Because he supports education." Here are two reasons to vote for Bush: He believes in family and he supports education. Most voters would agree that family and education are important and should be supported by the president, so these statements are clearly acclaiming some of Bush's positive qualities. Vice-President Al Gore also praised himself in his television spots:

> Al Gore has fought to put 100,000 new teachers in the classroom; for tougher standards to make sure our children are learning; to give parents more choice in choosing public schools. Now, for the first time, reading scores in the key grades of 4th, 8th and 12th are going up across America.

This commercial also discussed education, detailing several steps he had taken (new teachers, tougher standards, more choice) to improve it and the subsequent results (reading scores going up). Again, these are aspects which voters are likely to view as positive. Acclaims emphasize a candidate's pros, advantages, strengths. They persuade by giving people reasons to vote for the candidate who is being acclaimed.

Attacks: criticism of opponent

A second function of political campaign discourse is to **attack**, persuading voters about an alleged weakness or drawback of an opponent. In 2000, this television ad attacked Gore: "Al Gore's prescription plan forces seniors into a government-run HMO [Health Maintenance Organization]." This passage attacks Gore's prescription drug proposal, saying that it would put senior citizens into HMOs. Many voters dislike HMOs and would not want to be forced to use them for health care. This attack could raise serious questions about Gore among voters.

The following excerpt from another ad attacks Bush's social security proposal for promising the same money to two different groups: "Bush promises the same trillion dollars to younger workers and the elderly at the same time." These are charges that would probably create an unfavorable impression of Bush. We know that we can only spend a certain sum of money in one place, so these contradictory promises cannot both be fulfilled. Thus attacks point out weaknesses, disadvantages, or problems with a candidate: They persuade by giving reasons for the audience to vote against one's opponent.

Defenses: responses to attacks

The third function, **defending**, is to respond to an attack, attempting to refute or reject it. For example, the following television spot defends Gore against Bush's attack on his prescription drug plan. Remember that Bush charged that Gore's proposal put senior citizens into HMOs: "Newspapers say George Bush's prescription drug ad misrepresents the facts. In fact, Al Gore's plan covers all seniors through Medicare, not an HMO." This utterance is designed to refute Bush's attack (that Gore proposed forcing senior citizens to join HMOs). If it is persuasive, it should repair the damage done to Gore's eligibility by Bush's attack. Similarly, an ad supporting Bush rejects Gore's criticism of his social security plan, according to which Bush would have promised to spend the same trillion dollars for younger and older workers: "The press calls Gore's Social Security attacks "nonsense." If voters agree that Gore's attacks are wrong ("nonsense"), this defense should restore Bush's reputation with those who were persuaded by Gore's attack. So defenses reject or refute attacks. They are intended to reduce or eliminate the damage inflicted by an attack.

These three functions are intended to persuade voters to support one candidate over another. They work like an informal version of the cost–benefit analysis. Candidates attempt to persuade voters by stressing their own benefits (through acclaims), by exposing their opponent's weaknesses or costs (through attacks), and by reducing their own alleged costs (by defending their image against attacks). The candidate who persuades voters that he or she is preferable to the opponents by using these functions is likely to receive most votes.

Topics of Political Campaign Messages

It is fairly common to discuss three bases for voting decisions: political party, policy stands, and character. It is rare for a candidate to switch political parties, so the primary ways to appeal to voters in a political campaign message are to discuss policy (that is, issues) and character (that is, image). In other words, political candidates attempt to persuade voters that their policy proposals and their character are preferable to the policy and character of their opponent(s). The three functions just identified – acclaim, attack, defense – can occur at either policy or character level.

Policy issues

Candidates discuss **policy** (government action and problems that might be addressed by government action) whenever they address issues like education, taxes, inflation, the environment, or foreign policy. The debates of the 2000 presidential campaign provide illustrations of these topics. In the first debate, Gore attempted to persuade voters to prefer him over Bush by acclaiming his policy proposals:

> I will balance the budget every year. I will pay down the national debt. I will put Medicare and Social Security in a lockbox and protect them. And I will cut taxes for middle-class families.

It should be obvious that a balanced budget, the national debt, Medicare, social security, and taxes – all concern policy. Similarly, Bush attacked Gore's policy proposals in the following excerpt from that debate:

> Under Vice-President Gore's plan, he's going to grow the federal government in the largest increase since Lyndon Baines Johnson in 1965, and we're talking about a massive government, folks. We're talking about adding to – or increasing 200 new programs – 200 programs 20,000 new bureaucrats.

Again, this passage concerns governmental policy, attempting to persuade voters to reject Gore and his plans to increase the size of the federal bureaucracy.

Character: image

At other times, the candidates discussed their **character**, which refers to the personal characteristics of the candidates (e.g. honesty, compassion, leadership, values). President Bush tried to persuade voters of Gore's drawbacks in the first debate, by declaring that "It's fuzzy math. It's a scaring – trying to scare people in the voting booth. Obviously tonight we're going to hear some phony numbers." The phrases "fuzzy math" and "phony numbers" suggest that Gore is attempting to deceive voters. Accusing him of trying to scare the voters is another criticism of his character. In the second debate, Gore's inaccuracies were discussed. The following statement from Gore sounded very humble, trying to persuade voters to adopt a positive view of his character:

> I can't promise that I will never get another detail wrong. I can promise you that I will try not to anymore. But I will promise you this, with all the confidence in – in my heart and in the world, that I will do my best, if I'm elected president, I'll work my heart out, to get the big things right for the American people.

The Vice-President admits to making a mistake and promises to work hard for the American people. These second two messages focus on character; neither actually discusses policy (e.g. taxation, social security, national defense). Thus candidates discuss both policy and character in their campaign messages as they work to persuade voters to prefer them over their opponent.

The Nature of Political Campaign Messages

Campaigns move through three major phases. First, candidates compete for their party's nomination in the primary campaign. Then the Republican and Democratic parties announce and celebrate their nominee in the nominating conventions.

The general election campaign occurs in the Fall (traditionally starting after Labor Day) and features the Republican and Democratic nominees, as well as some minor party candidates (e.g. in 1992 and 1996, Ross Perot represented the Reform Party; in 2000, Ralph Nader was the Green Party candidate). A great deal of research has investigated into the nature of presidential campaign messages: there have been studies of presidential primary debates (Benoit, Pier, Brazeal, McHale, Klyukovski, and Airne 2002), of presidential primary television spots (Benoit 1999, 2001), of convention nomination acceptance addresses (Benoit, Wells, Pier, and Blaney 1999; Benoit, McHale, Hansen, Pier, and McGuire, in press), of general presidential debates (Benoit and Brazeal 2002; Benoit and Harthcock 1999; Wells 1999), and of general presidential television spots (Benoit 1999, 2001). We will first discuss the frequency with which candidates use these functions (acclaims, attacks, defenses) to persuade voters. Then we will discuss the frequency of the topics (policy, character) of those messages.

Functions of political campaign messages

Table 14.1 reports the relative frequency of the three functions of presidential campaign messages. Despite the impression held by many, presidential campaign messages are not mostly negative. In every message form, acclaims are most common, attacks come second, and defenses are the least common function. Acclaims have no drawback as a persuasive approach: They tell the candidate's strengths or benefits and, in general, are inoffensive (of course, false or ridiculous acclaims can backfire). However, one disadvantage to attacks as a persuasive function is that many voters say they do not like mud-slinging or negative campaigning (Merritt 1984; Stewart 1975). This encourages candidates to avoid attacking too often. Defense, the least common persuasive function, has several drawbacks. First, it makes a candidate look reactive (defensive) rather than proactive. Second, defending oneself against an attack probably takes a candidate "off-message." Usually, attacks occur on topics that favor the attacker rather than the target of attack. Responding to an attack probably means that the defending candidate is spending less time on the issues that favor him or her. Finally, it is impossible to respond to an attack without identifying it. There is a danger that the defending candidate might remind or even inform some voters of a potential weakness. So it makes sense for acclaims to outnumber attacks, which in turn are more frequent than defenses.

Table 14.1 Functions of presidential campaign messages, 1948–2000 (%)

	Acclaims	Attacks	Defenses
Primary debates	68	28	4
Primary TV spots	71	28	1
Acceptances	75	24	1
General debates	55	35	10
General TV spots	60	39	1

There are also some differences between campaign messages. First, persuasive campaign messages in the primary are more positive (have more acclaims and fewer attacks) than general campaign messages. This is true for debates (68 percent acclaims in the primary, 55 percent in the general campaign; 28 percent attacks in the primary, 35 percent attacks in the general campaign) and for television spots (71 percent acclaims in the primary, 60 percent in the general campaign; 28 percent attacks in the primary, 39 percent attacks in the general campaign).

There are several reasons why persuasion in the primary campaign, generally, should employ fewer attacks and more acclaims. First, the candidates' opponents are the other members of their own political party. For example, in the 2000 campaign, George W. Bush, John McCain, Steve Forbes, Alan Keyes, Orrin Hatch, and Gary Bauer contended for the Republican nomination. However, because they are all Republicans or conservatives, there are fewer differences between these candidates in the primary (and more differences between Bush and Al Gore in the general campaign). Fewer differences means fewer opportunities to attack.

Second, each candidate knows that, if he/she wins the nomination, he/she will want the support of the other candidates. That is, Bush knew he would want the support of John McCain (and the other candidates) and the support of the Republican voters who preferred McCain. This is a reason to moderate one's attacks. If Bush attacked the other Republican candidates too viciously, he might forfeit their support, and the support of their adherents, in the Fall.

Another difference we can see from table 14.1 is that campaign persuasion in debates had more defenses than the other message forms. Defenses formed 1 percent of both television spots and acceptance addresses, but 4 percent of primary debate statements and 10 percent of general debate remarks. Why would defenses be more frequent in debates?

First, it is surely easier to resist the temptation to respond to an attack (to defend oneself) when reading the script of an acceptance address or doing repeated takes of a television spot. But in a debate, when one has just been attacked, candidates probably feel a natural urge to respond. Second, in a debate there is no need to worry that responding to an attack will inform or remind the audience about it: If the audience was paying attention, then they definitely heard the attack. Thus defenses are less common in campaign persuasion than acclaims or attacks, but more common in debates than other message forms.

Topics of political campaign messages

Table 14.2 summarizes the results of previous research into the topics of presidential campaign discourse. Many people think that campaigns are all about image, not about substance (or policy). However, we can see that every persuasive message form emphasizes policy over character. General debates are most heavily tilted toward policy. Three quarters of the statements and comments in debates concerns policy; only one fourth concerns character. Primary television spots are almost evenly split: 53 percent policy and 47 percent character.

Table 14.2   Topics of presidential campaign messages, 1948–2000 (%)

	Policy	*Character*
Primary debates	63	37
Primary TV spots	53	47
Acceptances	55	45
General debates	75	25
General TV spots	61	39

Why would policy comments predominate in presidential campaign messages? Public opinion poll data from every campaign from 1976 until 2000 reveal that more voters claim that the most important factor in determining their vote for the president is policy, not character (see Hansen and Benoit 2002). Presumably presidential candidates are aware of voter sentiments (candidates do extensive polling) and have adapted their messages to reflect voter interests.

A second pattern that emerges in table 14.2 is that, even though every persuasive message form emphasizes policy, general campaign messages discuss policy more, and character less, than primary campaign messages. There are two reasons for this difference. First, in the primary campaign, candidates are less well known, which means they need to introduce themselves to voters (discuss their character). For example, in 2000, George W. Bush and Al Gore, who ran in the general campaign, were better known that other candidates, who ran (and lost) in the primary campaign: Gary Bauer, Orrin Hatch, or Alan Keyes. Furthermore, even Bush and Gore were probably better known to most voters in the general campaign than in the primary. The fact that candidates are not as well known to voters in the primary campaign encourages them to discuss character more than in the general campaign.

Furthermore, the primary campaign pits members of the same political party against one another. That is, in the Republican primary, George Bush's opponent was not Al Gore; Bush ran against Bauer, Hatch, Keyes, Steve Forbes, and John McCain. Similarly, Al Gore ran against Bill Bradley, not against George Bush, in the Democratic primary. In general, there are more similarities in the policy positions of candidates from the same party than of candidates from different parties. This means there are more policy differences between candidates in the general than in the primary campaign, and therefore more opportunities to discuss policy in the persuasive messages of the general campaign.

Incumbent and challenger party messages

An important distinction between presidential candidates is that some are **incumbents,** who belong to the party in control of the White House, whereas other candidates are **challengers,** candidates who seek to take control of the Oval Office from the other party. Sometimes the incumbent party candidate is the president, seeking re-election or a second term in office. For example, in 1996 Bill Clinton was president and he ran for re- election as incumbent. In other cases, another political party member – usually the Vice-President – is the incumbent party candidate. In 2000, Vice-President Al Gore ran for election as the incumbent party candidate. However, incumbency is typically only a factor in the general election campaign. Oftentimes the incumbent is not challenged in the primary (no one contested the Democratic nomination in 1996). Furthermore, in the most recent campaign, it is not clear who was the incumbent in the Republican primary (George W. Bush was the front-runner, but he was not an incumbent). Because incumbency is most meaningful in the general campaign, table 14.3 does not include primary debates or primary television spots.

Table 14.3 reveals that, in all three message forms, incumbents persuade with more acclaims and defenses and challengers persuade with more attacks. In accept-ance addresses, given at the nominating convention to "kick off" the general campaign, incumbent party candidates acclaimed more than the challengers did (79 percent to 70 percent) and defended themselves more often too (1 percent to 0.3 percent); whereas the challengers attacked more often than the incumbents (30 per-cent to 19 percent). In (general) television spots, the incumbents acclaimed more (66 percent to 54 percent) and defended themselves more (2 percent to 1 percent); the challengers attacked more than the incumbents (45 percent to 33 percent). In (general) debates, the incumbents acclaimed more (57 percent to 53 percent) and defended themselves more (1 percent to 7 percent); the challengers, once again, attacked more than the incumbents did (40 percent to 31 percent).

These findings can also be explained. Incumbents have a record in the office being sought in the election. Candidates seeking re-election, like President Bill Clinton in 1996, have been running the government for most of the past four years and defi-nitely have established a record in office. Even vice-presidents, like Al Gore in 2000, tend to run on records like the Clinton–Gore record from 1992 to 2000. This record is an important resource. However, it is used differently by the two candidates. Incumbent candidates, of course, look for bright spots in the record and acclaim their successes when persuading the voters; challengers seek unsolved problems and

Table 14.3   Incumbency and message function (%)

	Acclaims	Attacks	Defenses
Acceptances			
Incumbent	79	19	1
Challenger	70	30	0.3
General TV Spots			
Incumbent	66	33	2
Challenger	54	45	1
General Debates			
Incumbent	57	31	12
Challenger	53	40	7

attack the incumbent's failures when they persuade the voters. So, incumbent party candidates have records in office which can support acclaims from the incumbents and attacks from their challengers.

Of course, the challenger party candidate has a record of some sort as well. In 2000, George W. Bush was the Governor of Texas, just as challengers Clinton (1992), Reagan (1980), and Carter (1976) had been governors. In 1996, challenger Bob Dole was the Senate majority leader. While these candidates acclaimed their own records in office and their incumbent opponents attacked their record, a record in the White House is the most relevant and most powerful evidence (for example, governors have no foreign policy experience to speak of). This means that the record favors acclaims from the incumbent and attacks from the challenger.

Furthermore, some voters tend to display inertia; they think: "If it isn't broken don't fix it" or "Don't change horses in the middle of the stream." They need to be persuaded to switch from the incumbent party to the challenger party. That reason to change can come from attacks by the challenger, reasons to "throw the rascals out of office." So incumbents tend to acclaim more than challengers, whereas challengers attack more than incumbents. Finally, incumbents defend themselves more than challengers do, because they have more opportunities to defend themselves, given that challengers attack more than incumbents.

Planning the Political Campaign

Candidates and their advisors need to make three key decisions. They rely heavily on their understanding of voters, which is reinforced with polling to the extent the campaign can afford polls.

Who is the target audience?

It is important to realize that a candidate for elective office does not have to persuade everyone, or to win every vote cast in the election. Winning a majority of the votes (or a plurality, if there are more than two candidates) is sufficient. In fact, as a practical matter, it is not possible to win every vote. For example, in the 2000 presidential campaign, George W. Bush favored allowing some people the opportunity to invest from their social security funds in the stock market, whereas Al Gore did not support this proposal. Some voters prefer one option and others prefer the other. Neither candidate could satisfy every voter. Our world has limited resources and people have different goals or priorities, so it is unreasonable to expect that a single candidate could please everyone. However, in our system of government it is not necessary for political candidates to persuade every citizen. In fact, because some people are not eligible to vote and others chose not to participate in the election, the candidate only needs to persuade the largest group among those who actually vote. This means that candidates can concentrate on trying to persuade only certain segments of the population.

What is the message?

Each campaign should develop a campaign message. The overall persuasive message should stress the policy positions and character of the candidate. The policy positions should be selected so as to attract voters and be consistent with the candidate's political party and persona. For example, in 2000, one candidate favored private school vouchers and the other opposed them. Private school vouchers are more consistent with the Republican than the Democratic Party, and it made perfect sense that Bush supported vouchers while Gore did not. Similarly, Republicans are more likely to favor larger tax cuts than the Democrats, so it was reasonable that Bush campaigned for tax cuts for all, whereas Gore wanted to target tax cuts to the middle class. One's policy positions should be consistent with that candidate's persona, including his/her political party.

Occasionally, a candidate can attempt to "poach" an issue from the other party. It was unusual that the Republican Bush spent as much time discussing education in 2000 as he did; this is traditionally considered a Democratic issue. In 1992, Democrat Bill Clinton discussed moving people from welfare to work, even though welfare reform is often thought to be a Republican position. If a candidate advocates too many positions that "belong" to the other party, this could create problems (voters might wonder if the candidate had any core values or was "really" a Republican or "really" a Democrat).

Candidates should also consider what they want to stress about their character in order to persuade voters. Character is important for at least two reasons. First, we know from chapter 3 that credibility can influence the persuasiveness of messages from candidates. Second, many voters consider character a reason to vote for or against a candidate. For example, Governor Bush in 2000 could have stressed his experience in government (as governor), or he could have campaigned as a "Washington outsider," because he had never held office in the federal government. Should a candidate stress that he or she cares about "regular folks," or that he or she is a hard worker? Should a candidate stress morality or honesty? Of course, these traits are not contradictory: one can be compassionate, hard working, moral, and honest. However, a candidate may choose to stress some aspects of character more than others.

It is important for the candidate to remain "on message." This is more easily accomplished in carefully prepared materials, like television spots or speeches delivered with the aid of a Teleprompter. However, in debates, interviews, talk show appearances, or press conferences, questions and statements from others may tempt a candidate to address other topics. The candidate's "message" is developed according to the belief that this group of topics (policy stands and character traits) has the potential to persuade the most voters. Straying too far off message, or staying off message for too long, undermines the benefits of having a message. Candidates do not want to create an unpleasant impression (ignoring a question due to rudeness or stupidity), but they should make an effort to stay on message.

A campaign may decide – particularly if it lags behind opponent(s) in public opinion polls – to revise the candidate's message. This should not be done lightly, because it might appear that the candidate is inconsistent or pandering to shifts in public opinion. However, at times, a campaign needs to adjust its message.

What is the optimal mix of media?

The modern campaign makes use of many different media, including television spots, debates, radio spots, speeches, printed brochures distributed or mailed to voters, webpages, talk show appearances, buttons, yard signs, and bumper stickers. While there is certainly overlap here, none of these media reaches precisely the same audience. Clearly these media vary in cost. Some are ephemeral, like speeches or appearances on Oprah or Letterman (some campaign speeches are preserved on the candidates' webpages, but it is unlikely that voters will encounter a speech more than once). Television and radio ads usually are broadcast repeatedly, which means that voters can see or hear them multiple times (although, once the campaign stops paying to air an ad, it will disappear). The campaign has to decide which topics to include in which messages at what time. When – and with which speeches, which advertisements, which brochures – should education, or taxes, or the environment, or prescription drug coverage, be mentioned? Should early speeches and ads focus more on education and less on taxes than later messages? How much detail should the message contain? For example, should the candidate devote an entire 30 second ad (not that long!) to taxes, or briefly mention taxes, education, and social security in one spot? In some instances all voters have the opportunity to see the same message (e.g. nationally televised debates or talk show appearances, webpages). In other cases (e.g. direct mail, television, or radio spots), the campaign must decide when and where to send the message and how often to repeat it.

Evaluating Political Campaign Messages

We want to end this chapter with some advice about how you should evaluate political campaign messages. Few of you will be political candidates yourselves, but almost everyone who reads this book will be eligible to vote. Our elected officials make decisions about taxes and airport security and many other matters that affect us personally, so it is in our best interest to make a good decision. If nothing else, the 2000 campaign between Governor George W. Bush and Vice-President Al Gore, with the recounts and the close vote in Florida, taught us that elections can be incredibly close and that every vote can count. First, we encourage you not to avoid candidate messages. Some people prefer to learn about candidates from the news media. One advantage of the news is that it is more objective than the candidates themselves. However, as discussed earlier, the news tends to focus on reporting the campaign as a horse race. You should keep this in mind as you read, watch, or listen to campaign news, to try to find information that will allow you to compare and contrast the candidates. The candidates discuss policy more often than most people think. Of course, candidates are not objective: They are trying to maximize their benefits and minimize their costs. This is a reason to listen to both candidates (or to more than two). Each candidate has an incentive to identify the opponents' weaknesses and to puncture unrealistic claims made by them. In a very real sense, we can compare a political campaign with a trial. The competing attorneys present the best case possible – identifying weaknesses in the opponent's case – so that the judge or jury can decide. So, too, voters should listen to, or read about, both candidates to make an intelligent vote choice. Notice that this advice assumes that you will use central processing for campaign messages!

Second, take some time to reflect on what matters most to you in your vote choice. We identify five questions to help you make an informed voting decision.

Box 14.1 How to evaluate a political campaign

1 Which matters most to you when deciding how to vote, policy or character (or both)?
2 If Policy matters to you, which issue(s) is(are) most important to you (e.g. taxation, education, health care, national security and terrorism)?
3 If Character matters to you, which aspect(s) of character is(are) most important to you (e.g. honesty, compassion, morals)?
4 How do the candidates compare on the same grounds (i.e. if taxes are important, you need to know what each candidate will do about taxes to make an informed decision)?
5 Can the candidates accomplish their goals (e.g. do they have the ability and/or experience to get legislation passed in congress, to negotiate with foreign leaders)?

Some voters believe that character is the most important factor, others believe that their vote should go to the candidate with the most acceptable policy proposals (some consider both to be equally important). Once you decide what matters the most for you, that choice can be refined further. If character is important, reflect on what that means to you: honesty, or compassion, or morality, or some other personality trait (or a combination of traits). If you value policy, consider which issues matter most to you: education, taxes, national security, the environment (or several issues). Once you have decided what is most important to you, compare both candidates to see which one is preferable on what matters most to you.

It should be clear that you can make the best decision when you know the same thing about both candidates, so you can compare them. For example, if you are choosing a car, it is very difficult to decide when you have one set of answers about one car (gas mileage, leg room, price) and a different set of answers about the other car (cargo room, color, safety features). So, too, with political candidates: to make an informed choice, you need to know about the morality (or honesty, compassion, and so on) of both candidates, and/or about the environmental policies (or social security proposals, economic policies, and so on) of both candidates. Also, as noted earlier, learning about both candidates can be important because each one may try to exaggerate strengths and gloss over weaknesses. But the opponent may puncture inflated claims and point out weaknesses. Knowing what both candidates have to say can provide a more complete and accurate picture than listening to only one.

We are not saying that everyone must become a political "junkie," watching, reading, and discussing nothing but politics. However, we urge you to make the effort to decide how to vote on the basis of what matters most to you and to make a comparison between the candidates. Keep in mind that the news media, with its emphasis on horse race, may not inform you about the candidates as much as you might think. You may want to watch a debate or visit the candidates' website or seek information elsewhere, but you should spend at least some time on this important decision. Your vote could make a difference, and governmental policies affect us all. Use the persuasive messages aimed at you to make an informed choice at the polls.

Glossary

Acclaim: praise or statement about the positive qualities of a candidate.
Attack: exposure or statement about the weaknesses or drawbacks of a candidate.
Challenger: candidate who seeks to win an office currently held by the opponent.
Character: the personal characteristics of a candidate.
Defense: a statement that refutes an attack on a candidate.
Incumbent: candidate who holds the office and is seeking re-election.
Policy: governmental action or problems that might be addressed by governmental action.

References

Ajzen, I. (2006). "Theory of planned behavior." <http://www.people.umass.edu/aizen/tpb.html> (accessed 8/17/06).

Ajzen, I., and Fishbein, M. (1980). *Understanding Attitudes and Predicting Social Behavior.* Englewood Cliffs, NJ: Prentice-Hall.

Alan Guttmacher Institute (1999, September). "Teen sex and pregnancy." <http://www.agi-usa.org/pubs/fb_teen_sex.html> (accessed 4/7/03).

Allen, M. (1991). "Comparing the persuasiveness of one-sided and two-sided messages using meta-analysis." *Western Journal of Speech Communication*, 15, 390–404.

Allen, M. (1993). "Determining the persuasiveness of one and two-sided messages." In M. Allen and R. Preiss (eds), *Prospects and Precautions in the Use of Meta-Analysis* (pp. 101–25). Dubuque, IA: Brown and Benchmark.

Allen, M., and Preiss, R. W. (1997). "Comparing the persuasiveness of narrative and statistical evidence using meta-analysis." *Communication Research Reports*, 14, 125–31.

Alm, R. (2002, October 29). "Surveys show that ethics crisis extends to nation's classroom." *Kansas City Star.* <http://www.kansascity.com/mld/kansascity/business/438924.htm>.

American Diabetes Association (n.d.). "Facts and Figures." <http://www.diabetes.org:80/main/application/commercewf?origin=*.jsp andevent=link(home)> (accessed 7/26/02).

Andrews, J. C., and Shimp, T. A. (1990). "Effects of involvement, argument strength, and source characteristics on central and peripheral processing in advertising." *Psychology and Marketing*, 7, 195–214.

Arens, W. F. (1999). *Contemporary Advertising.* Boston: Irwin/McGraw Hill.

Aristotle. (1954). *The Rhetoric,* trans. W. R. Roberts. New York: Random House, Modern Library.

Aronson, E. (1969). "The theory of cognitive dissonance: A current perspective." In L. Berkowitz (ed.), *Advances in Experimental Social Psychology* (vol. 4). New York: Academic Press.

Astor, A. (2001, April 4). "Top 10 meals coming to McDonald's." <http://dir.salon.com/people/satire/2001/04/04/mchaggis/index.html> (accessed 8/17/02).

"Athletes claimed fake injuries" (1999, July 10). *Columbia Daily Tribune*, p. A9.

Bagdikian, B. H. (2000). *The Media Monopoly* (6th edn). Boston, MA: Beacon Press.

Baron, R. M., and Kenny, D. A. (1986). "The moderator–mediator variable distinction in social psychological research: Conceptual, strategic, and statistical considerations." *Journal of Personality and Social Psychology*, 51, 1173–82.

Benoit, P. J. (1997). *Telling the Success Story: Acclaiming and Disclaiming Discourse*. Albany: State University of New York Press.

Benoit, W. L. (1987). "Argument and credibility appeals in persuasion." *Southern Speech Communication Journal*, 52, 181–97.

Benoit, W. L. (1991a). "A cognitive response analysis of source credibility." In B. Dervin and M. J. Voigt (eds), *Progress in Communication Sciences* (vol. 10, pp. 1–19). Norwood, NJ: Ablex.

Benoit, W. L. (1991b). "Two tests of the mechanism of inoculation theory." *Southern Communication Journal*, 56, 219–29.

Benoit, W. L. (1999). *Seeing Spots: A Functional Analysis of Presidential Television Advertisements from 1952–1996*. New York: Praeger.

Benoit, W. L. (2001). "The functional approach to presidential television spots: Acclaiming, attacking, defending 1952–2000." *Communication Studies*, 52, 109–26.

Benoit, W. L., and Brazeal, L. M. (2002). "A functional analysis of the 1988 Bush–Dukakis presidential debates." *Argumentation and Advocacy*, 38, 219–33.

Benoit, W. L., and Harthcock, A. (1999). "Functions of the Great Debates: Acclaims, attacks, and defense in the 1960 presidential debates." *Communication Monographs*, 66, 341–57.

Benoit, W. L., and Kennedy, K. A. (1999). "On reluctant testimony." *Communication Quarterly*, 47, 367–87.

Benoit, W. L., and Wells, W. T. (1996). *Candidates in Conflict: Persuasive Attack and Defense in the 1992 Presidential Debates*. Tuscaloosa: University of Alabama Press.

Benoit, W. L., Blaney, J. R., and Pier, P. M. (1998). *Campaign '96: A Functional Analysis of Acclaiming, Attacking, and Defending*. New York: Praeger.

Benoit, W. L., Hansen, G. J., and Holbert, R. L. (2002). *Effects of Information Sources on Issue Knowledge and Issue Salience in the 2000 Presidential Campaign*. New Orleans, LA: NCA.

Benoit, W. L., Hansen, G. J., and Holbert, R. L. (2004). "Presidential campaigns and democracy." *Mass Communication and Society*, 7, 177–90.

Benoit, W. L., McKinney, M. S., and Holbert, R. L. (2001). "Beyond learning and persona: Extending the scope of presidential debate effects." *Communication Monographs*, 68, 259–73.

Benoit, W. L., Wells, W. T., Pier, P. M., and Blaney, J. R. (1999). "Acclaiming, attacking, and defending in nomination convention acceptance addresses, 1960–1996." *Quarterly Journal of Speech*, 85, 247–67.

Benoit, W. L., McHale, J. P., Hansen, G. J., Pier, P. M., and McGuire, J. P. (in press). *Campaign 2000: A Functional Analysis of Presidential Campaign Discourse*. Lanhan, NH: Rowman and Littlefield.

Benoit, W. L., Pier, P. M., Brazeal, L. M., McHale, J. P., Klyukovksi, A., and Airne, D. (2002). *The Primary Decision: A Functional Analysis of Debates in Presidential Primaries*. Westport, CT: Praeger.

Berscheid, E. (1985). "Interpersonal attraction." In G. Lindsey and E. Aronson (eds), *Handbook of Social Psychology* (3rd edn, vol. 2, pp. 413–84). New York: Random House.

Berscheid, E., and Walster, E. (1974). "Physical attractiveness." In L. Berkowitz (ed.), *Advances in Experimental Social Psychology* (vol. 7, pp. 157–215). New York: Academic Press.

Black, J. W. (1998, December 8). "Heroin use going up among US teen-agers." *Orange County Register*. <http://www.mapinc.org/drugnews/v98.n1139.a05.html> (accessed 4/7/03).

Bochner, S., and Insko, C. A. (1966). "Communicator discrepancy, source credibility, and opinion change." *Journal of Personality and Social Psychology*, 4, 614–21.

Boninger, D. S., Brannon, L. A., and Brock, T. C. (1993). "Effects of transmitter tuning on attitude change persistence: An examination of alternative explanations." *Psychological Science*, 4, 211–13.

Boninger, D. S., Brock, T. C., Cook, T. D., Gruder, C. L., and Romer, D. (1990). "Discovery of reliable attitude change persistence resulting from a transmitter tuning set." *Psychological Science,* 1, 268–71.

Bramucci, R. (2003, September 19). "Cheating prevention in college classrooms." <http://www.tcc.cc.fl.us/about_tcc/academic_affairs/division_of_library_services/faculty_library_resources/cheating_prevention_in_college_classrooms>.

Brehm, J. W., and Cohen, A. R. (1962). *Explorations in Cognitive Dissonance.* New York: Wiley.

Brians, C. L., and Wattenberg, M. P. (1996). "Campaign issue knowledge and salience: Comparing reception from TV commercials, TV news, and newspapers." *American Journal of Political Science,* 40, 172–93.

Bryant, J., and Zillmann, D. (1989). "Using humor to promote learning in the classroom." *Journal of Children in Contemporary Society,* 20, 49–78.

Burghart, T. (2003, May 29). "Suspended New York Times reporter resigns." *Chicago Sun-Times.* <http://www.suntimes.com/output/news/cst-nws-nyt-129.html>.

Burke, K. (1966). *Language as Symbolic Action: Essays on Life, Literature, and Mthod.* Berkeley, CA: University of California.

Burke, K. (1989). "Poem." In Simons, H. W., and Melia, T. (eds), *The Legacy of Kenneth Burke* (p. 263). Madison: University of Wisconsin.

Bush, B. (1990, June 1). "Text of Mrs. Bush's remarks at Wellesley College commencement." <http://bushlibrary.tamu.edu/biographies/firstlady/wellesleyspeech.html>.

Cacioppo, J. T., and Petty, R. E. (1985). "Central and peripheral routes to persuasion: The role of message repetition." In L. F. Alwitt and A. A. Mitchell (eds), *Psychological Processes and Advertising Effects: Theory, Research, and Application* (pp. 91–111). Hillsdale, NJ: Lawrence Erlbaum.

Cacioppo, J. T., Petty, R. E., and Kao, C. F. (1984). "The efficient assessment of need for cognition." *Journal of Personality Assessment,* 48, 306–7.

Cacioppo, J. T., Petty, R. E., and Morris, K. (1983). "Effects of need for cognition on message evaluation, recall, and persuasion." *Journal of Personality and Social Psychology,* 45, 805–818.

Cacioppo, J. T., Petty, R. E., Feinstein, J. A., and Jarvis, W. B. G. (1996). "Dispositional differences in cognitive motivation: The life and times of individuals varying in need for cognition." *Psychological Bulletin,* 119, 197–253.

Calder, B. J., Insko, C. A., and Yandell, B. (1974). "The relation of cognitive and memorial processes to persuasion in a simulated jury trial." *Journal of Applied Social Psychology,* 4, 62–93.

Callahan, N. (1997, June 15). "San Francisco drug peace rally speech." <http://www.november.org/razorwire/rzold/03/0303.html>.

Cantor, J., and Venus, P. (1980). "The effect of humor on recall of a radio advertisement." *Journal of Broadcasting,* 24, 13–22.

Chaiken, S. (1979). "Communicator physical attractiveness and persuasion." *Journal of Personality and Social Psychology,* 37, 1387–97.

Chaiken, S. (1980). "Heuristic versus systematic information processing and the use of source versus message cues in persuasion." *Journal of Personality and Social Psychology,* 39, 752–6.

Cicero. (1921). *The Orator,* tr. G. L. Hendrickson. Cambridge, MA: Harvard University Press.

Clark, R.A. (1984). *Persuasive Messages.* New York: Harper and Row.

Clinton, W. J. (1998, September 11). "President Bill Clinton speaks at the annual White House prayer breakfast for clergy following his testimony and address to the nation on the Monica Lewinsky affair." <http://www.pbs.org/greatspeeches/timeline/clinton_prayer_s.html>. Also as:

Clinton, W. J. (1998). "Remarks by the president at religious leaders' breakfast." <www.whitehouse. gov> (=White House Documents).

Coen (2002). "Ad Spending to Grow at Slightly Slower Rate." <http://login.vnuemedia. com/>.

Coleman, R. P. (1983, December). "The continuing significance of social class in marketing." *Journal of Consumer Research*, 10, 265–80.

Collier, M. J. (1994). "Cultural identity and intercultural communication." In L. Samovar and R. E. Porter (eds), *An Introduction to Intercultural Communication* (pp. 36–45). Belmont, CA: Wadsworth.

Cotton, J. L., and Hieser, R. A. (1980). "Selective exposure to information and cognitive dissonance." *Journal of Research in Personality*, 14, 518–27.

D'Alessio, D., and Allen, M. (2002). "Selective exposure and dissonance after decisions." *Psychological Reports*, 91, 527–32.

Day, L. A. (1991). *Ethics in Media Communications: Cases and Controversies*. Belmont, CA: Wadsworth.

DeGroat, T. J. (2002, October 30). "The bottom line: Understanding your market." <http:// www.asiandiversity.com/articles/97073056.htm>.

Derks, P., Kalland, S., and Etgen, M. (1995). "The effect of joke type and audience response on the reaction to a joke: Replication and extension." *Humor*, 8, 327–37.

"Diet drug-maker paid for favorable articles" (1999, May 24). *Columbia Daily Tribune*, p. 7A.

"Disaster notes: terror hits home" (2001, May 24). *Columbia Daily Tribune*, p. 2A.

Dobrow, L. (2002, February). "How old is old enough? As marketers go younger and younger, ethical and legal concerns sand out." *Advertising Age*, 73.5, 4.

Donnelly, J. H., and Ivancevich, J. M. (1970). "Post-purchase reinforcement and back-out behavior." *Journal of Marketing Research*, 7, 399–400.

Downey, K. (2002, October 21). "Ethnic men use media differently." <http://209.61.190.23/ news2002/oct02/oct21/1_mon/news3monday.html>.

Eagly, A. H., and Chaiken, S. (1975). "An attribution analysis of the effect of communicator characteristics on opinion change: The case of communicator attractiveness." *Journal of Personality and Social Psychology*, 32, 136–44.

Eagly, A. H., and Chaiken, S. (1993). *The Psychology of Attitudes*. Fort Worth: Harcourt Brace Jovanovich.

Eagly, A. H., and Telaak, K. (1972). "Width of the latitude of acceptance as a determinant of attitude change." *Journal of Personality and Social Psychology*, 23, 388–97.

Elliott, S. (1993, September 22). "27 attorneys general oppose Joe Camel." *New York Times*, p. D21.

Farnsworth, S. J., and Lichter, S. R. (2003). *The Nightly News Nightmare: Network Television's Coverage of US Presidential Elections, 1988–2000*. Lanham, MD: Rowman and Littlefield.

Fazio, R. H., and Zanna, M. P. (1981). "Direct experience and attitude–behavior consistency." In L. Berkowitz (ed.), *Advances in Experimental Social Psychology* (vol. 12, pp. 161–202). New York: Academic Press.

Festinger, L. (1957). *A theory of Cognitive Dissonance*. Stanford, CA: Stanford University Press.

Festinger, L. (1964). *Conflict, Ddecision, and Dissonance*. Stanford: CA: Stanford University Press.

Festinger, L., and Carlsmith, J. M. (1959). "Cognitive consequences of forced compliance." *Journal of Abnormal and Social Psychology*, 58, 203–10.

Fieser, J. "Ethics." In "The internet encyclopedia of philosophy." <http://www.iep.utm.edu/e/ ethics.htm> (accessed 6/22/07).

Fieser, J., and Dowden, B. (2004). *The Internet Encyclopedia of Philosophy*. <http://www.utm.edu/research/iep/e/ethics.htm>.

Fink, L. S. (1997, September 4). "Speech to first year students after outward bound afternoon." <http://gos.sbc.edu/f/fink.html>.

Fishbein, M., and Ajzen, I. (1975). *Belief, Attitude, Intention, and Behavior*. Reading, MA: Addison-Wesley.

Fishbein, M., Ajzen, I., and Hinkle, R. (1980). "Predicting and understanding voting in American elections: Effects of external variables." In I. Ajzen and M. Fishbein (eds), *Understanding Attitudes and Predicting Social Behavior* (pp. 173–95). Englewood Cliffs, NJ: Prentice Hall.

Fisher, M. (1992). "A whisper of AIDS: Address to the republican national convention." <http://gos.sbc.edu/> (= Gifts of Speech website) (accessed 7/26/02).

Ford, Harold. (2000, August 15). "Key note address. Online NewsHour: 2000 Democratic Convention." <www.pbs.org/newshour/election2000/demconvetion/ford.html>. Also as:

Ford, Harold (2000). "Remarks by the Honorable Harold Ford, Jr." <http://web.lexis-nexis.com/universe/document?_m=4d853950efe2fabb797905bc3479e978and_docnum=2and wchp=dGLbVzzzSkVAand_md5=62475e1d4d6dfdeb2f731a8d743756a1>.

Foss, S. K., Foss, K. A., and Trapp, R. (2002). *Contemporary Perspectives on Rhetoric* (3rd edn). Prospect Heights, IL: Waveland.

Freedman, J. L. (1965). "Confidence, utility, and selective exposure: A partial replication." *Journal of Personality and Social Psychology*, 2, 778–80.

Gable, M., Wilkens, H.T., Harris, L., and Feinberg, R. (1987). "An evaluation of subliminally embedded sexual stimuli in graphics." *Journal of Advertising*, 16, 26–30.

"Gambling everywhere? It's a sure thing" (1999, June 15). <http://www.cnn.com/US/9906/15/gambling/> (=CNN.com website) (accessed 8/17/02).

German, K., Gronbeck, B., Ehninger, D., and Monroe, A.H. (2000). *Principles of Public Speaking* (14th edn). Boston: Allyn and Bacon.

Gillig, P. M., and Greenwald, A. G. (1974). "Is it time to lay the sleeper effect to rest?" *Journal of Personality and Social Psychology*, 29, 132–9.

Gilligan, C. (1982). *In a Different Voice: Psychological Theory and Women's Development*. Cambridge, MA: Harvard University Press.

Greenberg, B. S., and Miller, G. R. (1966). "The effects of low-credible sources on message acceptance." *Speech Monographs*, 33, 127–36.

Greenwald, A. G. (1968). "Cognitive learning, cognitive response to persuasion, and attitude change." In A. G. Greenwald, T. C. Brock, and T. M. Ostrom (eds), *Psychological Foundations of Attitudes* (pp. 147–70). New York: Academic Press.

Hale, J. L., Householder, B. J., and Greene, K. L. (2002). "The theory of reasoned action." In J. P. Dillard and J. W. Pfau (eds), *The Persuasion Handbook: Developments in Theory and Practice* (pp. 259–68). Thousand Oaks, CA: Sage.

Hale, J. L., Lemieux, R., and Mongeau, P. A. (1995). "Cognitive processing of fear-arousing message content." *Communication Research*, 22, 459–74.

Hale, J. L., Mongeau, P. A., and Thomas, R. M. (1991). "Cognitive processing of one- and two-sided persuasive messages." *Western Journal of Speech Communication*, 55, 380–9.

Hamid, P. N., and Cheng, S.-T. (1995). "Predicting antipollution behavior: The role of molar behavioral intentions, past behavior, and locus of control." *Environment and Behavior*, 27, 679–98.

Hamilton, M. A., Hunter, J. E., and Boster, F. J. (1993). "The elaboration likelihood model as a theory of attitude formation: A mathematical analysis." *Communication Theory*, 3, 50–65.

Hansen, G. J., and Benoit, W. L. (2002). "Presidential television advertising and the public policy priorities, 1952–2000." *Communication Studies*, 53, 286–96.

Harkins, S. G., and Petty, R. E. (1981). "The multiple source effect in persuasion: The effects of distraction." *Personality and Social Psychology Bulletin*, 7, 627–35.

Hass, R. G. (1981). "Effects of source characteristics on cognitive responses and persuasion." In R. E. Petty, T. M. Ostrom, and T. C. Brock (eds), *Cognitive Responses in Persuasion* (pp. 44–72). Hillsdale: Erlbaum.

Haugtvedt, C. P., and Petty, R. E. (1992). "Personality and persuasion: Need for cognition moderates the persistence and resistance of attitude changes." *Journal of Personality and Social Psychology*, 63, 308–19.

Haugtvedt, C. P., and Strathman, A. J. (1990). "Situational product relevance and attitude persistence." *Advances in Consumer Research*, 17, 766–9.

Haugtvedt, C. P., and Wegener, D. T. (1994). "Message order effects in persuasion: An attitude strength perspective." *Journal of Consumer Research*, 21, 205–18.

Hausenblas, H. A., Carron, A. B., and Mack, D. E. (1997). "Application of the theory of reasoned action and planned behavior to exercise behavior: A meta-analysis." *Journal of Sport and Exercise Psychology*, 19, 36–51.

Heider, F. (1946). "Attitudes and cognitive organization." *Journal of Psychology*, 21, 107–12.

Heider, F. (1958). *The Psychology of Interpersonal Relations.* New York: John Wiley.

Heumann, J. E. (1997, June 4). "Remarks at the individuals with disabilities education act bill signing ceremony." <http://gos.sbc.edu/h/heumann.html>.

Holbert, R. L., Benoit, W. L., Hansen, G. J., and Wen, W-C. (2002). "The role of political ad recall, news use, political discussion, and debate viewing in campaign issue knowledge and salience." *Communication Monographs*, 69, 296–310.

Horn, J. (2002, October 28). "Point and bet." *Newsweek*.

Horowitz, B. "Stewart uploads her cause to website." *USA Today* (posted 6/6/2003.). <http://www.usatoday.com/money/industries/retail/2003-06-05-marthareact_x.htm>.

Hovland, C. I., Lumsdaine, A., and Sheffield, F. (1949). *Experiments on Mass Communication.* Princeton, NJ: Princeton University Press.

Human Genome Project (2001, May 29). "Human genome project information: Cloning fact sheet." <http://www.ornl.gov/hgmis/elsi/cloning.html> (= Human Genome Project website) (accessed 8/17/02).

Hunter, J. E., Danes, J., E., and Cohen, S. (1984). *Mathematical Models of Attitude Change, 1: Change in Single Attitudes and Cognitive Structures.* New York: Academic Press.

Igou, E.R., and Bless, H. (2003). "Inferring the importance of arguments: Order effects and conversational rules." *Journal of Experimental Social Psychology*, 39, 91–9.

Isocrates. (1976). *Antidosis*, tr. G. Norlin. Cambridge: Harvard University Press, Loeb Classical Library.

Jackson, J. (2002, July 29). "Jackson issues statement after meeting with President Arafat." <http://www.rainbowpush.org> (= Rainbow/PUSH Coalition website) (accessed 8/16/02).

Janis, I. L. (1967). "Effects of fear arousal on attitude change: Recent developments in theory and experimental research." In L. Berkowitz (ed.), *Advances in Experimental Social Psychology* (vol. 3, pp. 166–225). New York: Academic Press.

Jepson, C., and Chaiken, S. (1990). "Chronic issue-specific fear inhibits systematic processing of persuasive communications." *Journal of Social Behavior and Personality*, 5, 61–84.

Johannesen, R. L. (1996). *Ethics of Human Communication* (4th edn). Prospect Heights, IL: Waveland Press.

Johnson, B. T., and Eagly, A. H. (1989). "Effects of involvement on persuasion: A meta-analysis." *Psychological Bulletin*, 106.2, 290–314.

Johnson, B. T., and Eagly, A. H. (1990). "Involvement and persuasion: Types, traditions, and the evidence." *Psychological Bulletin*, 107.3, 375–84.

Jordan, N. (1952). "Behavioral forces that are a function of attitudes and of cognitive organization." *Human Relations*, 6, 273–87.

Kahle, L. R., and Homer, P. M. (1985). "Physical attractiveness of the celebrity endorser: A social adaptation perspective." *Journal of Consumer Research*, 11, 954–61.

Kellogg, A. P. (2001, July 6). "Pitchmen on campus." *The Chronicle of Higher Education*, p. A8–9.

Kern, M. (1989). *30 Second Politics: Political Advertising in the Eighties*. New York: Praeger.

Key, W. B. (1972). *Subliminal Seduction: Ad Media's Manipulation of a not so Innocent America*. Englewood Cliffs, NJ: Prentice-Hall.

Khouri, C. (1994, May 22). "Rules to live by: Dos, don'ts, and other fabulous tips from someone who's been there and done that." <http://gos.sbc.edu/k/khori.html>.

Kiesler, C. A., Collins, B. E., and Miller, N. (1969; reprinted 1983). *Attitude Change: A Critical Analysis of Theoretical Approaches*. Malabar, FL: Robert E. Krieger.

Kim, M. S., and Hunter, J. E. (1993a). "Attitude–behavior relations: A meta-analysis of attitudinal relevance and topic." *Journal of Communication*, 43, 101–42.

Kim, M. S., and Hunter, J. E. (1993b). "Relationships among attitudes, behavioral intentions, and behavior: A meta-analysis of past research. Part 2." *Communication Research*, 20, 331–64.

Kornblum, J. (2001, December 13). "Asian-Americans put lots of time into Web." <http://www.usatoday.com/life/cyber/tech/2001/12/13/ebrief.htm>.

Korzenny, F., and Lanusse, A. L. (n.d.). "Research uncovers Hispanic advertising impact. <http://www.cheskin.com/think/articles/quirks0497.html> (= Cheskin Market Insight Series).

"100 leading national advertisers" (2000, September 25). *Advertising Age*. <www.adage.com/daplace/archives/dp497.html>.

Leventhal, H. (1970). "Findings and theory in the study of fear communications." In L. Berkowitz (ed.), *Advances in Experimental Social Psychology* (vol. 5, pp. 119–86). New York: Academic Press.

Lichter, S. R., and Noyes, R. E. (1995). *Good Intentions Make Bad News: Why Americans Hate Campaign Journalism*. Lanham, MD: Rowman and Littlefield.

McDonald, M., and Lavelle, M. (2001, July 30). "Call it 'kid-fluence.'" *US News and World Report*, 131, p. 32.

McCroskey, J. C. (1970). "The effects of evidence as an inhibitor of counter-persuasion." *Speech Monographs*, 37, 188–94.

McGuire, W. J. (1964). "Inducing resistance in persuasion: Some contemporary approaches." In L. Berkowitz (ed.), *Advances in Experimental Social Psychology* (vol. 1, pp. 191–229), New York: Academic Press.

Macaulay, M. I. (1990). *Processing Varieties in English: An Examination of Oral and Written Speech Across Genres*. Vancouver: University of British Columbia Press.

Mamalade jokes (n.d.) <http://homepage.powerup.com.au/~mamalade/mamalade2.htmstart> (= Mamalade website) (accessed 8/17/02).

Maslow, A. (1970). *Motivation and Personality* (2nd edn). New York: Harper and Row.

Mehrabian, A. (1969). "Significance of posture and position in the communication of attitude and status relationships." *Psychological Bulletin*, 71, 359–72.

Merritt, S. (1984). "Negative political advertising: Some empirical findings." *Journal of Advertising*, 13, 27–38.

Miller, C. E., and Norman, R. M. B. (1976). "Balance, agreement, and attraction in hypothetical social situations." *Journal of Experimental Social Psychology*, 12, 109–19.

Miller, R. L. (1976). "Mere exposure, psychological reactance and attitude change." *Public Opinion Quarterly*, 40, 229–33.

Mills, J., and Harvey, J. (1972). "Opinion change as a function of when information about the communicator is received and whether he is attractive or expert." *Journal of Personality and Social Psychology*, 21, 52–5.

Mongeau, P. A. (1998). "Another look at fear-arousing persuasive appeals." In M. Allen and R. W. Preiss (eds), *Persuasion: Advances through Meta-Analysis* (pp. 53–68). Cresskill, NJ: Hampton Press.

Mongeau, P. A., and Stiff, J. B. (1993). "Specifying causal relationships in the elaboration likelihood model." *Communication Theory*, 3, 65–72.

Moser, H. R., and Rogers, W. B. (2002). "How the Federal Trade Commission helps to shape consumer behavior." *National Social Science Journal*, 18.2. <http://nssa.apsu.edu/NSSAJ/18-2/pdf/9.pdf>.

Nagle, J. (2002, August), "California Superior Court judge Ronald S. Prager has ordered R. J. Reynolds Tobacco Co., the nation's second-largest cigarette maker, to pay $20 million penalty for allegedly targeting teens with magazine ads for Camel and other cigarettes." *Consumers' Research Magazine*, 85, p. 38.

O'Keefe, D. J. (1987). "The persuasive effects of delaying identification of high- and low-credibility communicators: A meta-analytic review." *Central States Speech Journal*, 38, 63–72.

O'Keefe, D. J. (1990). *Persuasion: Theory and Research* (1st edn). London: Sage.

O'Keefe, D. J. (2002). *Persuasion: Theory and Research* (2nd edn). Newbury Park, CA: Sage.

O'Toole, J. (1981). *The Trouble with Advertising*. New York: Chelsea House.

Olson, J. M., and Zanna, M. P. (1979). "A new look at selective exposure." *Journal of Experimental Social Psychology*, 15, 1–15.

Osgood, C. E., and Tannenbaum, P. H. (1955). "The principle of congruity in the prediction of attitude change." *Psychological Review*, 62, 42–55.

Osgood, C. E., Suci, G. J., and Tannenbaum, P. H. (1957). *The Measurement of Meaning*. Urbana, IL: University of Illinois Press.

Osterhouse, R. A, and Brock, T. C. (1970). "Distraction increases yielding to propaganda by inhibiting counterarguing." *Journal of Personality and Social Psychology*, 15, 344–58.

Parisien, M. (2003, July). Personal communication.

Patterson, T. E. (1980). *The Mass Media Election: How Americans Choose Their President*. New York: Praeger.

Patterson, T. E., and McClure, R. D. (1976). *The Unseeing Eye: The Myth of Television Power in National Elections*. New York: G. P. Putnam's Sons.

Peeler, C. L, and Cohn, S. (1995). "The Federal Trade Commission's regulation of advertising claims for dietary supplements." *Food and Drug Law Journal*, 50.3. <http://www.fdli.org/pubs/Journal%20Online/50_3/art2.pdf>.

Perloff, R. M., and Brock, T. C. (1980). "...'And thinking makes it so': Cognitive responses to persuasion." In M. E. Roloff and G. R. Miller (eds), *Persuasion: New Directions in Theory and Research* (pp. 67–99). Beverly Hills: Sage.

Pessah, R. (2001, April 19). "Grads awaiting convocation." <www.conrnelldailysun.com/articles/2648/>.

Petras, R. and Petras, K. (1993). *The 776 Stupidest Things ever Said*. New York: Doubleday.

Petty, R. E. (1998, November 12). "Personal communication (e-mail): Questions about ELM research."

Petty, R. E., and Cacioppo, J. T. (1979). "Issue involvement can increase or decrease persuasion by enhancing message-relevant cognitive processes." *Journal of Personality and Social Psychology*, 37, 1915–26.

Petty, R. E., and Cacioppo, J. T. (1981). *Attitudes and Persuasion: Classic and Contemporary Approaches*. Dubuque, IA: William C. Brown.

Petty, R. E., and Cacioppo, J. T. (1984). "The effects of involvement on responses to argument quantity and quality: Central and peripheral routes to persuasion." *Journal of Personality and Social Psychology*, 46, 69–81.

Petty, R. E., and Cacioppo, J. T. (1986a). *Communication and Persuasion: Central and Peripheral Routes to Attitude Change*. New York: Springer-Verlag.

Petty, R. E., and Cacioppo, J. T. (1986b). "The elaboration likelihood model of persuasion." In L. Berkowitz (ed.), *Advances in Experimental Social Psychology* (vol. 19, pp. 123–205). San Diego, CA: Academic Press.

Petty, R. E., and Cacioppo, J. T. (1990). "Involvement and persuasion: Tradition versus integration." *Psychological Bulletin*, 107, 367–74.

Petty, R. E., Cacioppo, J. T., and Goldman, R. (1981). "Personal involvement as a determinant of argument-based persuasion." *Journal of Personality and Social Psychology*, 41, 847–55.

Petty, R. E., Cacioppo, J. T., and Schumann, D. (1983). "Central and peripheral routes to advertising effectiveness: The moderating role of involvement." *Journal of Consumer Research*, 10, 135–46.

Petty, R. E., Haugtvedt, C. P., and Smith, S. M. (1995). "Elaboration as a determinant of attitude strength: Creating attitudes that are persistent, resistant, and predictive of behavior." In R. E. Petty and J. A. Krosnick (eds), *Attitude Strength: Antecedents and Consequences* (pp. 93–130). Mahwah, NJ: Lawrence Erlbaum.

Petty, R. E., Wells, G. L., and Brock, T. C. (1976). "Distraction can enhance or reduce yielding to propaganda: Thought disruption versus effort justification." *Journal of Personality and Social Psychology*, 34, 874–84.

Petty, R. E., Cacioppo, J. T., Kasmer, J. A., and Haugtvedt, C. P. (1987). "A reply to Stiff and Boster." *Communication Monographs*, 54, 257–62.

Petty, R. E., Kasmer, J. A., Haugtvedt, C. P., and Cacioppo, J. T. (1987). "Source and message factors in persuasion: A reply to Stiff's critique of the elaboration likelihood model." *Communication Monographs*, 54, 233–49.

Petty, R. E., Schumann, D. W., Richman, S. A., and Strathman, A. J. (1993). "Positive mood and persuasion: Different roles for affect under high- and low-elaboration conditions." *Journal of Personality and Social Psychology*, 64, 5–20.

Petty, R. E., Wegener, D. T., Fabrigar, L. R., Priester, J. R., and Cacioppo, J. T. (1993). "Conceptual and methodological issues in the elaboration likelihood model of persuasion: A reply to the Michigan State critics." *Communication Theory*, 3, 336–62.

Petty, R. E., Ostrom, T. M., and Brock, T. C. (eds) (1981). *Cognitive Responses in Persuasion*. Hillsdale: Erlbaum.

Pratkanis, A., and Aronson, E. (1992). *Age of Propaganda*. New York: W. H. Freeman and Co.

Reeber, A. S. (1995). *The Penguin Dictionary of Psychology* (2nd edn). London: Penguin Group.

Reinard, J. C. (1988). "The empirical study of the persuasive effects of evidence: The status after fifty years of research." *Human Communication Research*, 15, 3–59.

Reyes, R. M., Thompson, W. C., and Bower, G. H. (1980). "Judgmental biases resulting from differing availabilities of arguments." *Journal of Personality and Social Psychology*, 39, 2–12.

Rhine, R. J., and Kaplan, R. M. (1972). "The effect of incredulity upon evaluation of the source of a communication." *Journal of Social Psychology*, 88, 255–66.

Ries, A., and Trout, J. (1986). *Positioning: The Battle for Your Mind*. New York: McGraw Hill.

Robinson, M. J., and Sheehan, M. A. (1983). *Over the Wire and on TV: CBS and UPI in Campaign '80*. New York: Russell Sage.

Rogers, M., and Seiler, C. A. (1994). "The answer is no: A national survey of advertising industry practitioners and their clients about whether they use subliminal advertising." *Journal of Advertising Research, 34,* 36–45.

Rogers, M., and Smith, K. H. (1993). "Public perceptions of subliminal advertising: Why practitioners shouldn't ignore this issue." *Journal of Advertising Research,* 33, p. 10–19.

Rogers, S. (1992). "How a publicity blitz created the myth of subliminal advertising." *Public Relations Quarterly, 37,* 12–16.

Rose, F. (2000, September 26). "Free speech doesn't apply only to loudest shouters." *Columbia Daily Tribune,* p. A.

Roser, C., and Thompson, M. (1995). "Fear appeals and the formation of active publics." *Journal of Communication, 45,* 103–21.

Rosseli, F., Skelly, J. J., and Mackie, D. M. (1995). "Processing rational and emotional messages: The cognitive and affective mediation of persuasion." *Journal of Experimental Social Psychology, 25,* 49–58.

Rossiter, J. R., and Percy, L. (1997). *Advertising Communications and Promotion Management* (2nd edn). New York: McGraw Hill.

Rothwell, D. (1982). *Telling It like It Isn't.* Englewood Cliffs, NJ: Spectrum.

Russell, J. T., and Lane, W. R. (1996). *Kleppner's Advertising Procedure* (13th edn). Upper Saddle River, NJ: Prentice Hall.

Samovar, L., and Porter, R. E. (1994) (eds). *An Introduction to Intercultural Communication.* Belmont, CA: Wadsworth.

Schiappa, E. (1991). *Protagoras and Logos: A Study in Greek Philosophy and Rhetoric.* Columbia: University of South Carolina Press.

Settle, R. B., and Alreck, P. L. (1989). *Why They Buy: American Consumers Inside and Out.* New York: John Wiley and Sons.

Shavitt, S., Swan, S., Lowrey, T. M., and Wanke, M. (1994). "The interaction of endorser attractiveness and involvement in persuasion depends on the goal that guides message processing." *Journal of Consumer Psychology, 3,* 137–62.

Shea, D. M. (1996). *Campaign Craft: The Strategies, Tactics, and Art of Political Campaign Management.* Westport, CT: Praeger.

Shenk, D. (1997). *Data Smog: Surviving the Information Glut.* San Francisco: Harper.

Sheppard, B. H., Hartwick, J., and Warshaw, P. R. (1988). "The theory of reasoned action: A meta-analysis of past research with recommendations for modifications and future research." *Journal of Consumer Research, 15,* 325–43.

Sherif, C. W., Sherif, M., and Negergall, R. E. (1965; reprinted. 1981). *Attitude and Attitude Change: The Social Judgment–Involvement Approach.* Westport, CT: Greenwood Press.

Sherif, M., and Hovland, C. I. (1961; reprinted 1980). *Social Judgment: Assimilation and Contrast Effects in Communication and Attitude Change.* Westport, CT: Greenwood Press.

Sherif, M., and Sherif, C. M. (1967; rpt. 1976). "Attitudes as the individual's own categories: The social judgment–involvement approach to attitude and attitude change." In C. W. Sherif and M. Sherif (eds). *Attitude, Ego-Involvement, and Change* (pp. 105–39). Westport, CT: Greenwood Press.

Simons, H. W. (2001). *Persuasion in Society.* Thousand Oaks, CA: Sage.

Sivacek, J., and Crano, W. D. (1982). "Vested interest as a moderator of attitude–behavior consistency." *Journal of Personality and Social Psychology, 43,* 210–21.

Smith, K. H., and Rogers, M. (1994). "Effectiveness of subliminal messages and television commercials: Two experiments." *Journal of Applied Psychology, 79.6,* 866–74.

Snyder, M. (1979). "Self-monitoring processes." In L. Berkowitz (ed.), *Advances in Experimental Social Psychology* (vol. 12, pp. 526–37). New York: Academic Press.

Sopory, P., and Dillard, J. P. (2002). "The persuasive effects of metaphor: A meta-analysis." *Human Communication Research*, 28, 382–419.

Spiegelman, A. (2002, January 10). "Sept. 11 gave birth to lots of new words." <www.namibian.com.na/2002/January/world/023893F3AB.html> (= World News website) (accessed 8/16/02).

Sternthal, B., and Craig, S. (1973). "Humor in advertising." *Journal of Marketing*, 37, 12–18.

Sternthal, B., Dholakia, R., and Leavitt, C. (1978). "The persuasive effect of source credibility: A situational analysis." *Public Opinion Quarterly*, 42, 285–314.

Stewart, C. J. (1975). "Voter perception of mud-slinging in political communication." *Central States Speech Journal*, 26, 279–86.

Stiff, J. B. (1986). "Cognitive processing of persuasive message cues: A meta-analytic review of the effects of supporting information on attitudes." *Communication Monographs*, 53, 75–89.

Stiff, J. B., and Boster, F. J. (1987). "Cognitive processing: Additional thoughts and a reply to Petty, Kasmer, Haugtvedt, and Cacioppo." *Communication Monographs*, 54, 250–6.

Suggs, W. (May 26, 2000). "Bob Knight survives to coach another day." *The Chronicle of Higher Education*, p. A58–9.

Swartz, J. M. "Retailers offer websites in Spanish." *USA Today* (posted 5/28/2003). <http://www.usatoday.com/money/industries/retail/2003-05-28-hispanics_x.htm>.

Tang, D. (2001, May 27). "Napalm display draws protests." *Columbia Daily Tribune*. <http://archive.showmenews.com/2001/May/20010527/News007.asp>.

Tasaki, K., Kim, M-S., Miller, M. D. (1999). "The effects of social status on cognitive elaboration and post-message attitude: Focusing on self-construals." *Communication Quarterly*, 47.2, 196–212.

Theus, K. T. (1994). "Subliminal advertising and the psychology of processing unconscious stimuli: A review of research." *Psychology and Marketing*, 11.3, 271–90.

Thomas, C. (1998, July 28). "Supreme Court Justice Clarence Thomas defends his conservatism before members of the National Bar Association." <http://mitglied.lycos.de/FrankGemkow/laku/usa/speeches/cthomas.htm>. Also as:

Thomas, C. (1998). "Speech before the National Bar Association." <http://www.voxygen.net/cpa/speeches/thomastxt.htm>.

Thomsen, C. J., Borgida, E., and Lavine, H. (1995). "The causes and consequences of personal involvement." In R. E. Petty and J. A. Krosnick (eds), *Attitude Strength: Antecedents and Consequences* (pp. 191–214). Mahwah, NJ: Erlbaum.

Tourtellote, B. (1998, October 15). "Curtain falls on US 'teen' writer's masquerade." <http://www.infobeat.com/stories/cgi/story.cgi?id=2556606533-0cb>.

Tracy, K. (2002). *Everyday Talk: Building and Reflecting Identities*. New York: Guilford.

Tronto, J. (1993). *Moral Boundaries: A Political Argument for an Ethic of Care*. New York: Routledge.

US Census Bureau, (2003). "Projections of the total population of states: 1995 to 2025." <http://www.census.gov/population/projections/state/stpjpop.txt> (accessed 4/9/03).

US Department of Labor, Bureau of Labor Statistics. (2007a). "Latest numbers." <http://www.bls.gov/> (accessed 6/20/07).

US Department of Labor, Bureau of Labor Statistics. (2007b). "Regional and state employment and unemployment summary." <http://www.bls.gov/news.release/laus.nr0.htm> (accessed 6/20/07).

Vanden Bergh, B. G., and Katz, H. (1999). *Advertising Principles: Choice, Challenge, and Change*. Lincolnwood, IL: NTC.

Vokay, J. R., and Read, J. D. (1985). "Subliminal messages: Between the devil and the media." *American Psychologist*, 40.11, 1231–9.

Walster, E., Aronson, E., and Abrahams, D. (1966). "On increasing the persuasiveness of a low prestige communicator." *Journal of Experimental Social Psychology*, 2, 325–42.

Ward, C. D., and McGinnies, E. (1974). "Persuasive effect of early and late mention of credible and non-credible sources." *Journal of Psychology*, 86, 17–23.

Weaver, R. (1953). *The Ethics of Rhetoric*. South Bend, IN: Henry Regnery.

Weinberger, M. G., and Gulas, C. S. (1992). "The impact of humor in advertising: A review." *Journal of Advertising*, 18, 43–4.

Wells, W. T. (1999). "An analysis of attacking, acclaiming, and defending strategies in the 1976–1984 presidential debates." Ph.D. Dissertation, University of Missouri, Columbia.

White, G. L., and Gerard, H. B. (1981). "Postdecision evaluation of choice alternatives as a function of valence of alternatives, choice, and expected delay of choice consequences." *Journal of Research in Personality*, 15, 371–82.

Wicker, A. W. (1969). "Attitudes versus actions: The relationship of verbal and overt behavioral responses to attitude objects." *Journal of Social Issues*, 25.4, 41–78.

Wicklund, R. A., and Brehm, J. W. (1976). *Perspectives on Cognitive Dissonance*. Hillsdale, NJ: Erlbaum.

Wilson, E. J., and Sherrell, D. L. (1993). "Source effects in communication and persuasion research: A meta-analysis of effect size." *Journal of the Academy of Marketing Science*, 21, 101–12.

Winters, J. (1998, February 17). *Columbia Daily Tribune*. <http://archive.columbiatribune.com/1998/feb.19980217news12.htm>.

Witte, K. (1994). "Fear control and danger control: An empirical test of the extended parallel process model." *Communication Monographs*, 61, 113–34.

"Women call the shots on buying and maintaining the family car" (n.d.). <http://www.vmrintl.com/Usedcars/Reference%20Articles/women_buy_family_cars.htm>.

Woodward, G. C., and Dentorn, R. E. (1996). *Persuasion and Influence in American Life* (3rd edn). Prospect Heights: Waveland.

Zanot, E.J., Pincus, J.D., and Lamp, E.J. (1983). "Public perceptions of subliminal advertising." *Journal of Advertising*, 12, 39–45.

Zarefsky, D. (1999). *Public Speaking: Strategies for Success* (2nd edn). Boston: Allyn and Bacon. Cing enim velit prat. Duis nis alis nonumsa ndipsusci bla core dolorem iuscing er illandre digna amconsed te mod magnisi.

Index

Printed and bound by CPI Group (UK) Ltd, Croydon, CR0 4YY
11/09/2022
03146907-0002